DATA ANALYSIS

for Comprehensive Schoolwide Improvement

VICTORIA L. BERNHARDT, Ph.D.

Executive Director
Education for the Future Initiative
Pacific Bell Foundation[1]

Professor
Department of Professional Studies in Education
College of Communication and Education
California State University, Chico, CA

[1] The SBC Foundation, along with the Southwestern Bell, Pacific Bell, Nevada Bell, SNET, and Ameritech Foundations, is the charitable foundation of SBC Communications and its family of companies, including Southwestern Bell, Pacific Bell, Nevada Bell, SNET, Ameritech, and Cellular One properties.

EYE ON EDUCATION
6 DEPOT WAY WEST
LARCHMONT, NY 10538
(914) 833-0551
(914) 833-0761 fax

Library of Congress Cataloging-in-Publication Data

Bernhardt, Victoria L., 1952-
    Data analysis for comprehensive schoolwide improvement / by
Victoria L. Bernhardt.
        p.   cm.
    Includes bibliographical references (p.).
    ISBN 1-883001-57-9
    1. Computer managed instruction--United States. 2. School
improvement programs--United States--Data processing.   I. Title.
LB1028.46.B47 1998
371.2'00973--dc21   98-9736
                                                          CIP

10 9 8 7

Also Available from Eye on Education

THE SCHOOL PORTFOLIO:
A Comprehensive Framework for School Improvement
By Victoria L. Bernhardt

PERFORMANCE ASSESSMENT AND STANDARDS-BASED CURRICULA:
The Achievement Cycle
By Allan A. Glatthorn with Don Bragaw, Karen Dawkins, and John Parker

INFORMATION COLLECTION:
The Key to Data-Based Decision Making
By Paula M. Short, Rick Jay Short, and Kenneth Brinson Jnr.

RESEARCH ON EDUCATIONAL INNOVATIONS 2/e
By Arthur K. Ellis and Jeffrey T. Fouts

RESEARCH ON SCHOOL RESTRUCTURING
By Arthur K. Ellis and Jeffrey T. Fouts

TEACHING IN THE BLOCK
By Robert Lynn Canady and Michael D. Rettig

BLOCK SCHEDULING
By Robert Lynn Canady and Michael D. Rettig

THE ADMINISTRATOR'S GUIDE TO SCHOOL COMMUNITY RELATIONS
By George E. Pawlas

INNOVATIONS IN PARENT AND FAMILY INVOLVEMENT
By J. William Rioux and Nancy Berla

TRANSFORMING EDUCATION THROUGH TOTAL QUALITY MANAGEMENT:
A Practitioner's Guide
By Franklin Schargel

THE PERFORMANCE ASSESSMENT HANDBOOK
Volume 1 Portfolios and Socratic Seminars
Volume 2 Performances and Exhibitions
By Bil Johnson

THE REFLECTIVE SUPERVISOR:
A Practical Guide for Educators
By Ray Calabrese and Sally Zepeda

LEADERSHIP THROUGH COLLABORATION: **Alternatives to the Hierarchy**
By Michael Koehler and Jeanne C. Baxter

ABOUT THE AUTHOR

Victoria L. Bernhardt, Ph.D., is Executive Director of the Education for the Future Initiative, and Professor in the Department of Professional Studies in Education, at California State University, Chico. Dr. Bernhardt received a Ph.D. in Educational Psychology Research and Measurement, with a minor in Mathematics, from the University of Oregon in 1981.

While working with schools in the Initiative, which she has directed since 1991, Dr. Bernhardt developed the concept of the school portfolio. In 1996, this work received the NOVA Corporation Global Best Award for Renewal and Economic Development. Dr. Bernhardt was the recipient of the 1995 McKee Foods Corporation Award for Partnership Leaders. In addition, she has made numerous presentations at professional meetings, and has conducted over 300 workshops on the school portfolio process, data analysis, and databases at regional, state, national, and international levels.

The author's first book, *The School Portfolio: A Comprehensive Framework for School Improvement*, published by Eye on Education, was written to disseminate the research behind the school portfolio. It assists schools with clarifying their purpose and vision—measures and ensures congruence of all parts of the organization to enable the attainment of their vision. *The Example School Portfolio—A Companion to the School Portfolio: A Comprehensive Framework for School Improvement*, and *The School Portfolio Toolkit* demonstrate the uses of the school portfolio as a continuous improvement tool and provide tools and support for schools as they design and create their own school portfolio. This companion book, *Data Analysis for Comprehensive Schoolwide Improvement*, was written to help schools learn how to deal with data that will inform them of where they are, where they want to be, and how to get there—sensibly and painlessly.

The author can be reached at — Education for the Future Initiative
400 West 1st Street, Chico, CA 95929-0230
Tel: (530) 898-4482 — Fax: (530) 898-4484
vbernhardt@csuchico.edu
http://eff.csuchico.edu

ACKNOWLEDGEMENTS

This book is dedicated with appreciation to the hard-working staff of the Education for the Future Initiative who "make me look good."

This acknowledgment only begins to convey my appreciation for your dedication, hard work, and willingness to do things a *little differently* for the benefit of schools and for the betterment of students. I am indebted to Lynn Varicelli, Mary Tribbey, Marlene Trapp, Leni von Blanckensee, Jonni Davenport, Brad Geise, Sally Withuhn, Lara Bunting, Fran Rebello, Marcy Lauck, and George Bonilla, for your assistance, above and beyond the call of duty, with this book and for all you do each day. Now that the task of documenting our data analyses work with schools is complete, our workload may ease somewhat, giving us additional time to touch even more schools. It is my hope that each of you will reap the benefits of having this product.

A note of thanks and appreciation to associates and friends from across the country who graciously took time from their full schedules to review the various versions of the book: Bob Birdsell, Sue Clayton, Barbara Conklin, Ron Cope, Laura Dearden, Carol Duley, Pat Gopperton, Jeanne Herrick, Pete Higgins, Jere Jacobs, Bena Kallick, Harriett Kelly, Kurt Larsen, Mary Leslie, Rick Light, Bob McNamara, Rick Normington, Ed Sansom, Elaine Skeete, Ken Shelton, Connie Smith, Jacque Stendel, Mike Szymczuk, Nancy Todd, Charles Vidal, Louise Waters, and Alison Watson. A particular thank you to the schools that provided data for the *Example Schools* in the book, and the very real interest shown by workshop attendees over the past four years. Please know that your comments, recommendations, and data were invaluable and were the driving forces for finishing this project. I am indebted to each and every one of you . . .

A meaningful thanks to Bob Sickles, Publisher, Eye on Education, for allowing us to break the rules and publish this work in just a little different way, and for his patience and diligent support with our first book, *The School Portfolio: A Comprehensive Framework for School Improvement*.

A personal message of appreciation to my husband, Jim Richmond, who encourages me to explore and live my mission; understands the dynamics of my goals; and, with only slight reservation, supports my frequent absences from home.

And last, but not least, a special thank you to the Pacific Bell Foundation—now the SBC Foundation[1]—whose interest, concern, and support for public education is unmatched. I can still say there hasn't been a day since my first association with the Pacific Bell Foundation that I didn't wake up in the morning or go to bed at night thinking that I was the luckiest person on earth to have the greatest job in the universe. I love what I do—largely because *you* have allowed me to make a difference. Jere Jacobs, newly retired President, Pacific Bell Foundation; Mary Leslie, Education Director, Pacific Bell Foundation; and Phil Quigley, President and CEO of Pacific Telesis Group—I truly appreciated the opportunity of working with each of you. Now, a new and exciting phase of my professional life begins as I look forward to working with the extraordinary people at SBC, which now includes Mary Leslie.

I sincerely appreciate the selfless efforts of each of you. I hope what follows exceeds your expectations. If it does, it is because of the continuous improvement that has resulted because of your insights, direction, assistance, and support all along the way.

---

[1] The SBC Foundation, along with the Southwestern Bell, Pacific Bell, Nevada Bell, SNET, and Ameritech Foundations, is the charitable foundation of SBC Communications and its family of companies, including Southwestern Bell, Pacific Bell, Nevada Bell, SNET, Ameritech, and Cellular One properties.

TABLE OF CONTENTS

FOREWORD

As a corporate philanthropic organization, Pacific Bell has many reasons for funding education initiatives. We've pledged our support to invest in the communities where we work and live. Like all businesses, we want to recruit our employees from a strong talent pool. We want to operate in a thriving economy, spend less on remediating basic skills, and spend more to promote the professional development of our employees.

At the Pacific Bell Foundation[1], we certainly targeted all of the above when we became involved with the Education for the Future Initiative almost ten years ago. Through ongoing active involvement, we have made a real difference in California schools—and, to us, that matters. We are pleased, of course, with the indirect benefits of a stronger system in education, but perhaps the most important benefits are the improvements we have made within the communities in which we live.

Educational Excellence

Our experience shows we can make a difference.

Each time we are approached by a school considering a major improvement effort, everyone involved shows great enthusiasm. Administrators, staff, and parents are excited. The project is launched; however, the partners quickly become frustrated. Everyone works so hard without seeing the results they expect. The traditional measurements in schools are hard to understand and are often disheartening.

Like our partners in these efforts, we look for results. As business people, however, we find ourselves asking different questions. We ask, "How are our resources being spent? What do your clients say about the service you provide?

[1] The SBC Foundation, along with the Southwestern Bell, Pacific Bell, Nevada Bell, SNET, and Ameritech Foundations, is the charitable foundation of SBC Communications and its family of companies, including Southwestern Bell, Pacific Bell, Nevada Bell, SNET, Ameritech, and Cellular One properties.

How can we track performance and isolate those things that make the greatest impact on performance?"

Our experience with the Education for the Future Initiative has been unique. Beyond standardized test scores—which are often the only tangible indicators of whether reform efforts are making a difference—the Initiative teaches schools how to use other types of data in decision making.

Through our involvement, we have become convinced that data can be used to determine why students are not learning, and it can help contributors like the Pacific Bell Foundation make informed decisions about the educational needs of communities.

Based upon our past successes, the Pacific Bell Foundation's Education for the Future Initiative is working closely with several state departments of education, the United States Department of Education Comprehensive Assistance Centers, and schools and school districts throughout the state of California and across the nation to build comprehensive, easy-to-use performance-tracking systems schools can implement to improve children's learning.

The forerunner for this book, *The School Portfolio: A Comprehensive Framework for School Improvement*, describes the exemplary work of the Education for the Future Initiative in helping schools rethink and reestablish their role in improving student learning. The school portfolio process clearly demonstrates the powerful role data can play in student learning at all grade levels. *Data Analysis for Comprehensive Schoolwide Improvement* takes the work which appears to be the most difficult for schools—data analysis—and provides further direction on how to apply the portfolio principles.

Pacific Bell began its work with the Education for the Future Initiative almost a decade ago. Most recently, Jere Jacobs, the former president of the Pacific Bell Foundation, who recently retired, led this pioneering partnership. Today, following the merger of Pacific Telesis with SBC Communications, the SBC Foundation has renewed the company's commitment to this unique and effective program.

We all recognize that our education system needs to be improved. We also recognize that the efforts required to make these improvements will be worthwhile work. This book, *Data Analysis for Comprehensive Schoolwide Improvement*, provides the tools needed to accomplish such a task. Schools and school districts will discover within its pages invaluable resources for finding solutions to the challenges they face in preparing children for the future. We are proud to support this award-winning program.

Gloria Delgado
President
SBC Foundation
San Antonio, Texas

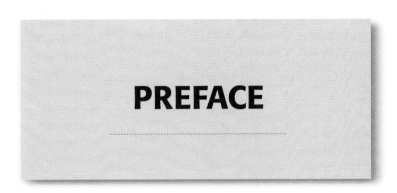

PREFACE

Schools are powerful organizations. Every day, across the United States, schools are impacting the lives of millions of children and the future of our very existence. Schools could, however, become even more powerfully efficient and effective learning organizations if data played a more active role in their daily existence.

I have become passionate about the impact data analyses make on building strong schools; teachers; administrators; and, district, county, regional, state and national education systems. Data not only tell us where we have been, where we are right now, and where we are going. Data inform us of the ways to get there, sensibly.

I have worked closely with teachers and schools on systemic change for more than a decade. The one area with which schools continue to have the most difficulty is data analysis. Consequently, they use it the least.

In this book, I want to show—

- why data make the difference in quality school improvement
- what data make the difference
- how gathered, analyzed, and properly used data make a difference in meeting the needs of every student in the school

> *Data provide the power to . . . make good decisions, work intelligently, work effectively and efficiently, change things in better ways, know the impact of our hard work, help us prepare for the future, and know how to make our work benefit all children.*

This book is not a statistics text. It takes data from real schools, and demonstrates how powerful data analyses emerge logically. It shows how to gain answers to questions to understand current and future impact.

Data can help identify and uncover powerful solutions to schools' biggest problems. I believe we have to look deeper than we are used to looking to get to analyses that make the difference. What I am professing is to take the data available to most schools and torture it until it confesses.

I want this book to contribute to the success of schools and districts throughout the United States and abroad, *because* . . . I want schools to prove that they can help *all* children to learn and to be all they want to be in the future.

Victoria L. Bernhardt, Ph.D.
Executive Director
Education for the Future Initiative
Chico, California

Visit our web site for additional information:
http://eff.csuchico.edu

Nearly every school in every state throughout the nation is attempting to reform, restructure, reengineer, or rethink the business of "school." What separates successful schools from those that will not be successful in their reform efforts is the use of one, often neglected, essential element—*data.*

Chapter 1

INTRODUCTION

Schools that analyze and utilize information about their school communities make better decisions about not only what to change, but how to institutionalize systemic change. Schools that understand the needs of their clientele—the students—are more successful in implementing changes and remain more focused during implementation. Further, schools that *use* data understand the effectiveness of their reform efforts—those that do not, can only assume that effectiveness.

Schools committed to improvement must not only analyze existing data. They must also collect and analyze additional data in order to understand—

- the current and future needs of the school, students, parents, teachers, and the community
- how well the current processes meet these clients' needs
- the ways in which the school and community are changing
- the root causes of problems
- the types of education programs and expertise that will be needed in the future

> *People without information cannot act. People with information cannot help but act.*
>
> Ken Blanchard

Types of data that assist schools in planning for and sustaining systemic reform include—

- demographics
- attendance/enrollment
- drop-out/graduation rates
- assessments of current teaching practices
- teachers', students', graduates', administrators', and parents' perceptions of the learning environment

+ in-house testing
+ student achievement
+ business and community needs
+ problem analyses
+ cost-benefit analyses
+ ongoing assessments of progress

The Importance of Data

We, in education, have a history of adopting one innovation after another as they are introduced. Very few of us take the time to understand the needs of the children we serve, the impact that our current processes have on children, the root causes of recurring problems, the solutions to alleviate the problems in the long run, and how to measure and analyze impacts after implementing new approaches.

The use of data can make an enormous difference in school reform efforts by improving school processes and student learning. Data can help us—

+ replace hunches and hypotheses with facts concerning what changes are needed
+ identify the root causes of problems, so we can solve the problem and not the symptom
+ assess needs to target our services on important issues
+ know if goals are being accomplished
+ determine if we are "walking our talk"
+ understand the impact of efforts, processes, and progress
+ answer the question for our community: "What are we getting for our investment in our children?"
+ continuously improve all aspects of the learning organization

. . . .

One small rural Northern California community learned a valuable lesson regarding the difference between hypotheses and fact while investigating why the majority of their high school graduates dropped out of college before the end of their first year. They learned that a great deal of money and time could have been spent in "solving a symptom" without ever getting to the real issue— the quality of their academic programs.

Each year, for several years, the community watched 80 percent of their graduates go off to college in the fall, 40 percent return to the community by Christmas, and almost 95 percent return by the end of spring—for good. This recurring problem was discussed widely among teachers and the community. Their hypothesis was that their students lacked experience and social skills. Their students simply did not have the social skills to function in other environments. Everyone "knew" that these students did not interact positively with people they knew, so they could not possibly know how to interact positively with strangers.

Based on this "knowledge," the school district began an extensive restructuring effort centered around working with all K-12 students to develop their social and communication skills. At the request of a consultant brought in to " . . . make this vision a shared community vision," the teachers reluctantly conducted a telephone survey of their graduates, asking them why they had dropped out of college. Almost without exception, graduates said the following: "They made me write. I can't write!" Based on this fact-finding survey, the focus of the restructuring effort changed immediately and the school district began using data on an ongoing basis to provide a challenging curriculum that kept students engaged in learning, enjoying school—and writing!

. . . .

One large Southern California elementary school learned the value of disaggregating their data to understand their students and to aid their reform efforts.

School personnel stated that because their population included so many "limited English-speaking children," the school's scores remained at a low level. They also reported that, because of these children, they could not become a mathematics, science, and technology magnet school.

The standardized achievement tests that had been given during the previous five years were analyzed. It was clear that while the reading and writing scores of the students with limited English-speaking abilities were lower than the other students, these same limited English-speaking students outscored English-proficient students in science and mathematics. With this and other information, the teachers researched strategies that could be used to everyone's advantage.

The research resulted in the school becoming a mathematics, science, and technology magnet school. It utilized hands-on activities in these areas to build language competence in their targeted population, while increasing all students' science, mathematics, and technology knowledge. The test scores of all students improved tremendously, in one year.

. . . .

Another elementary school in California's Central Valley learned through the use of empirical data that they were not "walking their talk." The data provided guidance in establishing a new purpose for the school and in understanding how to reach their goals.

The teachers stated that the purpose of their school was "to prepare students for middle school." As a means of gathering data to understand how well they were accomplishing this goal, a small group of teachers went to the middle and high schools and asked questions of teachers and former elementary school students. The elementary teachers were mortified to find that the majority of students who left their school with limited English-speaking skills were forever tracked in special programs that did not allow them to take college or career preparation classes. Some students had even dropped out of school.

The teachers came to the consensus that the purpose of their school, which served a mostly (about 85 percent) limited English-speaking population, was to do much more than prepare them for the middle school. The school needed to be preparing students for any career they might want to pursue in the United States.

These same teachers went back to their school understanding that their highest priority had to be to get their students speaking, reading, and writing English successfully before they left elementary school. They examined the processes used to teach students English. They were teaching English to non-English-speaking children for 20 minutes each day, and moving 35 children into English-speaking classrooms in one year's time—a process they had been using for the past four years. And, because the product of the process was the same every year, a process change was required in order to get different results.

By doubling the time spent teaching English to forty minutes each day, the number of students who became fluent in English by the end of that next semester more than doubled. Aside from learning how to measure their processes, the teachers learned the importance of tracking student performance on an ongoing basis, ensuring every student's success.

. . . .

Data Barriers

Schools do not ignore data deliberately. They often are just not aware of the wealth of information that could make their jobs easier (through knowing what works and what doesn't) and more satisfying (by learning how to get the results they want).

Some of the reasons schools may not use data regularly include the following:

- The work culture does not focus on data. Few people at schools and districts are adequately trained to gather and analyze data, or establish and maintain databases. Administrators and teachers do not think analyzing data is part of their job. District personnel have job definitions that do not include, as a priority, helping schools with data.

- Gathering data is perceived to be a waste of time; after all, we are here every day—we know what the problems are.

- Computer systems are outdated and inadequate; appropriate, user-friendly software is not available.

- Teachers have been trained to be subject oriented, not data oriented. Teaching has been an intuition-based profession which no longer works with our changing society.

- From the state level down to the regional and local levels, data are not used systematically, or are not used well.

- School personnel have only had negative experiences with data.

- There is a perception that data are collected for someone else's purposes.

- There are not enough good examples of schools gathering, maintaining, and benefiting from the use of data.

Many schools gather data. Doing something with the data is sometimes where the barriers begin. Perhaps it is pure optimism that gets in the way of analyzing data in schools—"we *hope* the process we are using is the best we can do for our children." Whatever it is that keeps us from assessing our progress and products adequately, we must learn to listen to, observe, and gather data from all sources, so we know where we are going and how we are doing.

The Purpose of this Book

The purpose of this book is to take a systems approach to supporting schools in overcoming these barriers by clarifying why data are important, what data to gather, how to use and analyze data for comprehensive schoolwide improvement, and how to communicate and report data results.

The Structure of this Book

This book begins with an overview of where we are in education and the barriers schools face with respect to data analysis. Chapter 2 describes how to get started, why we gather data, and to what end we use data. Chapter 3 defines multiple measures of data and the interactions of four major measures of data in terms of different levels of data analyses. Chapters 4, 5, 6, and 7 take each of the major measures of data described in Chapter 3 (demographics, perceptions, student learning, and school processes); defines each; describes their importance; and, explains how to gather, analyze, and use these data separately. Chapter 8 explores the interactions of these measures— two-way, three-way, and the all-important four-way interactions that allow schools to predict what they need to do to *prevent* failures. Chapter 9 describes how to put all the data analysis pieces together to know what changes are needed in the school for improved student learning. Chapter 10 talks about communicating the results of comprehensive data analyses to the community. Chapter 11 focuses on the databases behind the analyses. Chapter 12 discusses using the results of data analyses for schoolwide improvement and reviews the major elements of this book.

Most of the chapters contain examples of two fictional schools— one high school and one elementary school—using data from real schools. These data are used to illustrate the analyses that could be completed in your school.

At the end of each chapter is a set of questions that will assist school staff in thinking through their own data analyses. The intent is for staff to work through these chapters with their school teams as they design a comprehensive data analysis process that can be built upon each year to gain those powerful analyses that will help predict and prevent program failure—and to ensure that all students achieve success.

Three appendices and a References and Resources section appear at the end of the book. Appendix A presents the details of questionnaire construction, administration, and analysis. Appendix B consists of sample questionnaires. Appendix C offers the complete Education for the Future Initiative Continuous Improvement Continuums, a self-assessment tool for schools to use to measure and support their school processes and their continuous schoolwide improvement efforts.

Chapter 2

GETTING STARTED

How do you and others at your school know if what you are currently doing for students makes a difference with respect to what you want them to learn? It is assumed that you are clear on what it is you want students to learn (standards), and that your school standards are clearly reflected in the assessments you use.

If your school is like 95 percent of the schools in this country, my hunch is that you look at your standardized student achievement results each year, make statements about how these scores do not reflect what you are doing in the classroom, attempt to explain them to your school board, put the results in your desk drawer, and hope that the test will go away before your students have to take it again next year.

At the classroom level, in some schools, teachers have adopted rubrics and authentic assessment measures. They know their students are learning, but authentic assessment measures are not easy to talk about in terms of whole-class, let alone schoolwide, progress—it can be done, but it is difficult. Your school might also have a special externally funded program or two that requires the collection and analysis of data. You may have funders who want progress described. Questionnaires are then sent out each year and are analyzed *for the funders*.

> *It is hard to begin to move when you don't know where you are moving, how to move, or if you are going to get there.*
>
> Peter Nivio Zarlenga

Transforming Our Thinking About Data

Unfortunately, the scenario just described is all too familiar in schools across the nation. What needs to be included to that scenario is an understanding of how data can be used to improve what schools do for students and ensure that every student is learning—the school's ultimate purpose. We want to see data gathered throughout the school on a regular basis—not just when an external force requires it, and we want members of the school community to understand how to use data to accurately inform individuals, within and external to the school, of how the school is doing.

> *The real voyage of discovery consists not in seeking new landscapes, but in seeing with new eyes.*
>
> Marcel Proust

This chapter describes the process of gathering data to use for comprehensive schoolwide improvement. There are many ways to approach data analysis in schools. There are many ways to measure the effectiveness of school processes. The approach taken here is a systems approach—we want to gather and analyze data that will help us understand the system that produces the results we are getting. We also want to focus our schoolwide improvement efforts from random acts of improvement to ones focused on our ultimate purpose.

Contrary to most assumptions about data analyses, data are very logical—we merely need to think about what we want to know and why, and then think about the data we have, or need, to answer the questions.

To What End?

To guide the process, to keep it focused, and to ensure that it is used, it is important to understand from the beginning how data analysis information is going to be used and who is going to use it.

Typically, school data are analyzed to—

> *Without continual growth and progress, such words as improvement, achievement, and success have no meaning.*
>
> Benjamin Franklin

- improve instruction
- provide students with feedback on their performance
- gain common understanding of what quality performance is and how close we are to achieving it
- measure program success and effectiveness
- understand if what we are doing is making a difference

- make sure students "do not fall through the cracks"
- know which programs are getting the results we want
- get to the "root causes" of problems
- guide curriculum development and revision
- promote accountability
- meet state and federal requirements

If the focus of your data analysis efforts is on the comprehensive improvement of the entire learning organization, all other purposes will be met.

After determining why you analyze your school's data, think about how the data are used. Very often there is a "misconnect" between the answers to these two questions. We want the uses to align with the reasons for gathering the data.

Comprehensive data analysis is tied to schoolwide improvement, and there are some very important questions that must be answered in order to make the work we are doing worthwhile—not only the analysis work, but the work that is done for and with students every day.

Moving to a New Way of Thinking

The most important question is: *What is the purpose of the school?*

Other questions—

- What do you expect students to know and be able to do by the time they leave the school? (Standards)
- What do you expect students to know and be able to do by the end of each year? (Benchmarks)

> *If you don't know where you are going, anything you do will get you there.*
>
> Anonymous

- How well will students be able to do what they want to do with the knowledge and skills they acquire by the time they leave school? (Performance)
- Do you know why you are getting the results you get? Do you know why you are not getting the results you want?
- What would your school and educational processes look like if your school was achieving its purpose, goals, and expectations for student learning?
- How do you want to use the data you will gather?

The chapters that follow will help you think through all of these questions and their importance in our comprehensive data analysis journey.

Summary

Schools that are not using data in a purposeful way need to transform their thinking about data. If the focus of data analysis efforts is on comprehensive improvement of the entire learning organization, it is likely that other data analysis needs—such as external reporting requirements—will be met. Clarifying the purpose of the school sets the stage for all systems and data analysis work.

Getting Started Questions

As you begin your comprehensive data analysis journey, take some time with your school team to think through the following questions. Identify one person as the recorder—the other members contribute ideas.

What is the purpose of your school?

What is the purpose of collecting the data at your school?

How are the currently collected data used?

What are the roadblocks to *collecting* data at your school?

What are the roadblocks to *analyzing* data at your school?

What are the roadblocks to *reporting* data at your school?

What data will help us understand if we are meeting the purpose of our school, if we are being effective, if the purpose of our school benefits all students, and if the purpose translates into needed actions? What analyses will help us answer these questions?

Chapter 3

MULTIPLE MEASURES

Because learning does not take place in isolation, or only at school, multiple measures must be considered and used to understand the multifaceted world of school from the perspective of everyone involved, and to know if the school purpose is appropriate and being achieved effectively.

With student achievement, more than one method of assessment allows students to demonstrate their full range of abilities. Collecting data on multiple occasions allows students several opportunities to demonstrate their abilities. So it is with schools. If staff want to know if the school is achieving its purpose and how to continually improve all aspects of the school, multiple measures—gathered from varying points of view—must be used.

Since the major job of every school is student learning, let's begin by thinking through the factors that impact student learning. Most students learn faster when they are taught in a manner of learning they like. It follows, then, that we need to ask students what they like about the way they learn at school, and how they learn best. School processes, such as programs and instructional strategies, need to be described in order for all staff to meet the learning styles that will optimize all students' learning.

Because students neither learn only at school nor only through teachers, it seems necessary to know about the learning environment from the parent and community perspective. Schools may also need to know how employers feel about the skills of former students.

But, will these data provide enough information to determine how well the school is meeting the needs of all students? There are factors over which we have no control, such as background or demographics. These data are

> *Learning does not take place in isolation. Students bring to the learning setting what they have experienced and the values they have been taught at home and in their neighborhoods. This affects how they respond.*
>
> National Center for Education Statistics

crucial in our understanding of who we serve, and whether or not our educational services are reaching every student.

Together, these measures—demographics, perceptions, student learning, and analyses of school processes—can provide a powerful picture that can help us understand the school's impact on student achievement. These measures, when used together, give schools the information they need to get different results.

In Figure 1, the four major categories of measures discussed in this book are shown as overlapping circles. This figure illustrates the type of information that one can gain from individual measures and the enhanced levels of analyses that can be gained from the intersections of the measures.

One measure, by itself, gives useful information. Comprehensive measures used together and over time provide much richer information. Ultimately, schools need to be able to predict what they must do to meet the needs of *all* the students they have, or will have, in the future. The intersection of these four measures gives us that information.

Figure 1

Multiple Measures

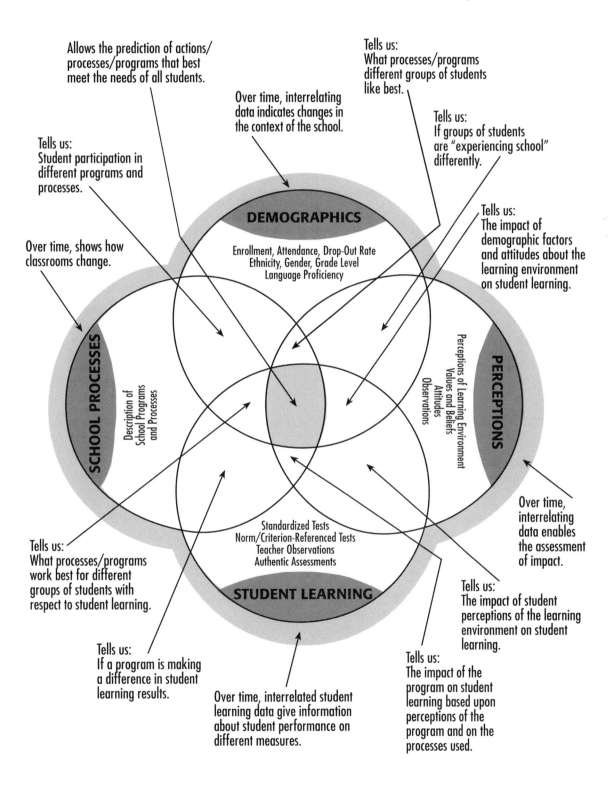

Allows the prediction of actions/ processes/programs that best meet the needs of all students.

Over time, interrelating data indicates changes in the context of the school.

Tells us: What processes/programs different groups of students like best.

Tells us: Student participation in different programs and processes.

Tells us: If groups of students are "experiencing school" differently.

Over time, shows how classrooms change.

Tells us: The impact of demographic factors and attitudes about the learning environment on student learning.

DEMOGRAPHICS

Enrollment, Attendance, Drop-Out Rate Ethnicity, Gender, Grade Level Language Proficiency

SCHOOL PROCESSES

Description of School Programs and Processes

Perceptions of Learning Environment Values and Beliefs Attitudes Observations

PERCEPTIONS

Standardized Tests Norm/Criterion-Referenced Tests Teacher Observations Authentic Assessments

STUDENT LEARNING

Tells us: What processes/programs work best for different groups of students with respect to student learning.

Over time, interrelating data enables the assessment of impact.

Tells us: If a program is making a difference in student learning results.

Over time, interrelated student learning data give information about student performance on different measures.

Tells us: The impact of student perceptions of the learning environment on student learning.

Tells us: The impact of the program on student learning based upon perceptions of the program and on the processes used.

Levels of Analysis

Different levels of analysis allow us to answer different questions at varying depths of understanding. Each of the four types of measures, alone, gives valuable descriptive information. Quality information can be found by digging deeper into the data through different levels of analysis in which one type of measure is analyzed with other measures, over time.

> *Analysis discourages inappropriate actions by filtering out the noise before potential signals are identified. Before you can detect signals within the data, you must first filter out the probable noise. And, to filter out noise you must start with past data.*
>
> Donald J. Wheeler

Below, ten levels of analysis are described, each one building on the previous, to show how past data and interactions of measures provide more comprehensive information than a single measure of data taken one time.

Level 1—Snapshots of Measures

At the first level of analysis, we look at the four major measures of data, shown in Figure 1, in their current state, and independent of each other.

Demographic data provide descriptive information about the school community—enrollment, attendance, grade level, ethnicity, gender, and native language. Demographic data are very important for us to understand as they are the part of our educational system over which we have no control, but from which we can observe trends and learn for purposes of prediction and planning. Demographic data assist us in understanding the results of all parts of our educational system through the disaggregation of other multiple measures, by demographic variables.

Perceptions data help us understand what students, parents, teachers, and others think about the learning environment. Perceptions can be gathered in a variety of ways—through questionnaires, interviews, and observations. Perceptions are important since people act in congruence with what they believe, perceive, or think about different topics. It is important to know what students, teachers, and parents think about school, so school personnel know how they are doing and what is possible!

Student Learning describes the results of our educational system in terms of standardized test results, grade point averages, standards assessments, and authentic assessments. Schools use a variety of student learning measurements—usually separately. Schools normally think of multiple measures as looking at multiple measures of student learning.

School Processes define what teachers are doing to get the results they are getting. For example, how is reading being taught at grade 2? School processes include programs, instructional strategies, and classroom practices. This is the measure that seems to be the hardest for teachers to describe. Most often, teachers say they do what they do unconsciously, and they are too busy doing it to systematically document and reflect on the processes. To change the results schools are getting, teachers and school personnel must begin to document these processes and align them with the guiding principles of the school.

Looking at each of the four measures separately, we get snapshots of data in isolation of any other data at the school level. At this level we can answer questions like—

- How many students are enrolled in the school this year? (Demographics)

- How satisfied are parents, students, and/or teachers with the learning environment? (Perceptions)

- How did students at the school score on a test? (Student Learning)

- What programs are operating in the school this year? (School Processes)

Level 2—Measures, Over Time

At the second level, we start digging deeper into each of the measures, by looking over time to answer questions such as—

- How has enrollment in the school changed in the past three years? (Demographics)

- How have student perceptions of the learning environment changed, over time? (Perceptions)

- Are there differences in student scores on standardized tests over the years? (Student Learning)

- What programs have operated in the school during the past five years? (School Processes)

Level 3—Two or More Variables Within Measures

Looking at more than one kind of data *within* each of the circles allows us to get a better view of the learning organization (e.g., 1996 standardized test subscores compared with performance assessment measures). We can answer questions like—

- What percentage of the students currently at the school are fluent speakers of languages other than English, and are there equal numbers of males and females? (Demographics)

◆ Are teacher, student, and parent perceptions of the learning environment in agreement? (Perceptions)

◆ Are students' standardized test scores consistent with teacher assigned grades and performance assessment rubrics? (Student Learning)

◆ How are the processes in the schools' three mathematics programs different? (School Processes)

Level 4—Two or More Variables Within One Type of Measure, Over Time

Level 4 takes similar measures as Level 3, across time (e.g., standardized test subscores and performance assessment measures compared from 1994 through 1996), and allows us to answer deeper questions such as—

◆ How has the enrollment of non-English-speaking kindergartners changed in the past three years? (Demographics)

◆ Are teachers, students, and parents more or less satisfied with the learning environment now than they were in previous years? (Perceptions)

◆ Over the past three years, how do teacher assigned grades and standardized test scores compare? (Student Learning)

◆ How have the processes used in the school's mathematics programs changed over time? (School Processes)

Level 5—Interaction of Two Types of Measures

Level 5 begins the interactions across two circles (e.g., 1997 standardized test results by ethnicity). Level 5 allows us to answer questions like—

◆ Do students who attend school every day get better grades? (Demographics by Student Learning)

◆ What strategies do third grade teachers use with students with native languages different from their own? (Demographics by School Processes)

◆ Is there a gender difference in students' perceptions of the learning environment? (Perceptions by Demographics)

◆ Do students with positive attitudes about school do better academically, as measured by teacher assigned grades? (Perceptions by Student Learning)

◆ Is there a difference in how students enrolled in different programs perceive the learning environment? (Perceptions by School Processes)

◆ Did students who were enrolled in interactive math programs, this year, perform better on standardized achievement tests than those who took traditional math courses? (Student Learning by School Processes)

Level 6—Interaction of Two Measures, Over Time

Looking at the interaction of two of the measures over time allows us to see trends as they develop. For example, standardized achievement scores disaggregated by ethnicity over the past three years can help us see if the equality of scores, by ethnicity, is truly a trend or an initial fluctuation. This interaction also begins to show the relationship of the multiple measures and why it is so important to look at all the measures together.

At Level 6 we are looking at the interaction of two of the circles over time. The kinds of questions we can answer at this level include—

◆ Has the difference in how students of different ethnicities scored on standardized tests changed in the past three years? (Demographics by Student Learning)

◆ Has there been a difference in student attendance rates for the different program offerings over time? (Demographics by School Processes)

◆ Have parent perceptions of the learning environment improved since the implementation of the new mathematics program? (Perceptions by School Processes)

Level 7—Interaction of Three Measures

As we intersect three of the measures at the school level, e.g., student learning measures disaggregated by ethnicity compared to student questionnaire responses disaggregated by ethnicity, the types of questions that we are able to answer include the following:

◆ Do students of different ethnicities perceive the learning environment differently, and do they score differently on standardized achievement tests consistent with these perceptions? (Demographics by Perceptions by Student Learning)

◆ What instructional process did the previously non-English-speaking students enjoy most in their all-English classrooms this year? (Perceptions by Demographics by School Processes)

♦ Is there a difference in students' reports of what they like most about the school, by whether or not they participate in extracurricular activities? Do these students have higher grade point averages than students who do not participate in extracurricular activities? (Perceptions by Student Learning by School Processes)

♦ Which program is making the biggest difference, with respect to student achievement for at-risk students, this year, and is there any one group of students responding "better" to the processes? (School Processes by Student Learning by Demographics)

Level 8—Interaction of Three Measures, Over Time

Looking at three measures over time allows us to see trends, to begin to understand the learning environment from the students' perspectives, and to know how to deliver instruction to get the desired results from and for *all* students.

Level 8 is Level 7 interactions over time (e.g., standardized achievement scores disaggregated by ethnicity compared to student questionnaires disaggregated by ethnicity, from 1994-96). Level 8 allows us to answer the following types of questions:

♦ What programs do all types of students like the most every year? (Demographics by Perceptions by School Processes)

♦ Have the processes used to teach English to English-learning students been consistent across grade levels, so each student is able to build on his/her abilities? (Demographics by Student Learning by School Processes)

Level 9—Interaction of All Four Measures

Our ultimate analysis is the intersection of all four measures, at the school level, e.g., standardized achievement tests disaggregated by program, by gender, within grade level, compared to questionnaire results for students by program, by gender, within grade level. These interactions allow us to answer questions like—

♦ Are there differences in achievement scores for 8th grade girls and boys who report that they like school, by the type of program and grade level in which they are enrolled? (Demographics by Perceptions by School Processes by Student Learning)

Level 10—Interaction of All Four Measures, Over Time

It is not until we intersect all four circles, at the school level and over time, that we are able to answer questions that will allow us to predict if the actions, processes, and programs that we are establishing for students will meet the needs of *all* students. With this intersection, we can answer the ultimate question:

◆ Are we achieving the purpose of our school, in all respects, for *all* students? (Student Learning by Demographics by Perceptions by School Processes)

Focusing the Data

Data analysis should not be about gathering data just because it is there. It would be very easy to get "analysis paralysis" by spending time pulling data together and not spending time using the data. School-level data analysis should be about helping schools understand if they are achieving their purpose and meeting the needs of *all* students—and, if not, why.

The data we gather and analyze must be focused on the purpose of the school—the core of everything that is done in the school—or the process will lead to nothing more than random acts of sporadic improvement, as opposed to focused improvement for better student results.

> *If you know why,*
> *you can*
> *figure out how . . .*
> W. Edwards Deming

Figure 2 on the following page shows how the benefits of a continuous improvement cycle could be missed altogether if the data analysis improvement process is not aimed at the school's guiding principles. A focused data analysis process will assist the continuous improvement process and provide comprehensive information about how the school is doing in relationship to its guiding principles.

Figure 2

Focusing the Data

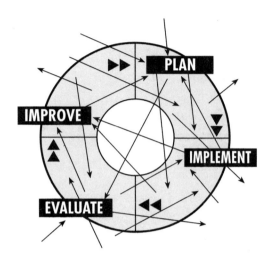

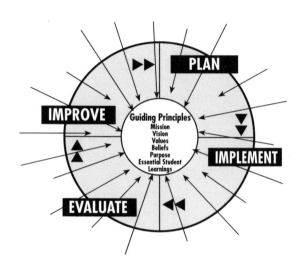

**Random
Acts of Improvement**

**Focused
Acts of Improvement**

Data analysis is easy when schools are clear on their purpose, on what they expect students to know, and what they expect students to be able to do. These analyses comfortably flow from questions that teachers and administrators naturally ask to learn if the purpose is being met. The good news is that, by looking at trends of the intersected four major measures, schools do not have to conduct complicated program evaluations or needs analyses. These intersections can tell them just about everything they would want to know, and the data are reasonably available.

Summary

Schools cannot use student achievement measures alone for continuous school improvement because the *context* is missing. Relying on one measure only can mislead schools into thinking they are analyzing student learning in a comprehensive fashion. Just looking at student learning measures could, in fact, keep teachers from progressing and truly meeting the needs of students.

The moral of the story is, if we want to get different results, we have to change the system that creates the results. When we focus only on student learning measures, we see school personnel using their time figuring out how to look better on the student learning measures. We want school personnel to use their time figuring out how to *be* better for *all* students. To do that, we must look at intersections of demographic, perception, student learning, and school processes data.

MULTIPLE MEASURES QUESTIONS

Think about the questions (grounded by the purpose) you would like to answer in your school. A matrix is offered to organize the kinds of data that will help you answer the questions. An example is shown below.

Purpose: Example: Provide learning for all students.

Questions	Standardized Math	Standardized Language Arts	Math GPA	Language GPA	Ethnicity	Gender	Language Fluency		
Are all student groups achieving at similar rates?	✓	✓	✓	✓	✓	✓	✓		

Demographics are typically known as the statistical characteristics of human populations (such as age or ethnicity). In education, demographic data translates to items such as—

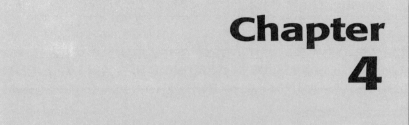

Chapter 4

DEMOGRAPHICS

- numbers of students in the school
- numbers of students with special needs
- ethnicities of the students in the school
- number of graduates
- number of students who drop out of school each year
- number of students living in poverty

Demographics clarify who our "clients" are. These data build the context of the school, and help us begin to predict future conditions so we can take an active approach to serving the needs of our future students.

Through the study of demographic trends, we can predict with some accuracy such things as the number of students and the ethnic diversity with which the school can expect to work in the future.

From an historical perspective, a school can use demographic data to analyze how well it has served its past and current population, and identify changes needed to meet the needs of its future clients.

Demographic information is crucial in data analysis as it helps us understand the context within which schoolwide change is planned and takes place. School variables, such as attendance and graduation rates, are included with other demographics mentioned in this section and shown in Table 1.

> *Because trends have clear direction, instead of causing turbulence, they actually help reduce it because they have a significant amount of predictability.*
>
> Joel Barker

Many school districts have these data available. The following list is offered to note the items that are usually available, upon request, at school and district offices.

Table 1

Demographic Data

Possible Existing Data at School and District Levels	
Student Demographics (disaggregated by subgroups, such as Ethnicity, Gender, English Fluency)	**School Level**
Numbers of Students	History
Parent Income Levels	Funding
Parent Education Backgrounds	Safety
Parent Employment	Physical Plan
Families on Public Assistance (AFDC%)	Uniqueness and Strengths
Free and Reduced Lunch (%)	Image in the Community
Drop-out Rates	Support Services for Students and Teachers
Graduation Rates	Number of Teachers and Administrators
Health Issues/Handicaps	Years of Teaching/Administering
Discipline Indicators (e.g., suspensions, referrals)	Ethnicity/Gender of Teachers and Administrators
Attendance Rates	Retirement Projections
Tardy Rates	Types of Certificates
Mobility	Student-Teacher Ratios
Number of Years at the School	Administrator-Teacher Ratios
School Community	Turnover Rates
History	Teacher Salary Schedule
Location	Support Staff
Population	**School District**
Race/Ethnicity	Description of District
Socioeconomic Status	History
Size	Number of Schools, Students, Teachers, and Administrators
Employment Status	Support Services for Students and Teachers
Educational Backgrounds	Organizational Structure
Housing Trends	**State Level**
Health Issues	Population
Crime Rate	Race/Ethnicity
Economic Base	Socioeconomic Status

Separating the results of different groups that make up the population is called disaggregation. Demographics play an important role in the disaggregation of data. Demographic subgrouping of any kind of achievement or perception measures allows us to isolate variations among different subgroups of students to understand if all students are achieving or experiencing school in the same way.

Disaggregation provides powerful information in the analyses of school variables, test scores, and questionnaire results. Schools need to disaggregate questionnaire data, e.g., attendance, drop-out rates, etc., to understand all aspects of the population of the school and to look for problems and their root causes.

Disaggregation

Disaggregation is not a problem-solving strategy. It is a problem-finding strategy.

Disaggregation helps us understand if we are truly meeting the purpose and mission of our school. If we are acting on the belief that all students can achieve, any breakdown of subgroups of students should show few differences. Disaggregation also helps us find subgroups that are not responding to our processes in the way that others are—enabling us to understand why and to search for new processes so all students can learn.

It is best to disaggregate for few rather than many subpopulations. When too many subpopulations are used, group sizes may become so small that individuals can easily be identified.

Choose general demographic variables that may be associated with student achievement, such as—

 ◆ gender
 ◆ ethnicity
 ◆ socioeconomic status
 ◆ grade level
 ◆ attendance
 ◆ number of years at the school

Disaggregation will be further explored in later chapters.

How to Disaggregate Demographic Information

Figure 3 shows two different examples of demographic charts for one high school. Each has been disaggregated by ethnicity. The charts display two variables for four years of data: enrollment numbers by ethnicity, and enrollment percentages by ethnicity for the years between 1994 and 1998. This disaggregation shows, in two ways, how the demographics of the school community have changed over the time period. The disaggregation for the first chart was made by calculating enrollment for each ethnicity for each of the years. Figure 3 shows that the number of Asian students has consistently increased during these four years, while the other ethnicities have fluctuated. Between 1994 and 1997, the total enrollment steadily increased. In 1997-98, the total enrollment decreased.

By converting the group enrollments to percentages in the second chart, one can see the relative percentage of each ethnic group to the total number of students. Note how important the total enrollment numbers are. Charts without numbers are useless when gauging perspective, especially when percentages are used.

Figure 3

Enrollment Over Time

This high school looked at enrollment over time, disaggregated by ethnicity, to confirm and depict the changing makeup of the school population. They then took these numbers and calculated percentages to get a relative idea of their numbers.

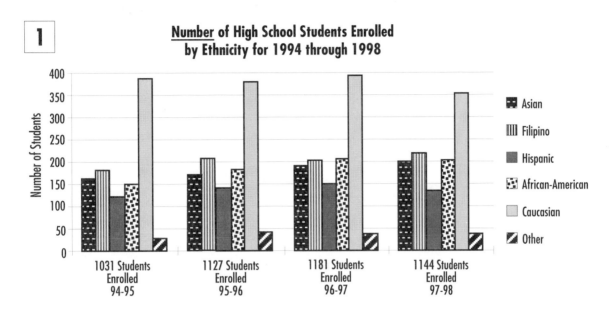

1

Number of High School Students Enrolled by Ethnicity for 1994 through 1998

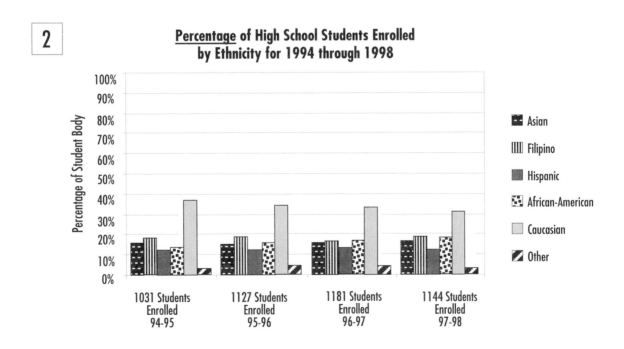

2

Percentage of High School Students Enrolled by Ethnicity for 1994 through 1998

Figure 4 displays a three-way analysis in a bar chart—grade point averages, by ethnicity, for freshmen, sophomores, juniors, and seniors, for 1997-98. Each of the points on the chart were calculated as subgroups of a total. For example: The average grade points for all freshmen, sophomores, juniors, and seniors were calculated to represent all students (shown in the "all students" bars of Figure 4), then the average of each subgroup, such as African-American freshmen, was calculated, and so on. Note that in this case, there is not enough information to use these data because we do not know how many freshmen, sophomores, juniors, or seniors there are. It is unfortunate because this could be a very informative chart. With disaggregation we want to make sure that all information is placed in the chart so that there can be no misinterpretations. (Chapter 10 discusses effective graphing methods.)

Figure 4

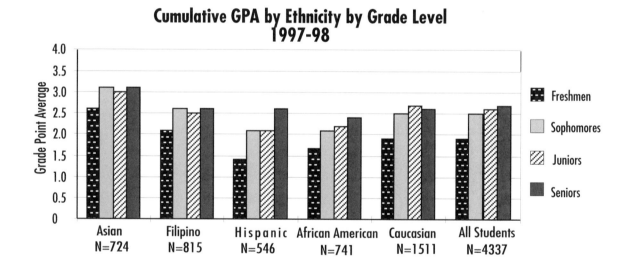

OUR EXAMPLE SCHOOLS

Starting with this chapter, we will follow Forest Lane Elementary and Valley High schools through all the levels of analysis for each of the four multiple measures. These two schools are fictional; however, actual data from several real schools were used for these examples. In this chapter, you will find examples of demographic charts which set the context for each school.

Level 1—Snapshot of Forest Lane Demographics

Demographic Descriptions for Forest Lane Elementary

Forest Lane Elementary School is a K-5 school in Mountain Union Elementary School District that served 992 students in 1997-98.

Forest Lane's student constituency is—

- American Indian/Alaska Native, 48, (5%)
- Asian, 309, (31%)
- Pacific Islander, 4, (<1%)
- Hispanic, 44, (4%)
- Black, 17, (2%)
- Caucasian, 570, (58%)

Figure 5 shows this breakdown in a pie chart.

Figure 5

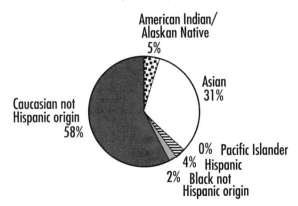

Forest Lane Elementary School Enrollment for 1997-98
(N = 992)

Of the 992 students at Forest Lane in 1997-98—

◆ 674 (68%) students qualified for AFDC

◆ 833 (84%) qualified for Free and Reduced Lunch

◆ 258 (26%) were children in migrant families

Level 2—Snapshot of Forest Lane Demographics, Over Time

Located in a rural setting in Northern California, Forest Lane Elementary School experienced an unanticipated influx of immigrant children during the past 10 years. In 1986, Forest Lane School began to receive immigrant children from countries such as Laos, Cambodia, and Vietnam. Figure 6 shows how the population changed over time.

Figure 6

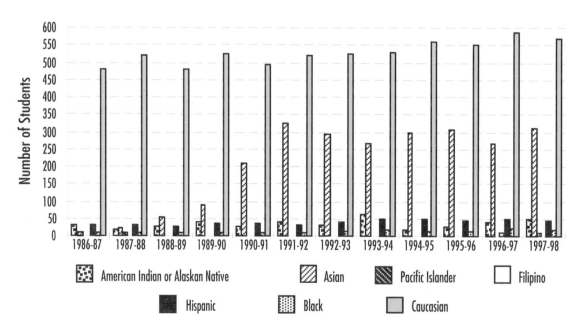

Essentially the Asian population increased sharply between 1986 and 1990, while the other ethnicities fluctuated slightly over time.

Level 3—Two or More Variables Crossed within Demographics

Figure 7 shows the English Language Learner (ELL) population for Forest Lane, by ethnicity for the 1997-98 school year. It is apparent from this chart that the majority of ELL students were Hmong, followed by much smaller numbers of Mien and Hispanic students.

Figure 7

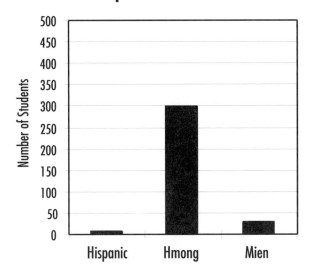

Forest Lane English Language Learner Population for 1997-98

Level 4—Two or More Variables Crossed within Demographics, Over Time

Figure 8 shows how the ELL population increased overall, over time, while decreasing slightly for Hispanic students. The number of Hmong students increased considerably since 1990. The Mien population peaked in 1991 and then decreased over time.

Figure 8

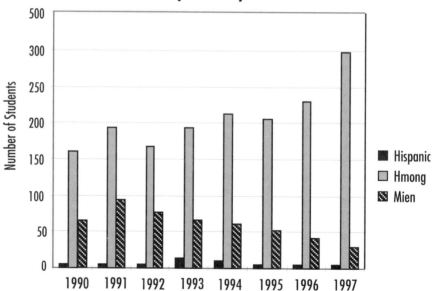

Forest Lane English Language Learning Students by Ethnicity Over Time

Level 1—Snapshot of Valley High School Demographics

Valley High School is a performing arts school and is one of three high schools in the California Unified School District, a district that serves approximately 20,000 students of a diverse population of families representing over seventy different nationalities. Much of this diversity is reflected in Valley's school population of approximately 1543 students—59 percent of whom are Hispanic, 29 percent Caucasian, 5 percent Asian, 3 percent Black, 2 percent Filipino, and 1 percent each American Indian and Pacific Islander.

Demographic Descriptions for Valley High School

Figure 9

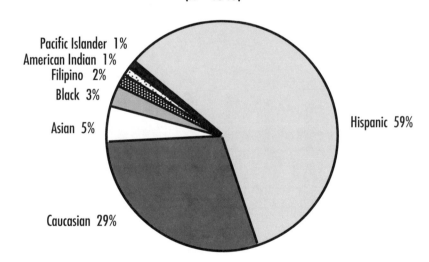

**Valley High School
Enrollment for 1997-98 by Ethnicity**
(N = 1543)

Pacific Islander 1%
American Indian 1%
Filipino 2%
Black 3%
Asian 5%
Caucasian 29%
Hispanic 59%

*Level 2—Snapshot of Valley High School Demographics,
Over Time*

Looking over time, in Figure 10, one can see how the ethnic makeup of Valley High changed dramatically since 1985. In 1985, the majority of students were Caucasian, followed by Hispanic and Asian. Over the years, the Caucasian population steadily decreased as the Hispanic population steadily increased at almost the same rate. By 1996, Hispanic students were the majority, followed by Caucasian students. The Asian population increased slightly.

Figure 10

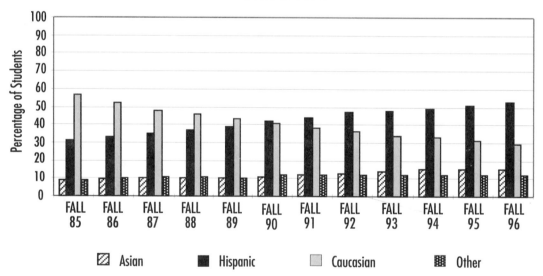

Level 3—Two or More Variables Crossed within Demographics

In 1996, a total of 533 Valley High students were eligible for Title I services, identified by the percentage of students qualifying for Free and Reduced Lunch. The chart below (Figure 11) shows the percentage breakdown of Title I students, by ethnicity.

Figure 11

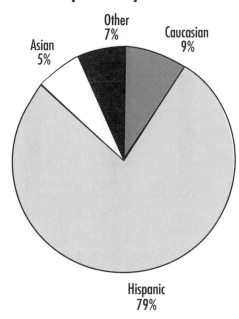

Valley High Students Eligible for Title I by Ethnicity in 1996

Other
7%

Caucasian
9%

Asian
5%

Hispanic
79%

Level 4—Two or More Variables Crossed within Demographics,
Over Time

The overall number of students eligible for Title I services at Valley High School decreased over time, from 571 in 1994, 583 in 1995, 533 in 1996, to 447 in 1997—from 46 percent of the population to 30 percent. Figure 12 shows the fluctuations by ethnicity.

Figure 12

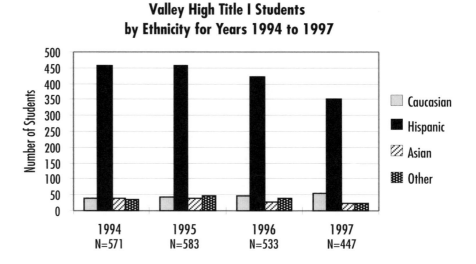

Valley High Title I Students
by Ethnicity for Years 1994 to 1997

Summary

Demographic data are very important to comprehensive data analysis for schoolwide improvement. Demographics establish the context of the school and describe the trends of the past which help staff understand all other measures with which they work in their schoolwide improvement efforts. Demographics allow the prediction of future conditions through a better understanding of "clients."

From our Forest Lane and Valley High examples, one can see how one year of enrollment data is valuable and informative. However, when we begin to look at enrollment over time, a different story appears. When we cross demographic variables, an even more comprehensive story of the conditions of our school begins to be told. One does not have to go back 10 years to get a complete look at the population changes; however, sometimes it is required—such as with Forest Lane and Valley High—to really understand when and how the population changed.

The comprehensive use of demographic data sets the stage for comprehensive data analysis.

Demographic and Disaggregation Questions

Below, think about the demographic data you have that will describe your school. How many years of complete and useable data do you have? How many years of data do you want to use in your analysis, keeping your school's guiding principles in mind?

Also, think about other demographic information you want to gather and how you will want to disaggregate and chart this information.

Demographic Data	Number of Years of Data Existing	Number of Years of Data Desired

The definition of perceptions and its synonyms provides almost enough information to understand why it is important to know the perceptions of our students, teachers, administrators, and parents.

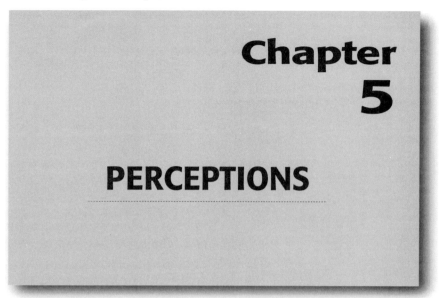

Chapter 5

PERCEPTIONS

The word perception leads us to such words as observation and opinion, with definitions that include—

- a view, judgment, or appraisal formed in the mind about a particular matter
- a belief stronger than impression and less strong than positive knowledge
- a generally held view
- a formal expression of judgment or advice
- a judgment one holds as true

Synonyms offered by Webster include opinion, view, belief, conviction, persuasion, and sentiment. The implications of these synonyms to comprehensive data analysis are discussed in the following text:

- *Opinion* implies a conclusion thought out yet open to dispute.
- *View* suggests a subjective opinion.
- *Belief* implies often deliberate acceptance and intellectual assent.
- *Conviction* applies to a firmly and seriously held belief.
- *Persuasion* suggests a belief grounded on assurance (as by evidence) of its truth.
- *Sentiment* suggests a settled opinion reflective of one's feelings.

All of us have perceptions of the way the world operates. We act upon those perceptions everyday as if they were reality. Basically, we do not act differently from what we value, believe, or perceive. In organizations, if we want to know what is possible (i.e., if we want to know how others are perceiving what is possible), we need to know the perceptions of the people who make up the organization. This might be the only way we can know that a shared vision truly exists.

> *Not to understand another person's way of thinking does not make that person confused.*
>
> Michael Quinn Patten

Changing Perceptions

Is it possible to change perceptions? Sure. How do we get perceptions to change? One way is through behavior changes. That means if a constituency does not believe in an approach we are taking in the classroom, one way to change the constituency's collective mind is to increase their understanding of the approach, possibly by giving them an opportunity to experience it. Awareness and experience can lead to basic shifts in attitudes and beliefs. That is why many schools have parent nights when there is a change in a math or technology curriculum. Giving parents an opportunity to understand and experience the approach helps them see a different perspective, which could make them more supportive of the program.

Another way to change perceptions is through "cognitive dissonance." Cognitive dissonance creates perception changes when people experience a conflict between what they believe and what they, or trusted sources, experience.

In order to change the way business is done, schools establish guiding principles which include the purpose and mission of the school, evolved from the values and beliefs of the individuals who make up the school community. Sometimes guiding principles are adopted that the school community *wants* and *hopes* to believe in, as opposed to those that they *do* believe in. Upon trying out behaviors that are consistent with these principles and observing positive impact, the individuals in the organization could change their internal thinking and begin believing in them. This is okay. Changed attitudes represent change at the deepest level of an organization's culture.

Too often, schools think of their guiding principles as being sacred and static. They might be sacred, but they should not be static. Even if a school keeps its guiding principles intact, their meaning evolves as people reflect and talk about them and as they are applied to guide decisions and actions.

An example of behavior changes preceding perception changes follows.

Blossom Middle School teachers were given a questionnaire about their values and beliefs about technology—how they believed technology would increase student learning, and in what ways e-mail, the Internet, and videoconferencing used in instructional units would impact student learning. Additionally, the students were given a questionnaire asking them similar questions and their impressions of the impact technology has had on their learning.

For two years, the results were almost the same; nothing was happening with respect to the implementation of technology or the attitudes about technology in the classroom. In the meantime, teachers were given professional development, and were strongly encouraged by administration to begin implementing technology in their curriculum. Then they were given a computer with an e-mail account.

During the following year, it became clear from the questionnaire results that the classrooms were different because teachers began using technology—first for their own benefit, and then with and for students. When their actions changed in the classroom and they actually started using the technology, their ideas and attitudes changed about the impact technology could have with respect to increasing student learning. It was also easy to see in the student questionnaire that their perceptions of the impact technology could have on their learning also changed—after the teachers' behaviors and attitudes changed.

Again, if we want attitudes to change—and we usually do as we implement new concepts and innovations—we need to change behaviors.

Assessing Perceptions

A common approach to understanding perceptions in schools is the use of questionnaires. Questionnaires are an excellent way to assess perceptions because they can be completed anonymously and readministered to assess the changes in perceptions over time. Appendix A focuses on the development and analysis of questionnaires. Appendix B contains several examples of questionnaires that work. There are other excellent ways to understand the perceptions of students, teachers, parents, and administrators. These include —

Do not underestimate the importance of helping people recognize what they already know.

Michael Quinn Patten

- ◆ observations
- ◆ person-to-person interviews
- ◆ telephone surveys
- ◆ focus groups

The advantages, disadvantages, and descriptions of when each questionnaire is most appropriate to use are summarized in Appendix A, Table A-1.

OUR EXAMPLE SCHOOLS

Perceptions of Forest Lane Elementary School

Forest Lane Elementary School chose to understand their students', teachers', and parents' perceptions of their school via questionnaires. Examples of their questionnaire results at different levels of analyses follow.

Level 1—Snapshot of Forest Lane Perceptions

1997 student perceptions of Forest Lane are shown in Figure 13 which follows. There are no items with which *all* students were in strongest agreement (i.e., all marking 5 on the five-point scale, with 1 being strongly disagree and 5 being strongly agree). From the questionnaire, one can see that the students were very much in strong agreement with the statements asking about their perceptions of the school. Only four items scored between 3 and 4 (in agreement), and none of the averages were in disagreement. The items that were the highest for this group of students were—

- My family wants me to do well in school
- My family believes I can do well in school
- My teacher believes I can learn
- My teacher is a good teacher
- My principal cares about me

Figure 13

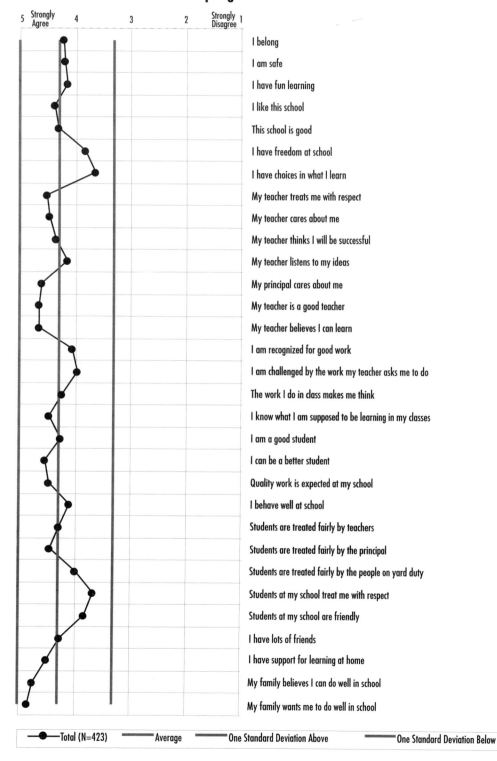

Forest Lane Total Student Responses
Spring 1997

Level 2—Snapshot of Forest Lane Perceptions, Over Time

Forest Lane surveyed the perceptions of students two years in a row, 1977 and 1998. Figure 14 compares the two years of data. As one can see, students were in stronger agreement with the statements in 1998 than they were in 1997. All of the 1998 response averages were in strong agreement (between 4 and 5).

Figure 14

Forest Lane Student Responses by Year
1997 and 1998

	Strongly Agree 5	4	3	2	Strongly Disagree 1	

I belong
I am safe
I have fun learning
I like this school
This school is good
I have freedom at school
I have choices in what I learn
My teacher treats me with respect
My teacher cares about me
My teacher thinks I will be successful
My teacher listens to my ideas
My principal cares about me
My teacher is a good teacher
My teacher believes I can learn
I am recognized for good work
I am challenged by the work my teacher asks me to do
I know what I am supposed to be learning in my classes
I am a good student
I can be a better student
Quality work is expected at my school
I behave well at school
Students are treated fairly by teachers
Students are treated fairly by the principal
Students are treated fairly by the people on yard duty
Students at my school treat me with respect
Students at my school are friendly
I have lots of friends
I have support for learning at home
My family believes I can do well in school
My family wants me to do well in school

■ Total Survey Respondents Spring 1997 (N=639)　　◇ Total Survey Respondents Spring 1998 (N=622)

Level 3—Two or More Perceptions of Forest Lane

In 1997, Forest Lane teachers responded to a questionnaire in terms of what they thought the students would say. The results of that questionnaire were compared to the student questionnaire results. Figure 15 shows that, in most cases, teachers thought students would be less positive in their responses to the questions. There were some significant differences between teacher predictions and student responses.

The greatest differences were in response to—

- Students are treated fairly by the people on yard duty
- I have support for learning at home
- I have choices in what I learn
- My family believes I can do well in school
- My family wants me to do well in school

In each of these cases, teachers predicted that students would respond less positive than they did.

Figure 15

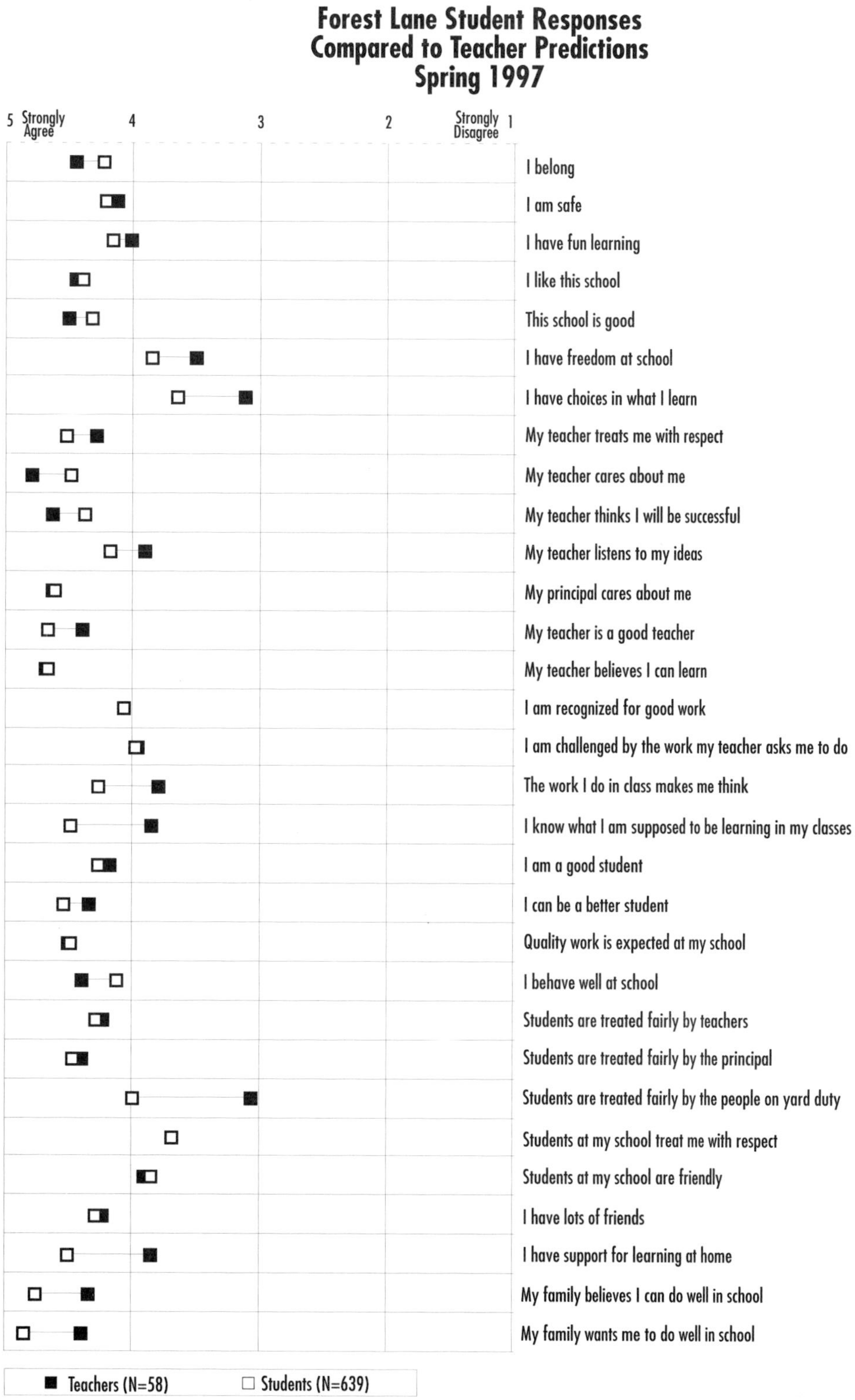

Forest Lane Student Responses Compared to Teacher Predictions Spring 1997

5 Strongly Agree	4	3	2	Strongly Disagree 1

I belong

I am safe

I have fun learning

I like this school

This school is good

I have freedom at school

I have choices in what I learn

My teacher treats me with respect

My teacher cares about me

My teacher thinks I will be successful

My teacher listens to my ideas

My principal cares about me

My teacher is a good teacher

My teacher believes I can learn

I am recognized for good work

I am challenged by the work my teacher asks me to do

The work I do in class makes me think

I know what I am supposed to be learning in my classes

I am a good student

I can be a better student

Quality work is expected at my school

I behave well at school

Students are treated fairly by teachers

Students are treated fairly by the principal

Students are treated fairly by the people on yard duty

Students at my school treat me with respect

Students at my school are friendly

I have lots of friends

I have support for learning at home

My family believes I can do well in school

My family wants me to do well in school

■ Teachers (N=58)　　□ Students (N=639)

Level 4—Two or More Perceptions of Forest Lane, Over Time

In Spring 1998, Forest Lane teachers and students completed the same questionnaire they took in 1997. Not only were the students in more agreement with the questions, as previously pointed out in Figure 14, the teachers were able to better predict student responses. Teachers predicted exactly what they thought students would say in fourteen items (see Figure 16).

Only two items had notable differences between the groups of respondents—

- I have freedom at school
- I have choices in what I learn

Teachers predicted that students would be in less agreement than they were.

Figure 16

**Forest Lane Student Responses
Compared to Teacher Predictions
Spring 1998**

5 Strongly Agree	4	3	2	1 Strongly Disagree	

I belong

I am safe

I have fun learning

I like this school

This school is good

I have freedom at school

I have choices in what I learn

My teacher treats me with respect

My teacher cares about me

My teacher thinks I will be successful

My teacher listens to my ideas

My principal cares about me

My teacher is a good teacher

My teacher believes I can learn

I am recognized for good work

My school work is challenging

I know what I am supposed to be learning in my classes

I am a good student

I can be a better student

Very good work is expected at my school

I behave well at school

Students are treated fairly by teachers

Students are treated fairly by the principal

Students are treated fairly by the people on yard duty

Students at my school treat me well

Students at my school are friendly

I have lots of friends

I have support for learning at home

My family believes I can do well in school

My family wants me to do well in school

■ Teachers (N=58)　　□ Students (N=649)

Perceptions of Valley High School

Level 1—Snapshot of Valley High School Perceptions

Valley High staff were concerned that too many freshmen students were receiving F's in their classes. In January 1997, they administered a questionnaire to understand freshmen student perceptions of the school. The results are shown in Figure 17.

The questionnaire showed that the students were in agreement with all but two statements—

- I would like help from a tutor
- The classwork/homework at Valley is easy

There were no items in which all freshmen responded to as "strongly agree."

Level 2—Snapshot of Valley High School Perceptions, Over Time

Valley High staff administered the same questionnaire to freshmen in January 1998. The results, also displayed in Figure 17, show that the freshmen responses in 1998 were almost identical to the freshmen responses in 1997.

Figure 17

Valley High School Freshman Student Responses by Year
January 1997 and 1998

5 Strongly Agree	4	3	2	Strongly Disagree 1	

I feel safe at Valley High

I feel like I belong at Valley High

I am treated with respect by teachers, security, administrators, and staff

I feel adequately informed about the support services at Valley High

I would like help from a tutor

The classwork/homework at Valley High is challenging

The classwork/homework at Valley High is at my level

The classwork/homework at Valley High is easy

I am trying my best at school

My teachers set high academic standards in the classroom

My teachers set high behavioral standards in the classroom

The students at Valley High are friendly

I have a regularly scheduled quiet time to do homework at home

I feel academically prepared for my classes at Valley High

■ Total Survey Respondents January 1997 (N=431)   ▲ Total Survey Respondents January 1998 (N=378)

Level 3—Two or More Perceptions

Valley High parents of freshmen responded to a questionnaire in Spring 1996 about their perceptions of Valley High School. The parents were in agreement with most items as shown in Figure 18.

They responded in strong agreement to the following five items:

- I feel welcome at my student's school
- I respect the school's principal
- The variety of elective offerings is important to my child's education
- I support my student's learning at home
- My student is happy at this school

Parents disagreed with the following four items:

- Class sizes are reasonable at this school
- Teachers communicate often with parents about their student's progress
- Teachers communicate with parents aside from grades
- I volunteer at this school

Figure 18 (Page 1)

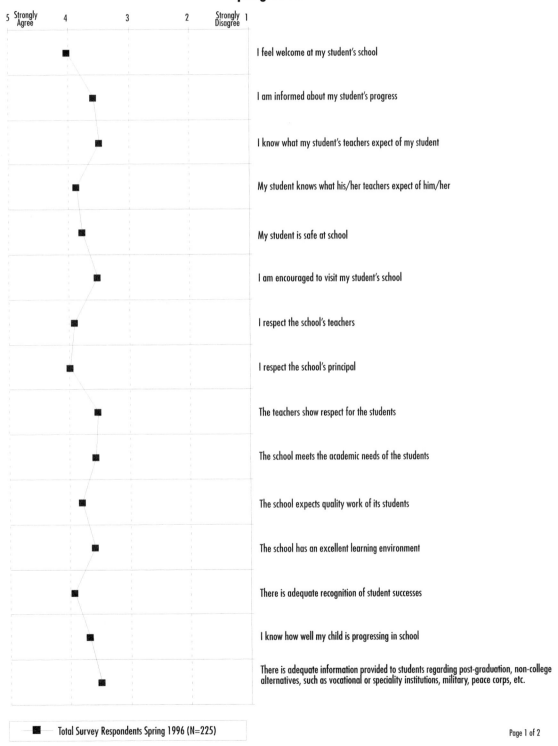

**Valley High School Parent Responses
Spring 1996**

| | | | | |
|5 Strongly Agree | 4 | 3 | 2 | Strongly Disagree 1 |

I feel welcome at my student's school

I am informed about my student's progress

I know what my student's teachers expect of my student

My student knows what his/her teachers expect of him/her

My student is safe at school

I am encouraged to visit my student's school

I respect the school's teachers

I respect the school's principal

The teachers show respect for the students

The school meets the academic needs of the students

The school expects quality work of its students

The school has an excellent learning environment

There is adequate recognition of student successes

I know how well my child is progressing in school

There is adequate information provided to students regarding post-graduation, non-college alternatives, such as vocational or speciality institutions, military, peace corps, etc.

■ Total Survey Respondents Spring 1996 (N=225)

Page 1 of 2

55

Figure 18 (Page 2)

Valley High School Parent Responses
Spring 1996 (Continued)

Level 4—Two or More Perceptions, Over Time

In 1997, parents of freshmen at Valley High were asked to respond to the parent survey to which the 1996 parents of freshmen also responded. The responses in 1996 and 1997 were charted together and are shown in Figure 19.

Overall, the responses were almost identical. The 1997 parents were in slightly stronger agreement where there were differences. One item with which parents were in disagreement in 1996, but parents were in agreement with in 1997 was, "I volunteer at this school."

Figure 19 (Page1)

Valley High School Parent Responses
1996 and 1997

5 Strongly Agree	4	3	2	Strongly Disagree 1	

I feel welcome at my student's school

I am informed about my student's progress

I know what my student's teachers expect of my student

My student knows what his/her teachers expect of him/her

My student is safe at school

I am encouraged to visit my student's school

I respect the school's teachers

I respect the school's principal

The teachers show respect for the students

The school meets the academic needs of the students

The school expects quality work of its students

The school has an excellent learning environment

There is adequate recognition of student successes

I know how well my child is progressing in school

There is adequate information provided to students regarding post-graduation, non-college alternatives, such as vocational or speciality institutions, military, peace corps, etc.

■ Total Survey Respondents Spring 1996 (N=225)   △ Total Survey Respondents Spring 1997 (N=170)

Figure 19 (Page 2)

Valley High School Parent Responses
1996 and 1997 (Continued)

Scale				
5 Strongly Agree	4	3	2	1 Strongly Disagree

There is adequate information for students concerning college selections, college requirements, scholarship opportunities, and testing

The variety of elective offerings is important to my child's education

Parent volunteer needs are clearly communicated to parents

There are well-organized extracurricular activities for my student to participate in

The school adequately uses technology in education

My student's amount of homework is appropriate for his/her grade level and class content

My student feels challenged by his/her courses

Class sizes are reasonable at this school

Teachers communicate often with parents about their student's progress

Teachers communicate with parents aside from grades

My student knows what staff members to approach for help

My student gets the support s/he needs from the staff

New students receive adequate orientation to the school and its program offerings

I support my student's learning at home

My student is happy at this school

I volunteer at this school

■ Total Survey Respondents Spring 1996 (N=225)   △ Total Survey Respondents Spring 1997 (N=170)   Page 2 of 2

59

Summary

It is important to understand what the individuals who make up the school community are thinking or perceiving—it informs us of what they believe should be changed—which tells us what is possible with respect to schoolwide change. If stakeholders in the community do not believe in the changes we want to make, the changes cannot be made.

It is important to ask the same questions over time in order to see change. Changing items on a questionnaire will keep schools from seeing progress and from understanding what changes need to be made. Looking only at one year of questionnaire data is interesting; however, looking over time gives staff valuable information about possibilities and progress. Comparing responses from different school stakeholders gives compelling evidence and reinforcement. Appendix A focuses on the questionnaire process—from writing the questions, to analyzing the results.

Questionnaire Questions

Think about the questionnaires that you want to design, administer, and analyze. What information do you want to glean from the questionnaires? Please review the chart in Appendix A entitled "Begin with the End in Mind" before you begin. The questions below are a starting point.

What is the purpose for administering a questionnaire? What information do you want to collect?

To whom do you need to give the questionnaires in order to get this information?

How do you want the results displayed (i.e., charts, graphs, tables, distributions, percentages, comparisons)?

By what categories will you want to disaggregate the responses?

How will you administer each of the questionnaires?

How will you get the information from the questionnaires into some form, such as a database, that will allow you to chart the results?

Who is going to do the work?

The focus of most comprehensive school improvement efforts is on increasing the learning of all students. Measures of student learning help us understand how students are performing and what students know as a result of instruction. Before thinking about *how* to measure student learning, however, schools must be clear on *why* they are assessing student learning. Only then can they gain the congruence needed in an assessment program and really achieve those student learning increases.

Chapter 6

STUDENT LEARNING

Purposes for Measuring Student Learning

The most commonly stated reasons schools give for measuring student learning include the following:

- make sure students "do not fall through the cracks"
- assess individual or group achievement
- diagnose learning problems
- certificate/graduate students
- guide curriculum development and revision
- improve instruction
- be accountable
- understand which programs are getting the results we want
- know if we are achieving our standards
- know how we compare to others in the nation

> *We need to spend more time, energy, and attention on asking the question: Why we are assessing students— rather than how.*
>
> National Leadership Network

Unclear in these reasons is whether the goal of measuring student learning is increased student learning or higher test scores. Schools need to be honest with themselves about which it is. The true purpose for measuring student learning is obvious in the manner in which a school uses its student learning results. The values and priorities of the organization are revealed in these uses.

Many of our workshop participants say student learning results get used at their schools as follows:

- A report is developed and presented to the school board.
- The superintendent is evaluated on the results and is replaced if the results do not improve within three years.
- Program longevity is determined.

Ways to Measure Student Learning

A student assessment program that truly meets the needs of every student must be congruent with its purposes, uses, and practices. The program can then begin to predict not only needs, but also the approaches required to meet those needs.

While we know that student learning measures must be interpreted in context, with the understanding of other variables that impact it, traditionally student learning has been measured by one or more of the terms listed below:

> *The way in which a local school assesses student outcomes accurately represents the educational outcomes that the school cares most about.*
>
> Lawrence Lezotte
> and Beverly Bancroft

- standardized tests
- norm referenced tests
- criterion referenced measures
- authentic assessments
- teacher-made tests
- teacher-assigned grades
- performance assessments
- standards-based assessments

Analyses of all types of student learning measures used in the school can help one know if all students are learning, and if true learning can be detected better with one measure rather than another. Looking across measures, teachers can determine how the different measures contrast in performance, and if students perform differently on one type of test versus another. Comparing results on different measures gives teachers insight into what teaching strategies, as well as testing strategies, work best with different students.

While it is impossible to obtain a perfect measure of any student's achievement, standardized tests are commonly used as indicators. If teachers know what is on the test, and if what is on the test is consistent with what and how they are teaching in the curriculum, they are not necessarily bad measures of student learning.

The word "standardized" in reference to testing describes tests that are uniform in content, administration, and scoring, and therefore allow for the comparison of results across classrooms, schools, school districts, and states. Standardized tests consist of items that assess the extent to which a student has acquired certain content or mastered certain skills.

With *standardized* tests we can look at individual student gains and the gains of groups of students disaggregated to understand the impact of educational programs on the students. Standardized achievement tests make it possible to compare an individual's score to groups of people, and groups to other groups, to understand if a program is making a difference.

Norm referenced standardized tests are based upon the assumption that any trait that we are trying to measure will resemble a normal curve (Figure 20), with the majority of scores falling in the center and then spreading out equally on either side. Norm referenced testing is based on relative standards and answers the question: "How are the students doing in comparison to others in the norming group?" (Normality is an idealization—measures can be meaningful without assuming normality.)

Criterion referenced tests assess definite instructional objectives. They are designed to measure the results of instruction to assess specific instructional or behavioral objectives. Criterion referenced testing is based upon absolute standards and answers the question: "What can the students do?" Criterion referenced tests can be standardized across large populations of students, or they can be classroom based. Teacher-made tests are criterion referenced, except when teachers grade "on the curve."

Standardized Achievement Tests

Interpreting Standardized Achievement Test Scores

The interpretation of standardized test scores involves comparisons of performance to a standard. Criterion referencing is an interpretation of scores with respect to a fixed performance level, while norm referencing is an interpretation of scores with respect to other people who took the test.

Most standardized aptitude tests use norm referenced scoring. The norming group, a representative sample of the group for whom the test is intended, serves as a comparison for score interpretation. Typical scores and their definitions follow. How they relate to each other on the normal curve is illustrated in Figure 20.

Figure 20

The Normal Curve

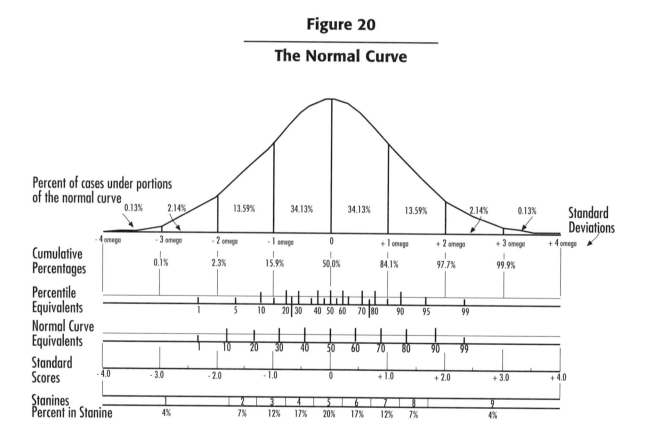

The Normal Curve, Percentiles, and Standard Scores

Raw scores are the numbers of questions answered correctly by the student. Raw scores are the basis for all other types of scores. Derived scores are interpretations of raw scores and provide information about the standing of a particular score relative to the norming group.

Derived scores include, but are not limited to, the following:

- *Percentile scores, or percentile equivalents* express the percentage of scores in the norming group that fall below a particular score.

- *Standard scores* compare a student's performance to that of other students at the same grade level on a normal curve.

- *Normal curve equivalent (NCE) scores* are normalized standard scores. NCE's were calculated by test publishers to have equal intervals that can be used for making comparisons. NCE's use a score of 50 to indicate an expected year's growth. In other words, an NCE score of 50 is what we expect an "average" student to achieve at any normed grade level. Therefore, a student who maintains the same score from one year to the next has achieved one year of growth.

- *Stanines* is a standard score system that divides the normal population on a nine-unit scale (standard nines from one to nine).

- *Grade-equivalent* scores express performance as the grade and month at which a particular score is thought to represent typical performance. A grade-equivalent score does not necessarily imply that the student possesses readiness for the grade level indicated. What it indicates is that the score is equivalent to the norming group average.

- *Age norms* express a number that would imply an equivalent score to the norming age group.

Standard deviation is another term often used with test scores. A standard deviation is a number that indicates the amount of variation across all scores and is also calculated for each item. A small standard deviation indicates that the scores are close together. A large standard deviation indicates that the scores that make up the average are quite varied.

Reporting Norm Referenced Performance

Test publishers send reports to schools that often look like the following Example Test Report (Figure 21).

Figure 21

Example Test Report

TBS/4

Tests of Basic Skills, Fourth Edition

District Evaluation Summary

Grade 1

	READING VOCAB.	COMPR.	TOTAL	MATHEMATICS C & A	WORD ANALYSIS
Number of Students	122	120	120	122	122
Grade Equivalent					
Grade Mean Equivalent	1.4	1.4	1.4	1.7	
Standard Deviation	0.6	0.8	0.6	1.0	
Normal Curve Equivalent					
Mean	43.7	42.6	43.0	53.3	47.3
Standard Deviation	18.9	19.8	18.1	26.3	20.4
NP of Mean NCE	38	36	37	56	45
SCALE Scores					
Mean	531.5	523.6	528.4	552.4	536.1
Standard Deviation	62.3	78.8	62.5	83.7	57.8

Which scores should schools use to report to the community and for the purposes mentioned earlier in this chapter?

Normal Curve Equivalent (NCE) scores were developed to avoid problems that often occur with other types of scores. School personnel frequently try to analyze percentile scores. However, percentile scores should never be added, subtracted, or averaged because the distance between points is not equal. At the upper and lower ends of the scale, the points are farther apart than in the middle because they represent a distribution where the majority of scores are found to be in the middle. NCE's were derived to have an average of fifty and a standard deviation of 21.06. This value was selected because it produces an exact match between NCE's of 1 and 99 and percentiles of 1 and 99. NCE's are an equal interval scale and can be aggregated and averaged. If you want to know how your students performed compared to other students, states, and the nation, you can convert the analyzed NCE scores to percentiles, by using Table 2. If you need to convert percentile ranks to NCE's, use Table 3. Note how the conversion can be more exact going from NCE scores to percentiles. A conversion in the opposite direction uses an average NCE. Standard scores also have equal intervals and can be used in the same way NCE scores can be used.

Table 2

NCE to Percentile Conversion

NCE Range	Percentile Rank	NCE Range	Percentile Rank	NCE Range	Percentile Rank	NCE Range	Percentile Rank
1.0 - 4.0	1	36.1-36.7	26	50.3-50.7	51	64.6-65.1	76
4.1 - 8.5	2	36.8-37.3	27	50.8-51.2	52	65.2-65.8	77
8.6-11.7	3	37.4-38.0	28	51.3-51.8	53	65.9-66.5	78
11.8-14.1	4	38.1-38.6	29	51.9-52.3	54	66.6-67.3	79
14.2-16.2	5	38.7-39.2	30	52.4-52.8	55	67.4-68.0	80
16.3-18.0	6	39.3-39.8	31	52.9-53.4	56	68.1-68.6	81
18.1-19.6	7	39.9-40.4	32	53.5-53.9	57	68.7-69.6	82
19.7-21.0	8	40.5-40.9	33	54.0-54.4	58	69.7-70.4	83
21.1-22.3	9	41.0-41.5	34	54.5-55.0	59	70.5-71.3	84
22.4-23.5	10	41.6-42.1	35	55.1-55.5	60	71.4-72.2	85
23.6-24.6	11	42.2-42.7	36	55.6-56.1	61	72.3-73.1	86
24.7-25.7	12	42.8-43.2	37	56.2-56.6	62	73.2-74.1	87
25.8-26.7	13	43.3-43.8	38	56.7-57.2	63	74.2-75.2	88
26.8-27.6	14	43.9-44.3	39	57.3-57.8	64	75.3-76.3	89
27.7-28.5	15	44.4-44.9	40	57.9-58.3	65	76.4-77.5	90
28.6-29.4	16	45.0-45.4	41	58.4-58.9	66	77.6-78.8	91
29.5-30.2	17	45.5-45.9	42	59.0-59.5	67	78.9-80.2	92
30.3-31.0	18	46.0-46.5	43	59.6-60.1	68	80.3-81.7	93
31.1-31.8	19	46.6-47.0	44	60.2-60.7	69	81.8-83.5	94
31.9-32.6	20	47.1-47.5	45	60.8-61.3	70	83.6-85.5	95
32.7-33.3	21	47.6-48.1	46	61.4-61.9	71	85.6-88.0	96
33.4-34.0	22	48.2-48.6	47	62.0-62.5	72	88.1-91.0	97
34.1-34.7	23	48.7-49.1	48	62.6-63.1	73	91.1-96.4	98
34.8-35.4	24	49.2-49.6	49	63.2-63.8	74	96.5-99.0	99
35.5-36.0	25	49.7-50.2	50	63.9-64.5	75		

Table 3

Percentile to NCE Conversion

NCE Range	Percentile Rank	NCE Range	Percentile Rank	NCE Range	Percentile Rank	NCE Range	Percentile Rank
1.0	1	36.5	26	50.5	51	64.9	76
6.7	2	37.1	27	51.1	52	65.6	77
10.4	3	37.7	28	51.6	53	66.3	78
13.1	4	38.3	29	52.1	54	67.0	79
15.4	5	39.0	30	52.6	55	67.7	80
17.3	6	39.6	31	53.2	56	68.5	81
18.9	7	40.1	32	53.7	57	69.3	82
20.4	8	40.7	33	54.2	58	70.1	83
21.8	9	41.3	34	54.8	59	70.9	84
23.0	10	41.9	35	55.3	60	71.8	85
24.2	11	42.5	36	55.9	61	72.8	86
25.3	12	43.0	37	56.4	62	73.7	87
26.3	13	43.6	38	57.0	63	74.7	88
27.2	14	44.1	39	57.5	64	75.8	89
28.2	15	44.7	40	58.1	65	77.0	90
29.1	16	45.2	41	58.7	66	78.2	91
29.9	17	45.8	42	59.3	67	79.6	92
30.7	18	46.3	43	59.9	68	81.1	93
31.5	19	46.8	44	60.4	69	82.7	94
32.3	20	47.4	45	61.0	70	84.6	95
33.0	21	47.9	46	61.7	71	86.9	96
33.7	22	48.4	47	62.3	72	89.6	97
34.4	23	48.9	48	62.9	73	93.3	98
35.1	24	49.5	49	63.5	74	99.0	99
35.8	25	50.0	50	64.2	75		

Reporting Standardized Testing Over Time

If at all possible, use the same assessment device and matched scores to look at growth of the same students over time. If matched scores are not possible, at least follow the same groups of students (cohorts) over time (e.g., first grade 1994, second grade 1995, third grade 1996, etc.). Figure 22 on the next page shows how to follow cohorts of students to understand their achievement, as measured by NCE's on a standardized test, over time.

Another common way to analyze test scores is to look at the percentage of respondents scoring above or below certain levels. You can use almost any derived score to chart this way, as long as you are careful with the interpretation. For the most part, it is wise to avoid grade-and age-equivalent scoring. Too many misinterpretations and misconceptions are made around these results.

Figure 22

Charting Standardized Achievement Scores

If the scores are matched, i.e., the, students are the same from one year to the next, we can make comparisons.

A NCE score of 50 is calculated by test publishers to be the average score from one year of teaching at any grade level.

A gain of zero does not mean that nothing was learned. It means that students achieved one year's growth in one year's time (as measured by this particular test).
(3rd grade to 4th grade scores)

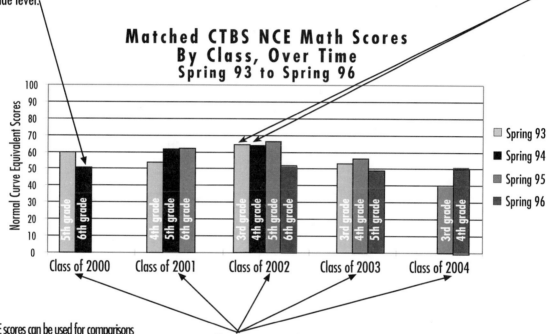

Matched CTBS NCE Math Scores
By Class, Over Time
Spring 93 to Spring 96

Follow the same students over time, or, at minimum, the same classes.

NCE scores can be used for comparisons because they:
- have equal intervals
- can be aggregated and averaged
- have a derived average of 50, and a standard deviation of 21.06
- can be compared from one test to another
- can be compared from one grade to another
- can be used to calculate gain scores
- match percentiles of 1 to 99
- can be converted to percentiles after analysis

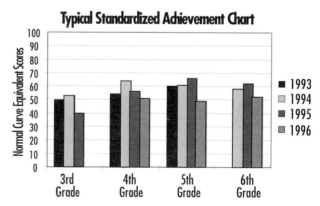

Typical Standardized Achievement Chart

Most often, Student Achievement scores are charted for one year, by grade level, implying that one could make meaningful comparisons from grade-to-grade, which we really cannot, because the scores do not represent the same students.

The first graph in Figure 23 shows the percentage of third graders reading 35 or more words per minute by October, for four years. The district's goal, or standard, is to have 80 percent of all third graders reading 35 or more words per minute by October. Unfortunately, this chart shows that in no year, in the past four years, did the district achieve its goal. This chart does not provide enough information for the district to act differently to get different results, so they created the second chart that looked at the average number of words students not meeting the standard were reading by the type of support program in which they were participating. This chart shows that students who were Title I eligible, limited-English proficient (LEP), and migrant were reading only 17 words a minute, on an average, while Title I students were reading 20 words per minute, and resource students were reading 25 words per minute.

Disaggregating further, the district found that male resource students read 25 words a minute, on an average, while girls in the resource program met the standard. Title I males read 23 words per minute, and Title I females read 19 words a minute. Of the group representing Title I, LEP, and migrant, females were reading more words per minute (20 wpm) than males (6 wpm). Disaggregating helped the district pinpoint where the lowest readers were programmatically.

Figure 23

Using District Standards

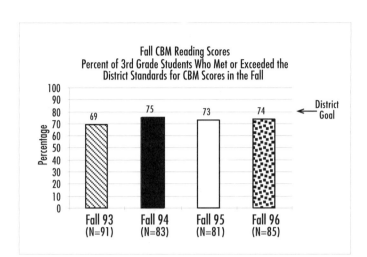

Using their standard of "80% of all 3rd grade students will read 35 or more words per minute by October," this district evaluated the fall reading scores for its 3rd graders for the current year and the previous three years.

Although the current year was slightly higher than the previous year, fewer than 80% of the students were reading at 35 words per minute or higher.

To try to determine where best to focus efforts, the district looked at the students who had not met the standards in the current year by the support services they receive.

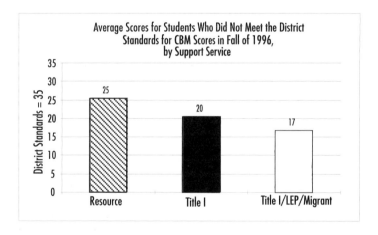

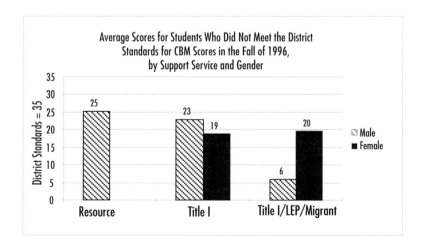

Next, the district looked at students who did not meet the district standards, by both support service and gender.

Measurement Error

We often hear people talk about sample sizes being too small to make any conclusions. Typically what this means is that the larger the number of students in a sample the more confidence we have that the score is an accurate reflection of that sample group's abilities. We also want to know if the increases showing up in a testing program in any year are because of "true" increases in learning. In order to understand a "true" gain resulting from an instructional program, we construct confidence bands that give each score a range as opposed to a single number. This range provides flexibility in understanding what the score would be if there were "errors" in the test. The table that follows (Table 4) gives the calculated standard error of measure for normal NCE's.

To construct a confidence band, consider that a group of five students had an average score of 40 on a reading test. We need to look at Table 4, the Give and Take Table, to see that the error of measurement associated with the five students in this group is 4.5—the smaller the number of students, the more likely it is that the average represents a chance occurrence or error. For example, if four students took a test with 100 points possible, three of them scored 90 points, and the fourth came in late, only finished part of the test, and scored 50 points, the average for that group would be 80. If the total number taking a test were 20, 19 of whom scored 90 points and one who scored 50, the average score would be 88—more reflective of the group average. The smaller the group, the more weight each individual pulls in the overall average. The confidence band would then be formed from 35.5 to 44.5 (i.e., 40 - 4.5 = 35.5; 40 + 4.5 = 44.5). The interpretation: We can feel confident (68 percent of the time—one standard deviation) that the average true score of these students would be somewhere between 35.5 and 44.5. We can feel 95 percent confident that the average true score would be between 31 and 49 (double the size of the band—two standard deviations—2 x 4.5 = 9) (i.e., 40 - 9 = 31; 40+ 9 = 49).

Table 4

Give and Take Table

Number of Students	Error (NCE's)	Number of Students	Error (NCE's)
1	10.1	20	2.3
2	7.1	25	2.0
3	5.8	30	1.8
4	5.1	35	1.7
5	4.5	40	1.6
6	4.1	45	1.5
7	3.8	50	1.4
8	3.6	75	1.2
9	3.4	100	1.0
10	3.2	200	0.7
15	2.6	300	0.6

Authentic Assessments

Authentic assessments refer to a variety of tools which are based upon the idea that a student's real work is the test of what the student knows and is able to do. While traditional testing requires that students answer questions correctly (often on multiple choice tests), authentic assessments require that students demonstrate knowledge and skills, including the process by which they solve problems.

Authentic assessment measures may include—

Exhibitions: Students present their knowledge and defend their work before an audience (peers, parents, school partners, etc.). Exhibitions usually include written work, visual aids, and an oral presentation. In some schools, students use multimedia for their presentations.

Portfolios: Student portfolios are purposeful collections of student work that are tied to standards students are striving to attain.

Performance assessments: These assessments measure applications of knowledge such as the ability to integrate knowledge across disciplines, contribute to the work of a group, and/or develop a plan of action when confronted with a new situation. Performance assessments may be the product of the student's actual work, as in projects, or may be designed as a separate assessment.

Projects: Students work on real problems which often cross subject areas. Projects generally involve several weeks or more of work usually in cooperative groups, are open-ended, and provide students with choices in how they will pursue the project. An exhibition may be the culminating experience of the project.

Developmentally appropriate assessments: This term refers to a variety of measures that allow students to demonstrate their knowledge at their level of development. Most authentic measures are developmentally appropriate in that they allow students to show what they know, rather than focus on what they don't know. Schools and districts need to be careful about developmental appropriateness in designing or choosing assessments, especially in the primary grades.

Rubrics: Rubrics are generally a scoring matrix in which levels of work are described. Rubrics are often used in combination with authentic assessments such as those mentioned above.

If there are numbers associated with these measures, they can be charted and disaggregated for fuller analyses. Figure 24, which follows, shows rubric scores for the writing assessment for cohorts of students, charted over time.

Standards-based Assessments

Standards-based assessments are based upon an agreement that students will demonstrate their learning in specified ways and at a clearly specified level of achievement.

There are different types of standards-based assessments. Content standards identify what students are to learn. Performance standards describe the work students must produce to demonstrate that they have met the standards. Standards-based assessments are criterion referenced, i.e., the standard is the criterion for measurement. A variety of measures from projects and exhibitions to standardized tests could be used to know whether students meet a standard.

Figure 24

Interpreting Teacher Level "Authentic Assessment" Charts and Analyses

1996 Writing Assessment

Ms. Smith's third grade writing assessment subscores compared
to the third grade average for the school and the district.

The school averages were lower than the district and Ms. Smith's class averages in the areas of Autobiography and Problem-Solving, and averaged slightly higher than the district in the area of Story Development.

Ms. Smith's class averages were higher than the school and the district averages on all four sections of the 1996 Writing Assessment.

The school outscored the district in the report of information writing subtest.

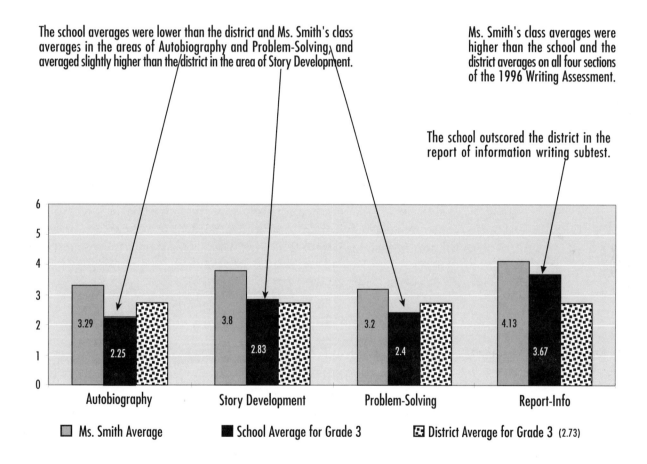

☐ Ms. Smith Average   ■ School Average for Grade 3   ⊞ District Average for Grade 3 (2.73)

Setting standards is a judgmental process. The standards are subjective by definition. It is important for local standards to yield measurements that—

- provide reliable selection or classification of individuals
- validly support inferences concerning the achievements, aptitudes, and performance capabilities of those assessed
- fairly and unbiasedly reflect the abilities of those assessed without regard to gender, ethnicity, and socioeconomic condition
- support classification of examinees into decision-relevant categories when necessary (e.g., beginning, proficient, advanced, graduation, certification)

Charting standards-based assessments can be tricky. Our goal is to provide quality information that will allow us to know not only how well all students are doing, but to also know how we can assist all students to improve their learning.

Figure 25 shows examples of standards-based assessment tables. The first chart shows average scores for the different groups of students, the numbers of students in each group, and the percentage of students meeting or exceeding the district standard. The chart shows that each of the subgroup averages are below the district standard of 4.0. Many interpretations by districts of this type of chart are misleading. When looking only at the averages, many say all students scored below the district standard—which is not correct— the *average* score is below the district standard. Many districts also want to jump to solutions and lower the standard when they see these kinds of results. As Figure 25 explains, this information is quite limiting to the district for schoolwide improvement. Many misinterpretations can be made. A much more effective manner of charting this same information would be to simply display the number of children in each of the groups who scored at the different levels. That way the district is able to see if all groups of students are having difficulty with the same concept, and determine how many students are performing above the district standard. In order to do something about the problem of students not meeting the district standard, this information must be dealt with at the school and classroom levels. The other important piece of information that this type of analysis can provide is a clear view of the quality of the standard and how it performs with the intended students.

Figure 25

Assessing Standards for Improvement

Departments of Education ask schools to provide an average score for each group of student, and to show the percentage of students meeting the standard.

Writing Assessment

Group	Average	Number of Students	Percentage of Students Meeting the Standard
GATE	3.84	40	70%
LEP	2.54	245	18%
Title I	2.56	900	18%
Special Ed	2.00	76	6%
Migrant	2.32	80	8%

District Standard = 4.0

Interpretations of this chart might include:
• The majority of students in this district have scored below the district standard
• Not even Gate kids are above the district standard
• We need to lower our standards

Before lowering your standards, consider different analyses, such as...looking at the numbers of students scoring in each rubric option. (Averages do not provide substantive information.)

Rubric Score	GATE	LEP	Title I	Special Ed	Migrant
6	2	0	1	0	1
5	12	9	31	1	0
4	14	36	126	4	5
3	8	75	293	11	27
2	2	83	312	38	32
1	2	47	137	22	15

From this analysis the school is able to locate "who" is falling below the district standard.

School 1, Grade 2

Rubric Score	GATE		LEP		Title I		Special Ed		Migrant	
	M	F	M	F	M	F	M	F	M	F
6										
5										
4				1		1				1
3			3	6	15	17				2
2			6	6	8	10			3	2
1				4	9	6				1

Further analysis such as looking at the scores by school, grade level, and gender, gets us closer to identifying which students need support, and, with the rubric ratings, what kind of support can be determined.

Determining Measurement Approaches

In determining the types of measures to use to assess student learning, there are considerations that guide our decisions, such as—

- What is the purpose for assessing student learning?

- What do you ask students to do every day?

- Is the product they produce daily enough to meet your school's purpose for assessing student learning?

- Are the general goals and content of the test similar to those of the setting in which the test is used?

- Are reliability and validity of the measures adequate?

Some contend that the response format does not allow students to demonstrate complex cognitive skills. Another allegation is that the test content may shape the classroom curriculum. A third contention is that tests may be biased—underrepresented groups tend to score lower than the majority population. Truth-in-testing laws require that results of standardized tests and exam questions and answers be released to the public upon request.

Disadvantages of authentic assessment are that they usually include fewer questions and call for a greater degree of subjective judgment than traditional testing methods. Since there are no clear right or wrong answers, teachers have to decide how to grade students and determine what distinguishes an average performance from an excellent one. This potential disadvantage can be avoided with an evaluation rubric (rating scale with several categories) that clearly defines the characteristics of poor, average, and excellent performances so teachers can score performances in a consistent manner. Again, the way one chooses their assessment practices depends upon the purposes of and uses for the results.

Looking Across Student Learning Measures

Even though one should not put more than one kind of measurement scale into one chart, charts of different measures can be generally compared, as shown in Figure 26. By looking at these charts, we can see different distributions and begin to understand about student motivation and learning styles.

Figure 26

Multiple Measures of Student Learning

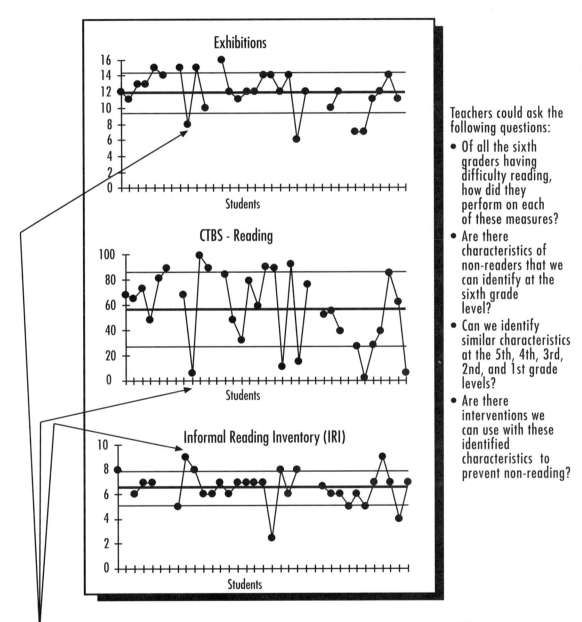

Teachers could ask the following questions:

- Of all the sixth graders having difficulty reading, how did they perform on each of these measures?

- Are there characteristics of non-readers that we can identify at the sixth grade level?

- Can we identify similar characteristics at the 5th, 4th, 3rd, 2nd, and 1st grade levels?

- Are there interventions we can use with these identified characteristics to prevent non-reading?

Looking at individual student measures gives teachers valuable information about how the different measures perform, learning styles and motivation of individual students, and begins to build a continuum of learning for students.

Other Common Testing Terms

Other common terms associated with testing are defined below. Please see the References and Resources section at the end of this book for further information about these terms.

Validity

The validity of a test or assessment refers to whether it provides the type of information desired. Validity can be enhanced by asking appropriate questions that get to what you want to know.

Different types of validity include the following:

+ *Content validity* relates to the appropriateness of the items with respect to the content, instruction, or the curriculum being measured.

+ *Predictive validity* refers to a test's ability to predict future performance in the area that the instrument is measuring.

+ *Face validity* relates to the appearance that the test measures what it claims to measure.

+ *Construct validity* refers to the degree to which the test actually measures the particular construct (trait or aptitude) in question.

+ *Concurrent validity* refers to the scores on a test being related to currently existing measures of the same content or behavior.

Reliability

The reliability of a test or assessment relates to the consistency with which knowledge is measured. Reliability tells us that if students were to take the test more than once they would get the same (or nearly the same) score.

Reliability is impacted by—

+ asking appropriate questions that would get to what you want to know (cannot be reliable if not valid)

+ the length of the test (with other things being equal)

+ the range of item difficulty (more variation of item difficulty tends to lower reliability and range restriction tends to lower reliability, i.e., the more varied the difficulty level of the test, the greater the reliability)

+ the consistency of the testing environment among test sites

OUR EXAMPLE SCHOOLS

Level 1—Snapshot of Forest Lane Student Learning

Forest Lane Elementary School is concerned about all students reading on grade level by grade 3. The teachers looked at the Spring 1998 results of the CTBS (Comprehensive Tests of Basic Skills) Reading Test for grade 3 (see Figure 27). With a district standard of 36 NCE, they could see from the overall chart that more students did not meet the standards on each subtest than did meet the standards.

Student Learning at Forest Lane Elementary School

Figure 27

**Forest Lane Elementary
Percentage of 3rd Grade Students Meeting CTBS Reading
Spring 1998 N=173**

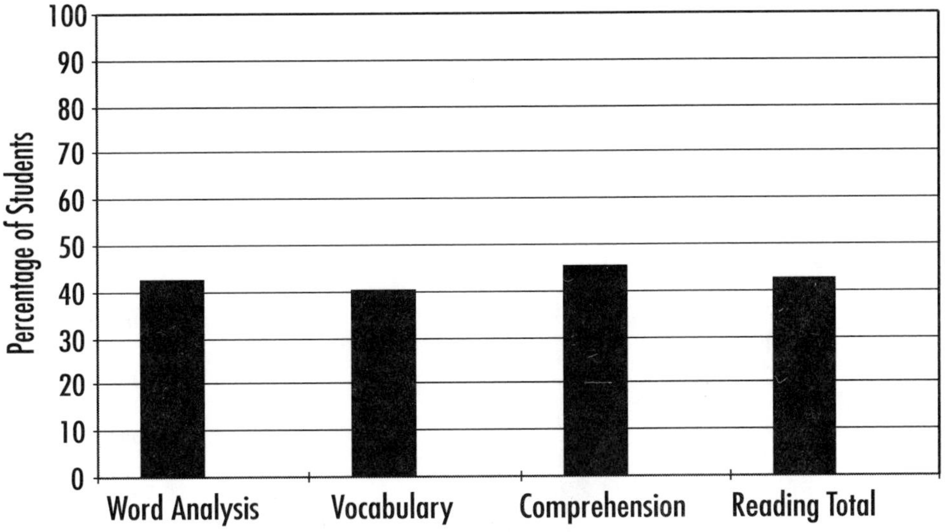

Level 2—Snapshot of Forest Lane Student Learning, Over Time

In order to get a bigger picture of how the school has been doing over time, Forest Lane teachers looked at school-level CTBS Reading Subscore Test results for the same set of third graders over three years (Figure 28). From this chart, the teachers could see that more students met the standards in 1996 than met it for the following two years. Some of the fluctuation is due to the change in numbers taking the test. In 1996, 120 students took the test. The increase in numbers taking the test in the following years was due to the increase in second language learners taking the test. This also explains the decrease in scores on the CTBS in 1997. The increase in scores in 1998 would show true gains with a population that could have difficulty with the English reading test.

Figure 28

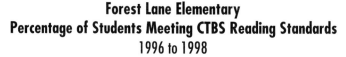

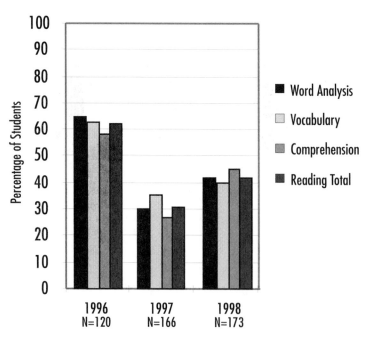

Forest Lane Elementary
Percentage of Students Meeting CTBS Reading Standards
1996 to 1998

Level 3—Two or More Student Learning Measures of Forest Lane

CTBS was only one way in which Forest Lane teachers were assessing their students in reading. They were also using text level scores. The teachers compared text level scores for Spring 1998 with the Spring 1998 CTBS scores. They could see, as shown in Figure 29, that proportionately more students met or exceeded the text level standard than the CTBS standard.

Figure 29

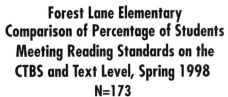

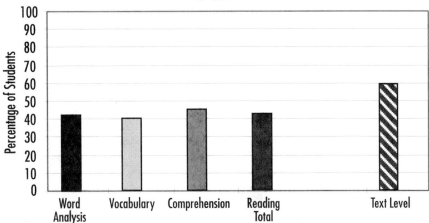

Level 4—Two or More Student Learning Measures of Forest Lane, Over Time

Wondering if the results were similar over time, the teachers plotted the results of their third graders on the same two tests for the three years that they had data. When teachers looked at the percentages of students meeting and not meeting the standards (Figure 30), they saw that over two times as many students did not meet the CTBS standards than those who did, starting in 1997. The proportion of students not meeting the CTBS standards decreased in 1998. The teachers could also see that the percentage of students meeting the text level standards steadily increased each year.

Figure 30

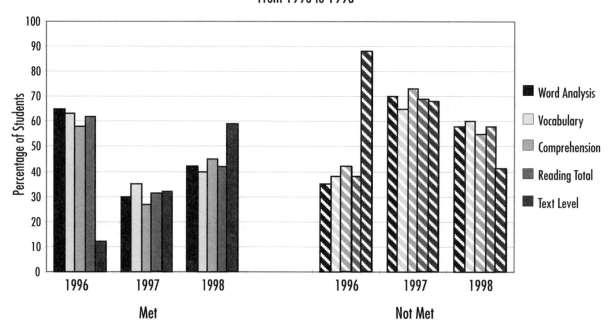

Forest Lane Elementary
Percentage of Third Grade Students Meeting and Not Meeting
Reading Standards for the CTBS and Text Level Tests
From 1996 to 1998

Level 1—Snapshot of Valley High School Student Learning

Valley High reviewed the NCE averages of their Comprehensive Achievement Tests, version V (CAT V), given in Spring 1997. As Figure 31 shows, it appears that, overall, Valley students performed better in mathematics than in reading and vocabulary. Mathematics Applications received their best score, although no subtest reached the normed average of 50. The lowest score is vocabulary.

Student Learning at Valley High School

Figure 31

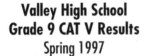

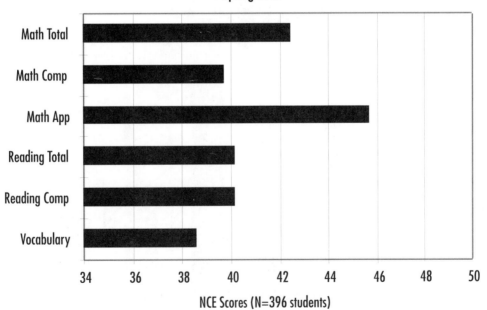

**Valley High School
Grade 9 CAT V Results
Spring 1997**

NCE Scores (N=396 students)

Level 2—Snapshot of Valley High School Student Learning, Over Time

Valley High gave the Comprehensive Achievement Tests to their 9th grade students in 1995, 1996, and 1997. Over the three years of testing, the CAT V scores showed only slight fluctuations within the subtests with no appreciable differences. Figure 32 charts the average NCE score for each subtest.

Figure 32

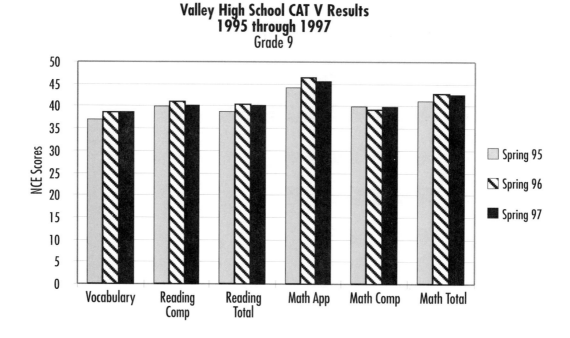

Level 3—Two or More Student Learning Measures

Valley High teachers wanted to learn more about how the ninth grade students getting two or more F's in coursework scored on the CAT V. Figure 33 shows the number of students from this subgroup who scored in each quarter of the CAT V Reading test distribution in 1997. The figure shows that the majority of these students scored in the second quarter of the distribution.

Figure 33

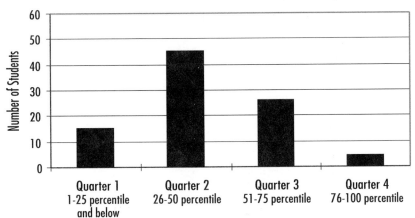

Valley High School CAT V 1997
9th Grade NCE — National Percentile Comparison

Level 4—Two or More Student Learning Measures, Over Time

Looking over time, Valley High teachers followed 10th graders who had Fs as 9th graders. They could see that between 1996 and 1997, the number of 10th graders scoring in Quarter 1 increased, in Quarter 2 decreased, in Quarter 3 increased, and in Quarter 4 increased slightly. Figure 34 shows this comparison over time.

Figure 34

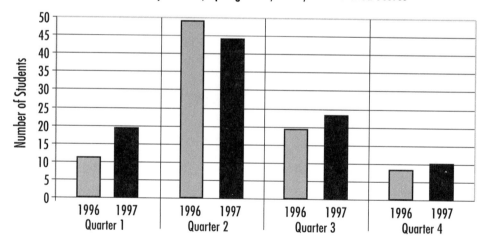

Valley High School
10th Grade Students with 2 or more F's
CAT V Reading Total Scores
By Quarter, Spring 1996, 1997, Not Matched Scores

School personnel typically think about multiple measures as being only in the area of student learning. These alone can give schools information with which to improve, but as you can see from the examples, schools must assess the *same* measures, grades, and students, *over time*, in order to use the information in a comprehensive fashion.

Used with other measures, these scores will become invaluable to school personnel in understanding what needs to change to get different results. These interactions will be explored in succeeding chapters.

Summary

Student Learning Questions

Think through your student learning assessment program and how it can be aligned. The following questions provide a guide for your thinking.

Questions	Current Status	Desired Status
Why do you measure student learning in your school?		
How is student learning measured in your school?		
How are student learning results used?		
How are student learning results disaggregated?		
How and to whom are student learning results reported?		

Of the four measures discussed in this book, school processes are the only measures that we actually have control over in the educational setting. Schools cannot control who the students are, where they come from, or, why they think the way they do. They can only control a portion of the student learning results— through their processes (i.e., programs, practices, and instructional strategies).

Chapter 7

SCHOOL PROCESSES

School processes are important to comprehensive schoolwide improvement because they are what produce school and classroom results. If different results are desired, processes must be changed. To change these processes—

- teachers have to be clear on what is being *implemented*
- study the results of these processes over time
- understand the relationship between the processes, results, mission/purpose, and actions
- study the research on effective processes
- build hypotheses and action plans to achieve different results

These hypotheses and understandings of the literature on student learning are crucial in the prediction of the types of processes schools will need to implement in order to get the results they want in the future. Looking at the data is only one piece of the puzzle. It helps teachers see what results they are getting, based upon what they are doing, but it does not give solutions or design new programs/processes.

School processes can refer to the educational and psychological events at the school and at the classroom level, i.e., the way schools "do" business. Work with school processes is analyzed descriptively or qualitatively. The description is usually easiest when the processes are mapped in the form of a flowchart. Schoolwide and classroom rubrics can assist with the qualitative assessment of where the school is with respect to the implementation of processes.

> *Where outcomes are evaluated without knowledge of implementation, the results seldom provide a direction for action because the decision maker lacks information about what produced the observed outcomes (or lack of outcomes).*
> Michael Quinn Patten

School Level Processes

At the school level, processes can be described and studied through a flowchart or a description or assessment of the implementation of the school vision. When studying our school's processes for improvement, teachers need to think about what they ask students to do, and how these requests align with the purpose and vision of the school. School processes are what teachers do to achieve that purpose—the vision. School processes are also those things that teachers do by habit, by custom, or inadvertently, and those things that may help or hinder progress.

> *Collecting data about a work process has little meaning to us until we use this data to predict and draw conclusions about the future, based on the past performance of this process. Data is value added only to the extent that it allows us to predict and draw conclusions about the future.*
>
> Neil Paulsen, Intel Corporation

Guiding questions that help create theoretical school processes are listed below:

- What do teachers want students to know and be able to do?
- How are teachers enabling students to learn, in terms of—
  - instructional strategies
  - learning strategies
  - instructional time
  - instructional location
  - student-teacher ratio
  - organization of instructional components
  - assessment
  - philosophies and strategies of classroom management
  - personal relationships between students, and between students and teachers
- How will teachers know if any given approach helps all students learn what they want them to learn?
- What will teachers do with the students who do not learn this way?
- What is the responsibility of all members of the school staff?
- What is the job of each member of the school staff?
- How will all parts of the curriculum relate?
- What learning strategies do good learners use?

In working with many schools, we have learned that articulating any given school process seems to be very hard for teachers to do. Process is a complex activity and not something that is often rigorously described—either philosophically or actually.

However, at the classroom level, teachers can be much more effective if they are able to describe the processes they are implementing—from their perspective and from the perspective of their students.

The first step in defining classroom processes is to identify what processes you want to use—the more specific, the more helpful in the end. The next step, to this end, is to describe what gets implemented in the classroom. It is then important to understand the discrepancies between actual and desired, and determine what has to change to get the desired results for students. Flowcharts and curriculum mapping approaches (see References and Resources) are helpful for describing processes used in classrooms. In many cases, processes vary widely from one classroom to another, and many depend as much upon an individual teacher's own educational experiences as a schoolwide philosophy. Examining and describing what actually exists helps everyone become clear on the processes that are and are not making a difference, which helps everyone become clear on what change to implement.

Classroom Level Processes

Our ultimate goal is to build a continuum of learning that makes sense for all students—one that builds upon itself through all classrooms, over the years, to create the cumulative effect we want for all students.

Understanding school processes is the first step in understanding if a school is achieving its school goals. Understanding the cumulative effect of the entire system, including classroom processes, is necessary for determining what needs to change for students.

School and Classroom Level Processes Working Together

A flowchart can help describe and visualize a process. Using this tool can help everyone see a process in the same way. A flowchart allows everyone to see the major steps in a process, in sequence, and then evaluate the difference between the theoretical and actual—first by describing what we would like to be doing, and then by describing what we are really doing.

Charting School Processes

Typical symbols used in flowcharting follow.

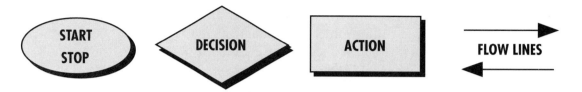

A flowchart is a visualization of a process—a process everyone can see and understand in the same way.

Steps in establishing flowcharts follow:

1. Define the beginning and the end of the process being charted.
2. Decide on the level of detail to be used.
3. Determine the major steps in the process and their sequence.
4. Label each symbol/step in the process.
5. Verify the flowchart. Is it clear?
6. Evaluate. Compare the charted version of the process to the "perfect" flow.

An example of a school's processes, with respect to reading instruction, is described through a flowchart, the Forest Lane example, which is displayed later in this chapter.

Another type of flowchart is called the top-down flowchart. This is probably the easiest and fastest way to chart processes. In a top-down flowchart, one simply follows the primary steps of the process being analyzed and under each primary process writes in the secondary steps, and so on. There should be no more than five-to-seven primary or secondary steps, or the process has not been identified enough. A top-down flowchart framework is shown in Figure 35.

Figure 35

Top-Down Flowchart

Title: Processes for Teaching Reading—Grade 1

1a	Instructional Strategies	2a	Assessment Strategies	3a	Groupings
1b	If reading at or above grade level—regular instruction with classroom teacher using Reading Recovery strategies.	2b	All students assessed at the beginning of first grade level using Clay's Observational Survey. All students assessed using the Text Level and Dictation subtests mid-year and at the end of the year.	3b	Regular students are grouped in the classroom by ability and by Family Learning Teams.
1c	If below grade level and in the bottom 20% of the class—individual instruction with resource staff as part of the formal Reading Recovery program.	2c	Same as above.	3c	Reading Recovery students are grouped in the classroom by ability and by Family Learning Teams.
1d	If below grade level and not in bottom 20% of the class—Literacy Group instruction using Reading Recovery strategies with resource staff.	2d	Same as above.	3d	Literacy Group students are grouped in the classroom by ability and by Family Learning Teams.
1e	If not able to graduate from Reading Recovery program into Literacy Group or regular classroom—referred to the resource or special education program staff for additional assessment, or to receive additional ESL instruction.	2e	Same as above.	3e	Students grouped by program.

Assessing School Processes

One approach to assessing the impact of school processes is to study the resulting flowcharts and note the discrepancies between theoretical and actual implementation. Another approach might be the use of rubrics that give schools an idea of where they started, where they want to be with respect to implementation, and where they are right now, such as with the Education for the Future Initiative Continuous Improvement Continuums (CIC), as described in *The School Portfolio: A Comprehensive Framework for School Improvement,* Second Edition (Bernhardt, 1998). These rubrics help schools assess their processes in seven categories which, when working together, have proven to lead to systemic change. (The CIC appear in Appendix C.)

Rubric assessments, like the CIC, also help build the discussion base for staff to know what they need to do to move ahead. These are assessments staff want to conduct over time to monitor progress. A Continuous Improvement Continuums assessment is shown in the Valley High example at the end of this chapter.

A key factor in moving implementation forward is identifying who is doing the assessment of school processes. Since teachers have the ultimate responsibility for implementing change at the classroom level, their assessment of school and classroom processes is crucial. However, a problem arises because many teachers tend to view the entire school in terms of their own classroom; they rarely get into other rooms. Giving teachers the opportunity to observe each other allows them to develop a schoolwide view of implementation, and to understand their role in moving the school forward. It also has the added benefit of allowing teachers to learn from their colleagues. Using rubrics to assess where the school is on implementation, and establishing next steps, is far more meaningful if teachers are able to see their colleagues in their classroom settings. To understand whether instructional strategies are being implemented, some schools send a teacher or a "critical friend" to take pictures of children working in their classrooms, gather samples of student work, and observe their colleagues teaching. The colleagues, together, analyze the information to understand whether the actual classroom strategies and work required of students are in line with the intended school processes. Only when schools know how well their processes have actually been implemented can they answer the question, "Does this process work for our students?"

Students' perceptions of school processes should not be ignored. When items on student surveys reflect the vision of the school, student responses give powerful information about their view of implementation. For example, Forest Lane Elementary School might include items such as:

I use computers in school as a tool for doing my class work.

I have access to a computer when I need one.

The results of the student survey can indicate to teachers the realities of student experience, which may be different from teachers' understandings.

OUR EXAMPLE SCHOOLS

School Processes at Forest Lane Elementary School

Forest Lane is especially proud of its reading and language arts program, which is based upon current research and uses strategies based on Reading Recovery teaching techniques, the foundation of the school's instructional program. Forest Lane staff are passionate about each student developing a self-extending system for literacy learning in the primary grades. This is accomplished through the regular assessment of literacy learning and, then, by grouping students across grade levels within their Family Learning Teams. These groupings allow for effective use of resource teachers and allow for accelerated student growth.

Level 1—Snapshot of Forest Lane Processes

As Figure 36 shows, beginning in 1998, Forest Lane teachers asked the district speech therapist to help them screen the kindergarten students who were not performing at grade level by mid-year. They also began to direct significant time from resource teachers to work with selected students, one-on-one, to help them gain literacy skills. By 1998, all of the classroom teachers had been trained and were either using or beginning to use Reading Recovery strategies in the regular classroom. Forest Lane also began to collect program level data for all K-3 students—from kindergarten students at mid-year and at the end of the year, and all first, second, and third grade students at the beginning and end of the year. Students in Reading Recovery and Literacy Groups were also tested mid-year. To determine if the process was creating a result that "sticks" with the students, the lead resource teacher was also working with the fourth and fifth grade teachers to ensure that text levels were assessed at those grades as well.

Figure 36

**Forest Lane Reading
Processes, 1996**

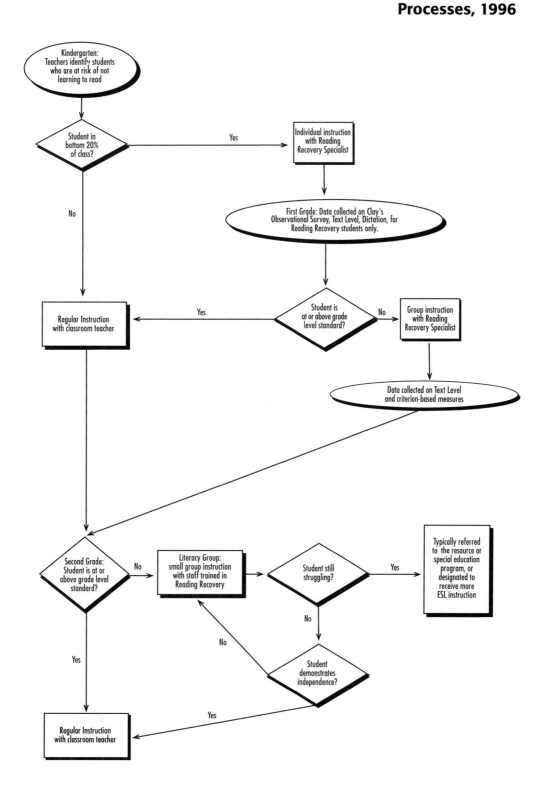

Level 2—Snapshot of Forest Lane Processes, Over Time

In 1997, as Figure 37 shows, several of the classroom teachers had been formally trained in Reading Recovery techniques. There were five resource teachers available to support students from kindergarten through second grade. The teachers who had been trained were now beginning to use Reading Recovery strategies in their regular classroom instruction. The Literacy Groups were still the responsibility of the resource teachers, but more Literacy Groups were offered as a result of the increased resource staff.

Data collected from the 1996 school year and during the 1997 school year reinforced the belief that this process was really making a difference with the students, who were doing much better. However, they still were not reading at levels that they needed to be. Upon studying the impact of their process, Forest Lane staff could see that they needed to start work even earlier to give these at-risk students the time and attention they needed to acquire the words and concepts necessary to read at grade level by third grade. They could also see that they needed to integrate the Reading Recovery strategies into every classroom.

Figure 37

Forest Lane Reading Processes, 1997

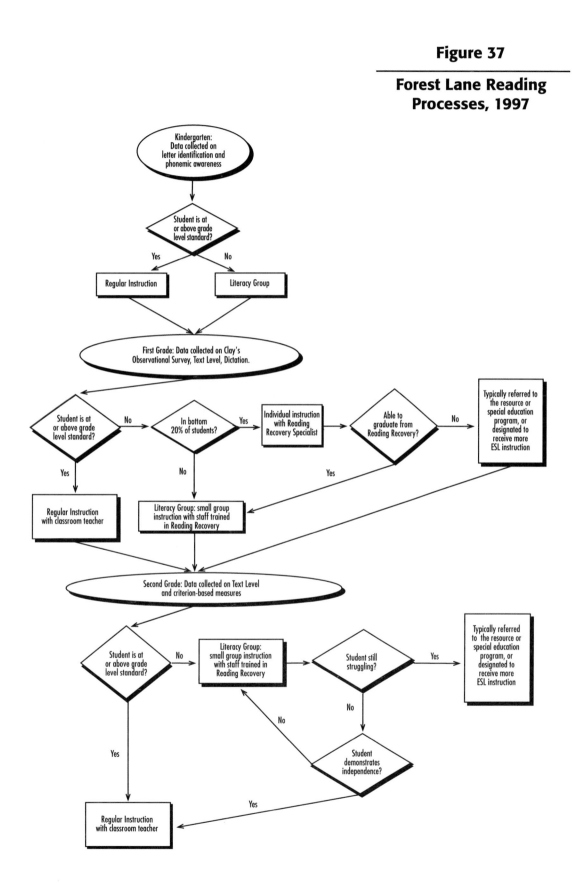

Figure 38 describes the process in place at Forest Lane during the 1996-97 school year. At that time, Reading Recovery was in its third year and had two resource teachers trained in Reading Recovery. The resource teachers, the principal, and several of the regular classroom teachers were committed to the use of Reading Recovery strategies. Because such a high proportion of the students attending Forest Lane came from homes that were not equipped to support the acquisition of literacy, these teachers wanted to figure out how to use those strategies with more of the students.

The previous year, Forest Lane had piloted Literacy Group instruction at the second grade level. In the Literacy Group, a resource teacher used Reading Recovery teaching strategies with small groups of five-to-six students at a time. The students chosen for Literacy Group participation were either students who were in the regular classroom, but were not reading at grade level, or students who had already been in the formal Reading Recovery Program and were doing better, but were still not reading at grade level. At the end of the pilot year, the resource and participating classroom teachers felt that this strategy had a significant impact on the students who had participated in the pilot. The principal supported the decision both to maintain the second grade Literacy Groups and to pilot the same strategy in some of the first grade classrooms. That year, the lead resource teacher also expanded a formal data collection effort to include the Literacy Group students.

Figure 38

Forest Lane Reading Processes, 1998

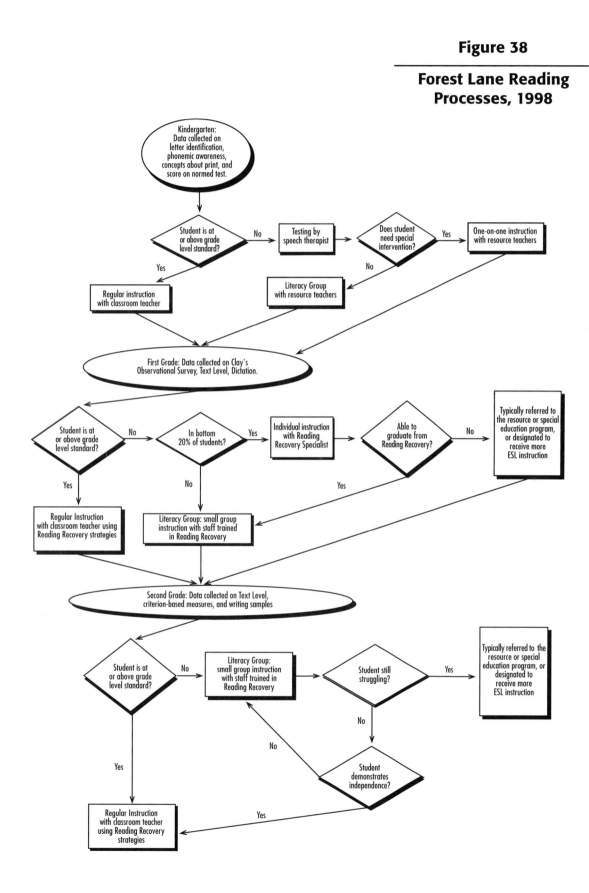

Level 3—Two or More Measures Crossed within School Processes

Forest Lane staff began assessing their learning organization on the Education for the Future Initiative Continuous Improvement Continuums in 1997. The results for 1997 and 1998 are shown in Figure 39. Forest Lane teachers' initial assessment found the following.

Information and Analysis

There was no systematic process for gathering and analyzing data. They tracked data to follow a few students at a time. Teachers were not able to access information for improvement on a consistent basis.

Student Achievement

Forest Lane teachers were proud that essential student learnings had been identified. No tracking of data had been done on a schoolwide basis, therefore, there were only minimal observable results.

Quality Planning

Forest Lane staff understood the importance of a mission, vision, and plan. They know they must revisit their efforts with the whole school community.

Professional Development

In 1996, Forest Lane's professional development approach was to allow individual teachers to determine what professional development they wanted to attend. It was unfocused and sporadic. The effectiveness of this approach was unknown because it was not evaluated for its effectivness.

Leadership

Forest Lane has a committed leadership team. School values and beliefs, mission and purpose have been identified, and staff are committed to continuous improvement. Staff realized they need to do more to study approaches they are taking with children and to communicate more effectively schoolwide.

<u>Partnership Development</u>
Forest Lane staff agreed that, as of 1996, they sought partnerships for money and things. They hope that when they align their curriculum they will be in a better position to recruit partners to "help" implement their curriculum.

<u>Continuous Improvement and Evaluation</u>
Until the data analysis system is put together and used comprehensively, changes made will not be comprehensive; they will be isolated.

Between 1997 and 1998, the staff at Forest Lane began gathering data about the impact of their processes on student learning, thus the increase in Information and Analysis. With this information, they learned what they needed to do to increase student learning, particularly in the area of reading. Although their full staff professional development days focused on their clarified vision, teachers were able to plan and implement new processes and partnerships that led to student achievement increases. The data analysis system allowed them to measure and improve on a continuous basis.

While the elements that make a difference with systemic school change are now in alignment, staff agree that they have to work to keep a systemic reliance on hard data, especially to build that continuum of learning across grade levels. At this next level, they will be in the position of being able to predict what they need to do to prevent all student failure in the future. The plan of action must help all classrooms implement the vision in the same way.

Figure 39

Forest Lane CIC Results
1997 and 1998

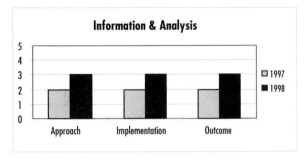

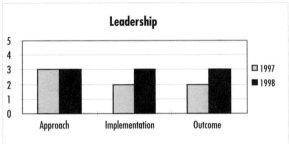

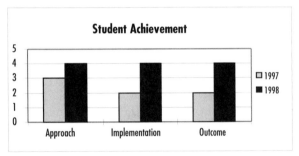

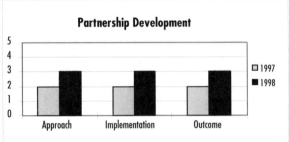

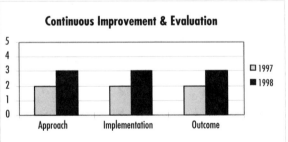

*Level 4—Two or More Measures Crossed within School Processes,
    Over Time*

Forest Lane assessed where they are on the EFF Initiative
Continuous Improvement Continuums two years in a row
as Figure 39 shows.

School Processes at Valley High School

Level 1—Snapshot of Valley High School Processes

Valley High staff conducted a baseline assessment of where they felt the school was on the Education for the Future Initiative Continuous Improvement Continuums on August 30, 1996. The results, taken from their school portfolio follow in Figure 40.

Figure 40

Valley High School Portfolio

VALLEY HIGH SCHOOL
CONTINUOUS IMPROVEMENT ASSESSMENT
August 30, 1996

On August 30, 1996, Valley High School staff met to conduct their baseline ratings on the Education for the Future Continuous Improvement Continuums. The ratings were reached by full staff consensus. The ratings and brief discussions follow.

Information and Analysis

Collectively, the staff believes that Valley High School is a 3 in Approach, 2 in Implementation, and 2 in Outcome for Information and Analysis. They believe that schoolwide data are being collected on student performance, attendance, and achievement, and surveys are being administered. However, they feel the information has not been implemented in such a way that it is being used for planning purposes. The data is also limited to some areas of the school, depending upon the teachers' involvement.

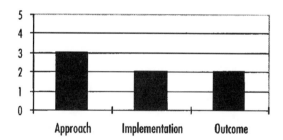

Next steps—
- We need to analyze and graph all existing data.
- We need to look at all data in a systematic way to help us plan strategically.
- We need to make sure that we get complete data.
- In October, we need to have a committee look at all the data that we have right now, begin to make some analyses based on what we have, and determine what additional information we need to gather.
- Following the meeting, the committee will bring back to the full staff this information, as well as the possibility of conducting a freshman survey that would ask such questions as: Why did you choose Valley? What are your goals for high school? What are your goals after high school? With these responses, we can begin to follow the students throughout their four years at Valley.
- The committee will also think about a survey that will follow students who left Valley, for whatever reason, to find out why they left.
- Additionally, we need to think about asking students these questions in the spring: Did we meet your needs, goals, and expectations? How could we better meet your needs, goals, and expectations?
- We need to use these data to feed the systemic plan, to analyze information to get to the root causes of problems, and to track data for improvement.

Figure 40 (Continued)

Valley High School Portfolio ^{V}H$_S$

Student Achievement

Valley staff rated themselves a 2 in Approach to Student Achievement, 2 in Implementation, and 3 in Outcome. The staff felt that until more data are collected, tracked, and analyzed, they cannot get beyond the 2 stage in Approach and Implementation. There has been a lot of effort, however, to start working on tracking bits of data which has led to an increase in communication between students and teachers regarding student learning. Staff are quite happy with these beginnings.

Student Achievement

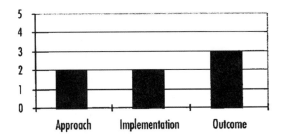

Next steps—
- We need to establish a schoolwide database that would allow a more systematic look at student achievement data and a closer look at the classroom data.
- We need to develop a comprehensive and consistent view of how students are evaluated at Valley.
- Schoolwide, we need to come to grips with the cross-curricular integration of the performing arts with core academics.
- We need to look back at the vision and mission and rethink the way courses are offered.

Quality Planning

Valley staff rated themselves a 2 in Approach, 2 in Implementation, and 3 in Outcome for Quality Planning. While staff realize the importance of a mission, vision, and comprehensive action plan, the current school plan is not a comprehensive representation of the vision for the school. Until it is, improvement cannot be systematic or schoolwide.

Quality Planning

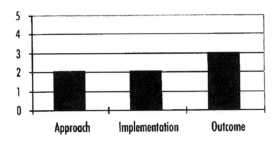

114

Figure 40 (Continued)

V**H**S **Valley High School Portfolio**

Next steps—
- We need to develop a systematic comprehensive schoolwide approach to planning that includes evaluation and continuous improvement.

Professional Development

Valley staff assessed themselves on Professional Development as 3 in Approach, Implementation, and Outcome. Staff felt that the school plan and analysis of student needs have been used to target appropriate professional development for teachers. In-service is helping them think through the entire school and to rethink the types of professional development that the entire staff need to engage in order to get to the vision.

Professional Development

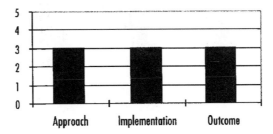

Next steps—
- We need the support to allocate more time for cross-curricular planning
- We need to follow through on the departmental policy forms that were established last spring.
- We need to evaluate staff development activities to make sure they are getting us to our goals.

Leadership

Valley staff rated the school a 3 in Approach, 2 in Implementation, and 2 in Outcome with respect to Leadership. The rationale, folded into next steps, follows:

Leadership

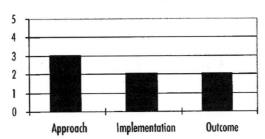

Next steps—
- We need to define a leadership structure for the school that is congruent with the school vision.
- We need to revisit the school vision to make sure it is congruent with staff's sense of where we want to go, especially as a performing arts school.

Figure 40 (Continued)

Valley High School Portfolio

Partnership Development

Collectively, staff believe, with respect to Partnership Development, that Valley High School currently is a 3 across the board in Approach, Implementation, and Outcome.

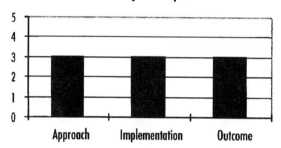

Next steps—
*   There needs to be documentation of the comprehensive partnerships that exist throughout the school.
*   This list of partnerships needs to be put out in a newsletter.
*   We need to take a serious look at how all of our partnerships affect student achievement and the school vision.
*   We need to plan how to establish partnerships with respect to our outcomes.

Continuous Improvement and Evaluation

Valley staff rated the school a 3 in Approach, 2 in Implementation, and 2 in Outcome with respect to Continuous Improvement and Evaluation.

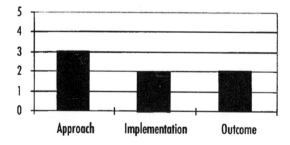

Next steps—
*   Staff determined that they need to research the impact of visual and performing arts on student achievement. This research will inform the vision for the school and how all the other pieces fit together.
*   We need to clarify our vision for congruence throughout all aspects of the school, and make sure we are "walking our talk."

116

Level 2—Snapshot of Valley High School Processes, Over Time

Valley High staff conducted their assessment of where they felt the school was on the Education for the Future Continuous Improvement Continuums for the second time on November 17, 1997. These results compared to the previous year's results follow (Figure 41).

Figure 41

Valley CIC Results
1996 and 1997

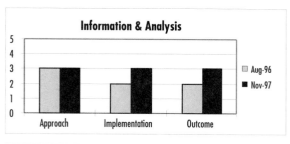

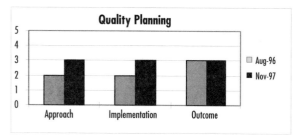

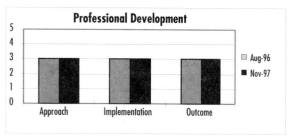

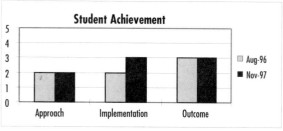

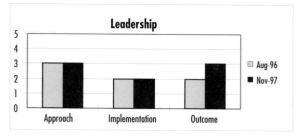

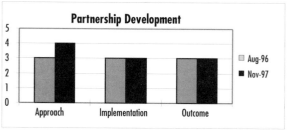

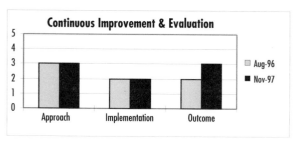

Overall, Valley High staff felt that they had made much progress with respect to systemic change during the past year. They especially improved in the areas of comprehensive data analysis and quality planning which led to increased partnerships and overall continuous improvement of the school. They know they must continue to track student achievement data, which is inconsistent, and build a database that would help them keep track of data in the future. Disappointingly, nothing different happened during the past year with respect to professional development. Staff know that until it does, nothing different will happen in the classroom and different student achievement will not result.

Level 3—Two or More Measures Crossed within School Processes

In 1997, the process for ensuring a successful freshman experience at Valley High included the following.

Figure 42

Pathway to a Successful Freshman Experience at Valley High School 1997

1. Recruitment Tour
2. Shadowing a current Freshman to experience Valley firsthand
3. Choice of High School
4. Curriculum Advisory Meeting at current Middle School and at the High School for parents and students
5. Coursework decisions made with respect to graduation requirements and plans after graduation: Parents, Student, Assistant Principal for Instruction involved
6. Auditions for performing groups, and elective placement/Spring prior to Freshman Year
7. Schedule assigned
8. Summer Orientation: School standards and expectations communicated, campus orientation/map, given buddy from the leadership class to help personalize the school
9. Bar-B-que for all Freshmen and parents
10. Organizational Binder given, complete with school discipline policy, time management guidelines, school calendar
11. School Starts
12. Principal's weekly
13. Students given classroom behavioral standards, absence policy, grading policy, course scope, standards and expectations, supply list, etc., for each class
14. Freshman orientation to Media Center and Career Center, and student support services
15. "With Distinction" option explained to all Freshman English classes
16. Homework Hotline begins
    - Homework posted by voicemail for all subjects
    - Message center enabling parents to contact teachers
17. Back-to-School night
    - Parents visit student's classes for overview of coursework and objectives, standards, grading, and absence policy
    - Orientation to school organizations for parent involvement
18. Six week, Twelve week, and Semester grading period
    - Parents come to school to pick up their student's grades. Faculty are on campus the entire day for consultation with parents about their student's progress
    - Students receive information about and invitation to join California Scholastic Federation and/or National Honor Society if GPA and student profile meets standards
19. If problems are developing:
    - D and F report given to Grade Level Advisors
    - Student with one or more D's and F's are contacted by their advisor and a path of action/remediation is determined
    - Teachers and/or administrators may refer students at any time to the Student Assistance Program, the Bilingual Tutorial Program, Individual Tutoring, or the Homework Center
20. Freshman survey given November/December to determine student adjustment to the school. Data analyzed by Administration and staff and action plan determined as appropriate
21. Curriculum advisors meet with all Freshman English classes in May to make schedule choices for Sophomore year. Schedule sent home to parents for input and revision

In looking at this process in conjunction with the EFF Continuous Improvement Continuums results, teachers could see that more data need to be used to inform the processes for better meeting the needs of freshman students.

Level 4—Two or More Measures Crossed within School Processes, Over Time

For the past three years, Valley teachers have used the same processes with freshman students. They looked at these processes in relationship to the results of the CIC, over time. At this point in time, there is not a strong relationship between schoolwide processes and freshman processes. Staff could see that until they dig deeper into the freshman processes (i.e., study past data and what is going on in the classroom), the results they are getting from freshmen will not change.

Summary

School processes might be the most important measure in understanding what needs to be done to improve student learning results in school organizations. It is often the last measure used and is seldom considered in schoolwide improvement efforts.

When schools understand their school processes, especially in relationship to the results they are getting, they can know exactly what they need to do differently to get different results.

Our first example showed how the processes impacted the reading scores Forest Lane was getting. The second example showed how Valley High School determined what they needed to do to implement systemic change. The examples also show how nothing changes until processes change.

School Processes Questions

Think about the processes your school is using to achieve its purpose and the results being achieved. Pick a specific teaching concept. Use one of the tools (i.e., flowchart, top-down flowchart, curriculum mapping, rubrics) to chart how you teach the concept.

Chapter 8

INTERACTIONS AND ANALYSES

Up to this point, we have taken Figure 1, Multiple Measures found in Chapter 3, and explored each of the four major measures—demographics, perceptions, student learning, and school processes. We have defined them, and given examples of what each measure looks like in a snapshot, over time, and crossed with like measures.

This chapter takes the four major measures and intersects each with one to three other measures for more complex analyses. On the next page is a table (Table 5) of possible two-way and three-way interactions across measures, and the all-important four-way interaction that gives us the ability to predict what we need to do to meet the learning needs of all students in the school. Each interaction shown is illustrated with an example of what the interaction of the measures can tell us. There are, of course, numerous other possibilities for intersecting these measures. As you read the table, keep in mind that complex interactions can mean different things depending upon the perspective from which one looks at the interactions—and what it is one wants to know.

These interactions become insights for use in comprehensive schoolwide improvement processes.

> *Interaction analysis helps us to understand what is going on in all parts of a program, and to assess the impact of our actions on the people we are trying to serve.*
>
> V. L. Bernhardt

Table 5

Interaction Analyses

INTERACTIONS	CAN TELL US—
Two-way Interactions	
• demographics by student learning	• if subgroups of students perform differently on student learning measures
• demographics by perceptions	• if groups of students are experiencing school differently
• demographics by school processes	• if all groups of students are represented in the different programs and processes offered by the school
• student learning by school processes	• if different programs are achieving similar student learning results
• student learning by perceptions	• if student perceptions of the learning environment have an impact on their learning results
• perceptions by school processes	• if people are perceiving programs and processes differently
Three-way Interactions	
• demographics by student learning by perceptions	• the impact demographic factors and attitudes about the learning environment have on student learning
• demographics by student learning by school processes	• what processes or programs work best for different groups of students measured by student learning results
• demographics by perceptions by school processes	• what programs or processes different students like best, or the impact different programs or processes have on student attitudes
• student learning by school processes by perceptions	• the relationship between the processes students prefer and learning results
Four-way Interactions	
• demographics by student learning by perceptions by school processes	• what processes or programs have the greatest impact on different groups of students' learning, according to student perceptions and as measured by student learning results

Interaction Analyses

Interaction analyses allow us to look closely and understand each piece of information we gather about a school. The first levels are easy to understand, but Table 5 demonstrates how much more information two and three measures together can provide rather than a single measure alone.

As you can see from the examples throughout this book, as the analyses get more sophisticated, answers to evaluation questions become evident. A caution as one starts these analyses: *Stay clear on the purpose of your analyses.* It is easy to keep gathering and analyzing and forget the questions one is striving to answer. If you keep sight of the goal, you'll know when to stop. A two-way interaction might answer the question just as well as a three-way.

> *Change is the law of life and those who look only to the past or present are certain to miss the future.*
>
> John F. Kennedy

Going back to Chapter 2, the purposes for conducting data analyses are to—

- improve instruction
- provide students with feedback on their performance
- gain a common understanding of what quality performance is and how close we are to achieving it
- measure program success and effectiveness
- understand if what we are doing is making a difference
- make sure students "do not fall through the cracks"
- know which programs are getting the results we want
- get to the "root causes" of problems
- guide curriculum development and revision
- "promote" or "measure" accountability
- meet state and federal requirements

The analyses we have been describing and working with throughout this book are not new, unique, or particularly difficult to perform. We have merely begun at the lowest level of analysis, and built upon each level to produce meaningful data that can be used for decision making and schoolwide improvement. These data can also be used within the context of commonly known analytical frameworks, such as needs assessment, program evaluation, and research. Occasionally some of the four major measures that would lead to accurate analyses in the traditional assessments get lost due to very focused evaluation questions—leading to erroneous conclusions. To conduct those analyses well, one needs to gather the data that are described within the four multiple measures and intersect them, just as we have done here.

How do interaction analyses relate to more traditional methods of analysis, such as program evaluation, needs assessment, and research? How do they all relate to comprehensive schoolwide improvement?

Traditional Analyses

Traditional analyses such as needs assessment, program evaluation, and research have distinct roles to play in comprehensive schoolwide improvement—some are more valuable than others.

> *It is easier to select a method for madness than a single best method for evaluation, though attempting the latter is an excellent way of achieving the former.*
>
> Halcolm

- *Summative program evaluation* addresses questions at the end of the program or year. What was done? What was it worth?

- *Formative program evaluation* asks questions about the current program. What is being done? Is it doing what it is intended to do?

- *Needs assessment* shows the discrepancies between the actual and the desired. What is our current status? What would we like it to be?

- *Research* answers questions of curiosity: Does Group A perform better than Group B?

Schools often conduct one or the other of these analyses when they should be conducting a combination of analyses. For instance, without program evaluation, needs assessment becomes *problem assessment* pointing to deficiencies without giving guidance to intervention strategies. Similarly, program evaluation depends upon needs assessment. If the worth of a program is to be judged, the needs of participants must be gauged. Without needs assessment, programs cannot really be evaluated; they can only be described. Research without elements of needs assessment and program evaluation is a "so what." It can be conducted by anyone, including people with only partial knowledge of the program.

Needs assessment helps decision making by clarifying what, and how important, the needs are. Within an educational setting, identifying needs requires uses of multiple measures—a knowledge of the population (demographics); values of the people to be served (perceptions); an idea of the success of the program or process in question (student learning); and, the services available to the population (school processes).

Needs Assessment

> *Whatever the combination of uses, the role of systemic analysis of need is reduction of uncertainty.*
>
> Jack McKillip

Needs assessment is sometimes described as the feedback process that enables us to learn about, and adapt to, the needs of our "clients." These assessments usually move beyond the identification of needs to solution identification. The key to doing that well is ensuring that comprehensive data have been gathered so that the solution is appropriate and that schools are not only dealing with a symptom.

Common steps in needs assessments are described below.

1. *Identify the uses of the needs assessment*
   Why are we conducting the assessment?

2. *Describe the target population*
   Demographics

3. *Identify needs*
   Define the discrepancy between expectations (what we expect students to know and be able to do) and current results (evidence of student learning) to define the problem. Consider your knowledge of student and teacher values (perceptions) and possible solutions (adaptation of existing or adoption of new school processes) may become obvious as a likely route to success.

4. *Assess the importance of the needs*
   Which are the most important and relate most to the purpose of the school?

5. *Communicate results*
   Measurements can be transformed to reflect the values, interests, or purposes of of those who make decisions.

Program Evaluation

There are many approaches to program evaluation. Just like any data analysis that we conduct, the type of evaluation depends upon the purpose. There are many purposes for conducting an evaluation within a school or school district. The most common are to—

* comprehensively understand how students are doing within the educational system the school/district is providing
* identify problems needing intervention
* understand cost benefits or cost effectiveness
* assess impact or monitor the program for improvement

The most often-heard terms associated with program evaluation are formative and summative. Formative simply refers to measuring how the program is doing while it is operating. Summative refers to assessments of overall program effectiveness, and usually takes place at the end of the year or program.

Typical steps in program evaluation are very similar to needs assessment. The steps, which follow, are focused a little differently.

> *Evaluating a program is like shooting at a moving target—it's hard as hell to hit and requires precise anticipation. The rare bull's eye brings uncommon satisfaction. Improving your aim means lots of practice and careful study of the non-random movements of the target.*
>
> Michael Quinn Patten

1. *Identify the purpose for the evaluation*
   Why are we conducting the analysis?
2. *Identify the audience*
   Who do you want to use the results?
3. *Identify sources of information*
   They could be from all four multiple measures of data.
4. *Conduct the assessment*
   It might be similar to interaction analyses, but is usually focused on questions of effectiveness.
5. *Communicate results*
   Communicate in a manner that targeted groups will understand and use.

Researchers study different phenomenon to make discoveries or to acquire information. This may not be useful in education. For example, researchers studying the impact of technology might want some children to have technology and others to not have technology to serve as a control group. Although there could be occasions when circumstances exist that allow this type of research, we would *never* want to deliberately keep children from having the opportunity to work with something that we think would increase student learning. Schools use their best judgment to implement what they think is best for children. Never could we, in good conscience, deny children opportunities we think will make a difference simply for the sake of methodological research purity.

Research

An evaluation that begins with an experimental design denies to program staff what it needs most: Information that can be used to make judgments about the program while it is in its dynamic stages of growth . . . We recognize that comparisons (of those receiving treatment versus those who didn't) have never been productive, nor have they facilitated corrective action. The overwhelming number of evaluations conducted in this way show no significant differences between "experimental" and "control" groups.

Provus

When selecting an analysis to use to determine whether or not an approach is working, school personnel often want to design an experiment. They believe that if there is no control group or tests of significance, the results are not valuable. Statistical significance is the probability that a given event will happen again, or that the given event did not occur as a function of chance. We want to use statistical significance only when it makes sense. In the analyses that we are conducting, statistical significance is not as important to us because we are not trying to generalize for the total population of learners or school. Instead, we are looking for analyses that are educationally significant.

I firmly believe that there is a place for applied research in education and in analyzing data for improving schools; however, the use of research is probably our least effective approach for comprehensive schoolwide improvement.

This section shows example charts for each interaction of the multiple measures, along with a description of their uses. Forest Lane data are used for these charts.

Example Charts

OUR EXAMPLE SCHOOLS

**Two-way
Interactions**

Student Learning by Demographics

Forest Lane Elementary School wanted to understand the differences in student performance by ethnicity. They also wanted to follow the same students, over time, to understand if all students were learning.

Figure 43, shows the percentage of students meeting the CTBS Reading Standards as first graders in 1996, second graders in 1997, and third graders in 1998. One can see the percentage of Caucasian students meeting the standards increased from the second year to the third year. A high percentage of Hispanic students did not meet the standards in 1996, which was reduced by almost half in the later years. The most students not meeting the Reading Standards on the CTBS, over time, were Hmong.

Figure 43

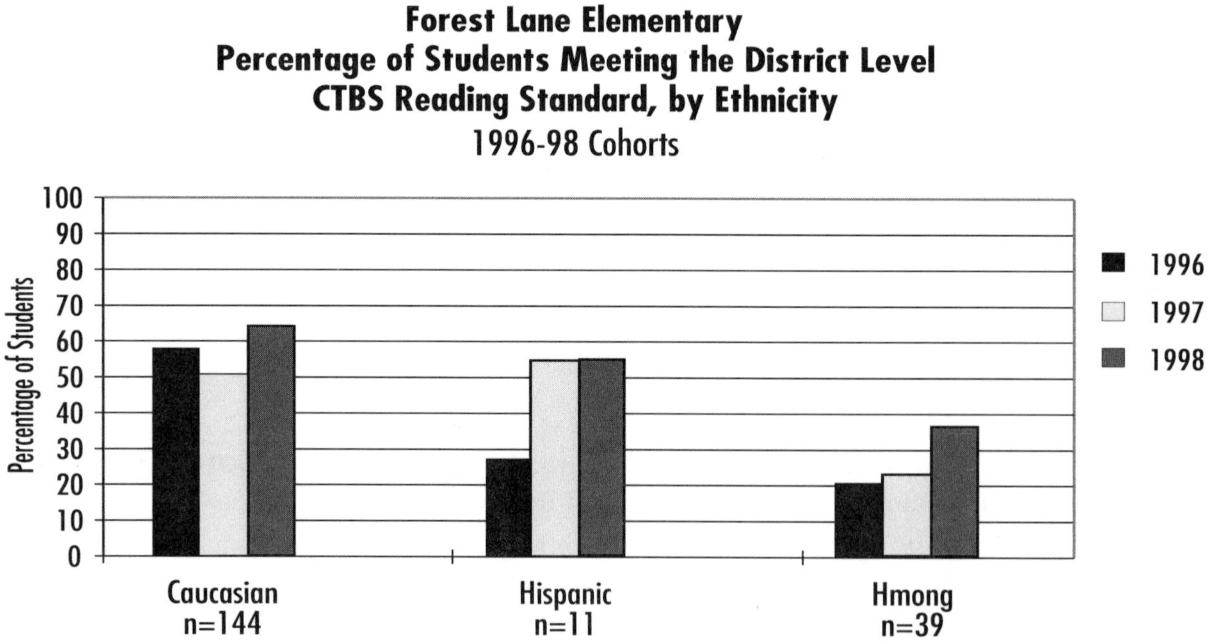

**Forest Lane Elementary
Percentage of Students Meeting the District Level
CTBS Reading Standard, by Ethnicity**
1996-98 Cohorts

Perceptions by Demographics

In 1996, Forest Lane student perceptions of the school were disaggregated by ethnicity to see how perceptions were different for different groups of students. Figure 44 shows that all ethnicities were in agreement with all items, with one exception. Asian students were neutral to the item, "Students at my school treat me with respect."

Figure 44

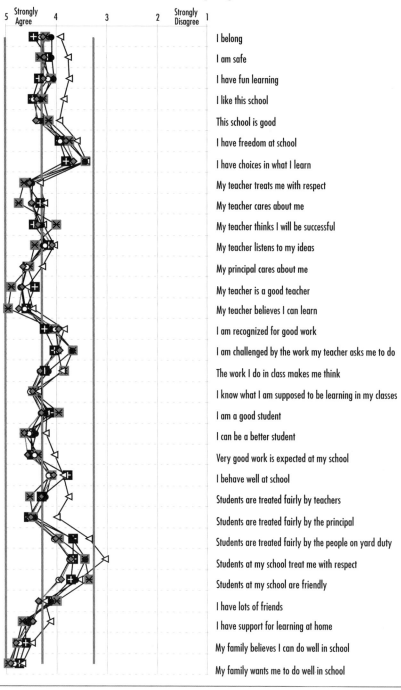

Forest Lane Student Responses Compared by Ethnicity
Spring 1997

*Total based on number of questionnaires. Students may select more than one category.

School Processes by Demographics

Looking at the number of Forest Lane students participating in Reading Recovery, by ethnicity, over time, Figure 45 shows that the total number of Reading Recovery students has increased overall, partially due to the fact that resource staff have increased and more students can be served. While the number of Reading Recovery students has decreased for all other ethnicities, the number of Caucasian students in Reading Recovery has more than doubled in the last year. Upon studying the first two years of data analyses on several measures, Forest Lane teachers and resource staff realized that the Hmong and Mien population did not benefit from the Reading Recovery program until they had an opportunity to acquire a fundamental level of concepts from the ESL teachers.

Figure 45

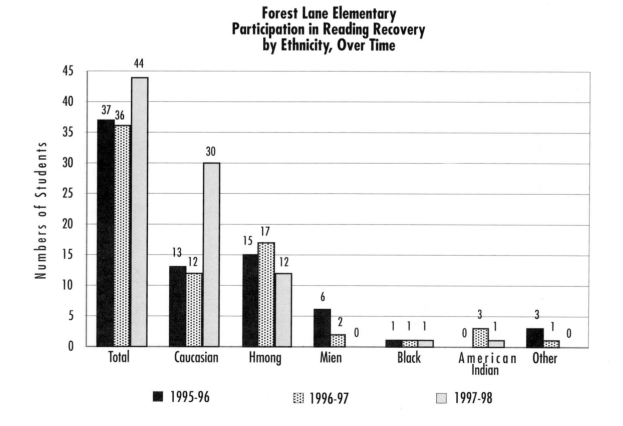

Forest Lane Elementary
Participation in Reading Recovery
by Ethnicity, Over Time

Student Learning by School Processes

Following cohorts of Reading Recovery students over time, one can see from the interaction chart below (Figure 46) that when the 1997-98 third graders were in first grade, the majority of students did not meet the first grade reading standards. Because of the gradual integration of Reading Recovery strategies into the classroom over the past two years in both the first and second grades, many of these students were able to meet the standard by second grade, and many more met the standard by third grade. The impact of more teachers understanding the strategies—and using them—may have caused the greater degree of success in the second group of cohorts.

Higher numbers of students who were second graders in 1997-98 did not meet the reading standard as first graders; however, by second grade, more students had met the standard than those who did not meet the standard. Overall, this chart suggests that the new school processes are making a difference with students meeting the standards.

Figure 46

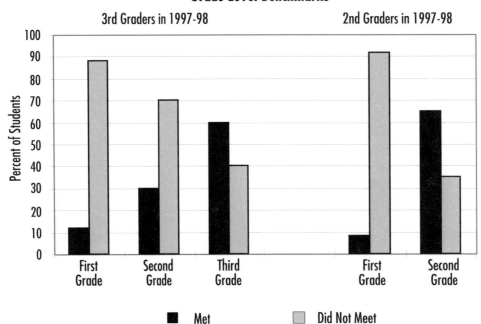

**Forest Lane Elementary
Text Level Scores Compared to
Grade Level Benchmarks**

Student Learning by Perceptions

Figure 14 in Chapter 5 showed student perceptions results for Forest Lane students over time, and Figure 30 in Chapter 6 showed student learning over time. Looking at the two together, one can see that, overall, student perceptions and student learning results increased over time, indicating a possible relationship.

Perceptions by School Processes

Teachers felt that Forest Lane students need a good deal of help in acquiring the words they need to learn in order to read. They felt that students were succeeding in those areas in which they had been able to put processes in place to meet the students' literacy acquisition needs—that is with those students who *stayed*.

When teachers were faced with a population consisting of large numbers of families being referred to Child Protective Services (CPS), and where the mobility factor was not good, there was a sentiment of "what can we do?" The teachers also discussed the need for a pre-school to enable early intervention with students.

Demographics by Student Learning by Perceptions

Using both two-way interaction charts on previous pages, Figure 43 (Percentage of Students Meeting and Not Meeting the District Level CTBS Reading Standards, by Ethnicity 1996-98 Cohorts) and Figure 44 (Total Student Responses, Spring 1997), Forest Lane teachers could see that in 1996, regardless of ethnicity, students felt that their families wanted them to do well in school and believed that their families thought they could do well in school. The charts indicate that the ethnic groups that did the best on the CTBS tests also had the strongest positive perceptions of the school. Students from the ethnic group not doing as well as the others felt less like they belonged, less safe, and less positive about the school in general. They also did not feel that students and adults treated them well.

Forest Lane Three-way Interactions

Demographics by School Processes by Student Learning

Figure 46 (previously displayed) could also be considered a three-way interaction chart. This chart shows that when we follow Forest Lane students from grades 1 through 3 (demographics), we can see their achievement scores (student learning) increasing because of their program participation (school processes).

Demographics by School Processes by Perceptions

Although the student questionnaire was not disaggregated by processes, the staff at Forest Lane believe that the use of Reading Recovery strategies by the classroom teacher, which is gaining greater acceptance in the first-through-third-grade levels, does a lot to improve students' self-esteem and ultimately improves their perceptions of the school. Next year, the school improvement questionnaire will be structured so that student responses can be identified by their participation in classrooms using these strategies.

School Processes by Student Learning by Perceptions

Looking at the total results in Figure 16, in Chapter 5, and Figure 30, in Chapter 6, one can see that, overall, the students are positive about the school. Unfortunately, the perceptions data were not broken down by school processes in previous years to know if there were differences in perceptions based on the program in which they were enrolled.

Forest Lane Four-way Interactions

Demographics by Student Learning by Perceptions by School Processes

Although there will be no formal, recorded perception data by processes until next school year, the Forest Lane teachers did make an attempt to intersect each of the four measures when looking at individual students. Using the data they had collected for the students who were formally involved in the Reading Recovery Program, Forest Lane teachers assessed individual student achievement results by Reading Recovery participation, by ethnicity, over the time period between grades 1 and 3. (See Figure 47) They also discussed as a group their perceptions of the students' perceptions of school and the students' reactions to processes used at the school. These data indicated to the teachers that, regardless of ethnicity, students can achieve and are able to meet the grade level standards. Because not all students were achieving, the teachers looked at every case and determined the conditions present when students did raise their student achievement scores above the performance that the teachers had expected in the past. The teachers felt that students placed in classrooms with teachers who were trained in Reading Recovery strategies, and who were able to continue to support student understanding of word concepts after the formal participation in the program ended, did better than students in classrooms with teachers who were not trained in and did not use the strategies. The teachers also determined that early placement in the Reading Recovery Program was not beneficial to the non-native English-speaking children. According to the data, these students received greater benefit from the Reading Recovery Program, or did not need the program, when they were allowed to receive ESL support first.

Figure 47

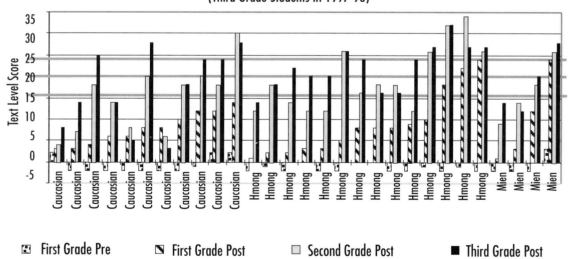

Forest Lane Elementary
Percentage of the Same Students Meeting Text Level Standards
From Grades One Through Three
(Third Grade Students in 1997-98)

☒ First Grade Pre   ◤ First Grade Post   ☐ Second Grade Post   ■ Third Grade Post

Summary

The analysis you choose depends upon the purpose for doing the analysis in the first place. Think about the questions you have that are related to the purpose of your school, and consider what you want to know related to comprehensive schoolwide improvement. You might choose different approaches to answer different questions. You might use elements of needs assessment, program evaluation, and research which might also be accomplished by simply looking at the interactions of the four major measures. Think through your questions logically. Most importantly, keep your focus on the purpose.

Interaction analyses allow one to understand data at an incremental level, and to see that one can create an analysis for any question. Interaction analyses are analyses that teachers and school personnel can do fairly quickly and easily. They can tell us different things depending upon the perspective and complexity of interactions.

Interactions and Analyses Questions

Think about the school improvement questions that you identified in Chapter 3. What interactions would give you information related to the questions?

Questions	Interactions

Chapter 9

PUTTING IT ALL TOGETHER

In the first eight chapters, multiple measures of school level data were gathered and analyzed, independently and inter-relatedly. Now the analyses need to be put together so they can be communicated and used for continuous improvement.

In Chapter 2, the focus for the data analysis work—the purpose of the school—is clarified and becomes a guide for all school analyses. Even when a problem has been identified, the problem is still grounded in the purpose of the school and what the school is attempting to do for children. With this clarity, schools can begin to ask questions and think about the data they need to collect to answer these questions, as was done in Chapter 3. Chapters 4 through 8 described the essence of the multiple measures of data, independently and then interactively.

Most of the time in education, staff want to rush their thinking as they endeavor to solve problems. It is worthwhile, however, to first think through what they know about the problem; think about the data that can assist with a better understanding of the problem; understand all that the data reveal; and, clarify goals and desired outcomes before identifying solutions.

In the beginning you think.
In the end you act.
In between you
negotiate the possibilities.
Some people move from
complexity to simplicity
and on into catastrophe.
Others move from
simplicity to complexity
and onward into full scale
confusion. Simplification
makes action possible in
the face of overwhelming
complexity. It also increases
the odds of being wrong.
The trick is to let a
sense of simplicity
inform our thinking,
a sense of complexity
inform our actions, and
a sense of humility inform
our judgments . . .

Michael Quinn Patten

Problem Solving Cycle

Problem identification and analyses help us think through the big picture and locate the root causes of problems. Steps in solving problems are shown in Figure 48, and are described below:

1. Identify the problem
2. Describe hunches and hypotheses
3. Identify questions and data to know if the hunches and hypotheses are fact or fiction
4. Analyze multiple measures of data
5. Analyze the political realities
6. Develop an action plan for solving the problem
7. Implement the action plan
8. Evaluate the implementation
9. Improve the process

Today's problems are yesterday's solutions.

Peter Senge

Figure 48

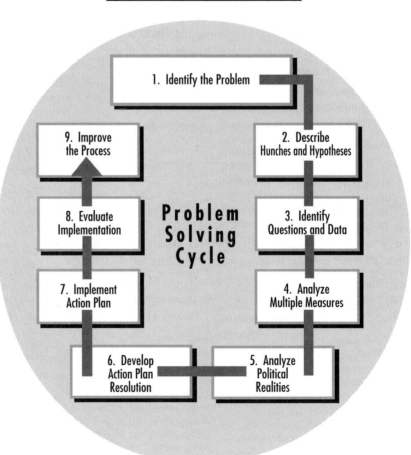

Identify the Problem

Identifying the "problem" helps focus the data analysis. Problems may be issues that arise from a directive from the district office. A problem might be the discrepancy between actual or desired results, or it might be a goal for improvement. Decide as you start if you are going to use neutral-, positive-, negative-, or solution-oriented questions or statements. An example problem is "All students are not reading at grade level by grade 3."

If your school does not have a problem to solve, this process can be effective using the purpose of the school as the focus statement.

Describe Hunches and Hypotheses

It is good for teachers to brainstorm their hunches and hypotheses about a problem before looking at the data. It allows them to see something they might otherwise miss. Group processes used to brainstorm hunches and hypotheses are shown in the examples that follow the discussion of working with problem analysis teams.

Working with Problem Analysis Teams

When working with a team on getting to root causes of problems, and looking for solutions to problems, conversations can get explosive. If ground rules are established, purposes kept clear, and time is focused on the issues at hand, teams can stay away from focusing on individual or group behaviors which usually cause conversations to lose focus. In defense of the best use of everyone's time, it is smart to—

> *Participation techniques are useless in the absence of leadership and purposeful goals.*
> Marvin Weisbord

- start with guidelines or ground rules of acceptable and unacceptable individual and team behavior
- determine how ground rules will be monitored
- determine how decisions will be made (e.g., by consensus or majority rule)
- identify a leader and roles for participation; how the process will be led
- make sure a "safe" room is established to enable threat-free, honest, open discussion

As the team works together, keep track of the agreements by writing down the points of agreement as they occur throughout the meeting. Because of a lack of personal involvement with the issues, sometimes an outside facilitator can help keep the interaction positive and productive, while managing conflicts that may arise out of the group's discussion.

The following examples for brainstorming, ground rules, and meeting etiquette are offered for working with problem analysis teams.

GUIDELINES FOR BRAINSTORMING

Brainstorming is used to create bigger and better ideas. It encourages open thinking and gets all members involved. Brainstorming allows team members to build on each other's creativity, while staying focused on the issue at hand. Brainstorming rules:

- Every idea is a good one
- No idea is ever criticized
- No person is ever criticized
- Ideas are written down so everyone can see
- Ideas are not discussed until brainstorming is complete

Brainstorming can be either structured or unstructured. With a structured process, each team member takes a turn after the brainstorming issue or item is clearly stated. Ideas are generated in turn until each person passes. With an unstructured process, team members volunteer ideas as the ideas come up.

Another way of brainstorming ideas would be to have everyone independently write down the first few ideas that come to mind, and then share those ideas, or, after writing three ideas on a sheet of paper, pass the paper to the next person who has five minutes to add three more ideas. This can be repeated as many times as there are team members. This forces team members to consciously build on other's perspectives and input.

GROUND RULES

- This is a safe room
- There is no rank in this room
- All ideas are valid
- Each person gets a chance to speak
- Each person gets a chance to listen
- What we decide here, everyone will implement
- We are here to focus on the future
- Our purpose is improvement, not blame

MEETING ETIQUETTE

- Raise your hand and be recognized before speaking
- Be brief and to the point
- Make your point calmly
- Keep an open mind
- Listen without bias
- Understand what is said
- Avoid side conversations
- Respect other opinions
- Avoid personal agendas
- Come prepared to do what is good for the organization
- Have fun

Cause and Effect Analysis

Also known as the fishbone analysis (named for the shape that results), the Cause and Effect Diagram (Figure 49) shows the relationship and the complexities between an "effect" or problem and all the possible "causes." It is good for staff to be able to describe what they think are possible causes of the problem before looking at what the data tell them. This approach helps staff sort out the issues that get in the way of achieving the ideal situation. These approaches are sometimes needed in order for some staff to get away from what they think are the causes when the data do not support the cause.

Steps in constructing a cause and effect diagram follow:

1. Identify the problem or the "effect" on the right-hand side of the diagram.

2. Brainstorm the possible major causes of the problem (might want to use the affinity analysis to identify the causes and the headings that result). You can use any categories that emerge to get people thinking creatively.

3. Place the causes in the boxes around the spine of the fish.

4. For each cause, ask, "Why does this happen?" and list the responses as branches off the major causes. (Could also create header cards from brainstormed causes.)

5. To find the most basic causes of the problem, look for the causes that appear repeatedly.

Figure 49

**Cause and Effect Diagram
Built on Teacher
Brainstorming**

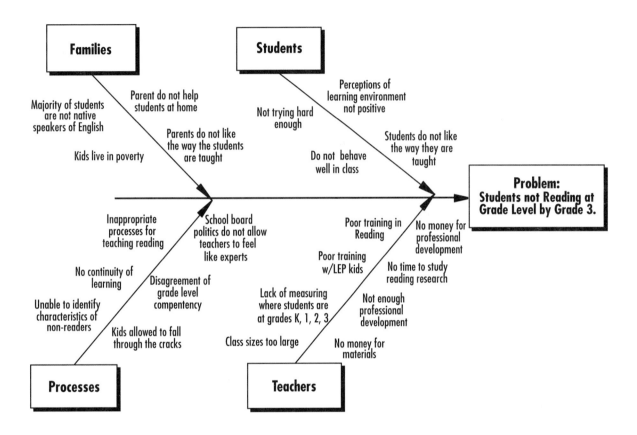

<u>The Affinity Diagram</u>

A tool that can be used in nearly all cycles of problem-identifying and problem-solving processes is the affinity diagram. The affinity diagram encourages creativity on everyone's part. It allows for comprehensive thinking concerning issues, encourages non-traditional connections among ideas and issues, often gets people talking about issues they normally might not, and allows breakthroughs to emerge naturally. The affinity diagram encourages ownership of the results that emerge to help overcome resistance to dealing with problems. This diagram is used when groups need a non-judgmental process for collecting ideas in a short period of time.

> *The evil is half-cured*
> *whose cause we know.*
>
> Shakespeare

Steps in building affinity diagrams follow:

1. *Clearly identify the problem*

   Problem: All students are not reading at grade level by grade 3

2. *Brainstorm hunches and hypotheses*

   Strive to capture the essence of *all* ideas. Record each idea on a self-adhesive note using at least a noun and a verb. Avoid using single words. Shortcuts here can greatly reduce the effectiveness of the final affinity diagram. Three to five minutes are often adequate.

Some of the issues that might surface, include the following:

- Inappropriate processes for teaching reading are being used
- Students' perceptions of the learning environment are not positive
- There is a lack of measurement concerning students at grades K, 1, 2, 3
- Students don't like the way they are taught
- Parents don't like the way the students are taught
- Parents do not help students at home
- Lots of kids are living in poverty
- Students don't behave in class
- School board desires

- The majority of students are not native speakers of English
- Class sizes are too large
- There is disagreement on grade level definition
- There is no time to study reading research
- There is not enough professional development for teachers
- Teacher abilities are not up to snuff
- There is no money for professional development
- There is no money for materials

3. *Without discussion, the group sorts the items into classifications*

   It is okay for some notes to stand alone. They might be as important as all the others that naturally fit into groups. If there is an idea that goes under more than one grouping, you might want to decide as a group to duplicate the idea.

4. *For each grouping create a header and agree on a concise sentence that combines the grouping's central idea*

5. *Divide large groupings into subgroups, if needed, and create subheadings*

6. *Draw the final affinity diagram connecting ideas to the header cards*

Figure 50 is an example of a typical affinity diagram that was built from the group brainstorm. The headings that emerged were Processes, Families, Students, and Teachers. The group lined up their brainstorming ideas under the header cards. This group was surprised that the majority of comments fell under two headers—Processes and Teachers. They also had a difficult time determining if the comments fell under the category of Processes *or* Teachers, which was quite informative to them. These teachers began to see that their level of training and their processes were the root cause of the problem.

Figure 50

Affinity Diagram

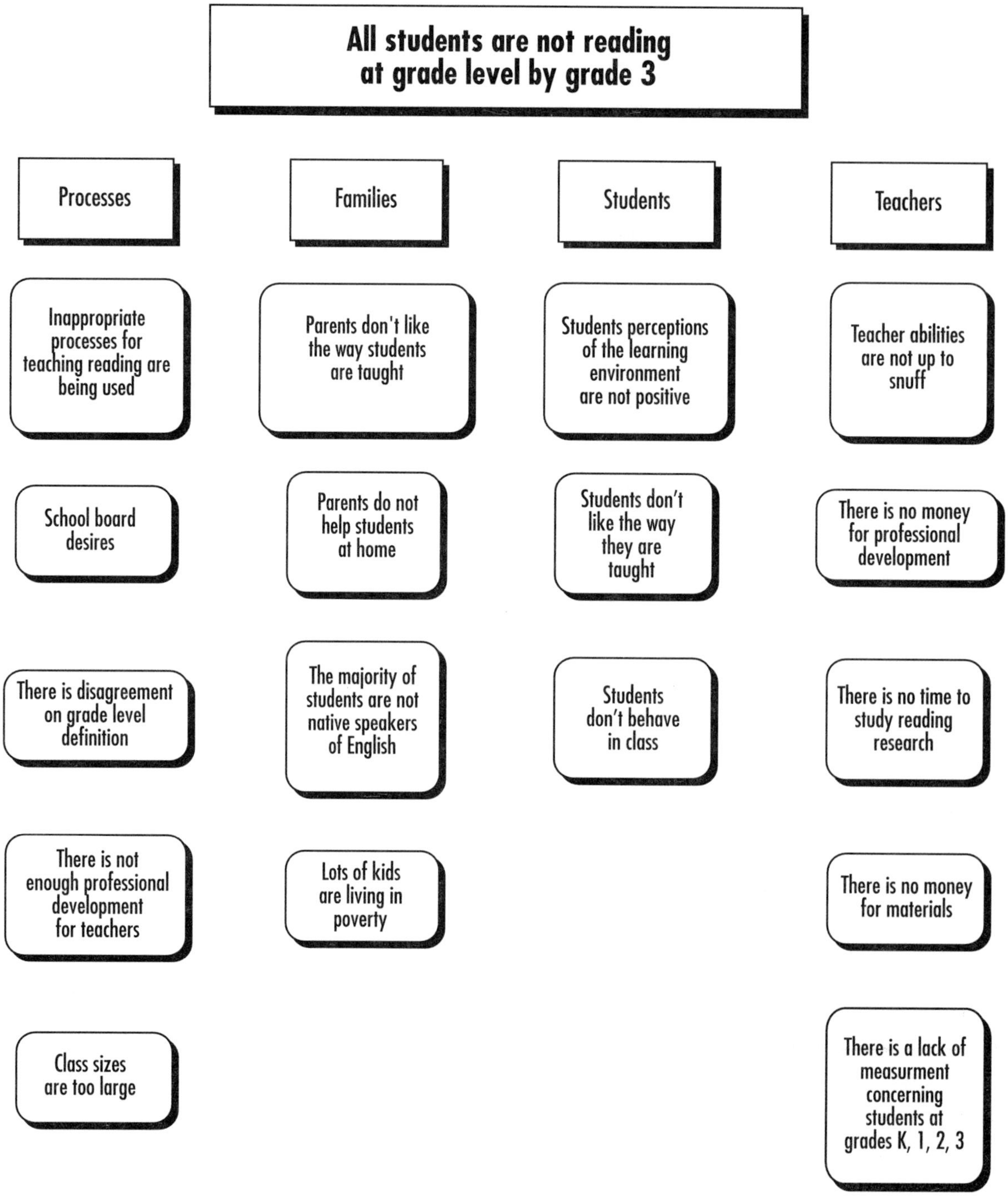

All students are not reading
at grade level by grade 3

Processes	Families	Students	Teachers
Inappropriate processes for teaching reading are being used	Parents don't like the way students are taught	Students perceptions of the learning environment are not positive	Teacher abilities are not up to snuff
School board desires	Parents do not help students at home	Students don't like the way they are taught	There is no money for professional development
There is disagreement on grade level definition	The majority of students are not native speakers of English	Students don't behave in class	There is no time to study reading research
There is not enough professional development for teachers	Lots of kids are living in poverty		There is no money for materials
Class sizes are too large			There is a lack of measurment concerning students at grades K, 1, 2, 3

Forcefield Analysis

Forcefield analysis is another way to think through all aspects of a situation so that solutions can be easily considered. Like the affinity diagram process, forcefield analysis forces people to think together about problems and desired changes, encourages honest reflection on the real underlying root causes of a problem and its solutions, and encourages people to agree on the factors. Forcefield analysis presents the positives and the negatives of a situation so they can readily be compared. It is another excellent way of looking at the *big picture*. Steps in a forcefield analysis follow:

1. Write the ideal state at the top of a flip chart or a piece of paper.
2. Brainstorm the forces that are *driving* toward this ideal state on the left.
3. Brainstorm the forces that are *restraining* movement from the ideal state on the right.

Figure 51 shows the brainstormed driving and restraining forces effecting the ideal state of all students reading at grade level by grade 3.

Figure 51

Ideal state — All students reading at grade level by grade 3.

Driving Forces	Restraining Forces
Fits with priorities	Our research does not support this possibility
What teachers want for kids	Class sizes are too large
Fits with the purpose of the school	Not enough money to incorporate the programs that are necessary
School board desires	No systematic measurements to know how we are doing
Reading Recovery can help	Reading specialist is needed
Parents do not like the way students are being taught	Families do not help with homework
We need better processes for teaching reading	Students are not native English speakers
Students like to go to school here	No agreement on what constitute reading at grade level
Teachers want to improve	Kids are living in poverty
We need strong measurements	Students do not behave
	Time
	No money for professional development
	No measurement of where students are with respect to reading at grades K, 1, 2, 3

Identify Questions and Data

Once the hunches and hypotheses are identified, staff can brainstorm a list of questions they might want to ask to determine if the hunches are fact or fiction. These questions and the list of data required to answer the questions flow logically from the hunches, like the sample below.

Questions about Hunches and Problem	Data
1. How do we define grade level reading for grades K through 3?	1. Staff Discussion.
2. How have students performed in reading in the past 3, or more years?	2. Student achievement data, by grade level, over time.
3. What are the characteristics of the students who are performing below grade level at any grade level?	3. Student achievement data, by grade level, over time, by gender and ethnicity.
4. What are the students' perceptions of the way reading is taught?	4. Student questionnaire results, disaggregated by gender, ethnicity, and grade level.
5. What are parents' perceptions of the way reading is taught, and how their child is learning at our school?	5. Parent questionnaire.
6. How are we teaching reading in the different grades?	6. Teacher report/process flow chart.
7. How are these data related?	7. Student learning by perceptions by demographics by processes.

Nine times out of ten, the data analysis is essentially designed through this list. At this point in the problem-solving cycle, teachers usually express shock at how much data is required to "problem solve." It is then that they realize that they have been acting on hunches to this point. Their options are to continue doing the same things and get the same results, or to gather the data and find out what the problem really is.

The Flow Chart

The flowchart was described earlier as a means of mapping school processes. The flowchart is also useful when thinking through the questions and the data that can answer the questions—a means of mapping out a data analysis plan, if you will.

Start with the focus of your data analysis. It might be a problem, or it might be the purpose of the school. For example, related to the problem of *students not reading at grade level by grade 3,* Figure 52 shows a flowchart of thinking through the questions and data analyses.

The flowchart starts with a definition of grade level reading for grades K, 1, 2, and 3, and then an understanding of how the students have been doing on student learning measures for the past three years, or more. Looking at the data, one can determine if there are subscores below grade level at the different grade levels. Those scores are disaggregated by what is thought to make a difference with student results (e.g., gender, level of poverty, ethnicity, English language proficiency, and length of time at the school). At the same time, data from the students' perspective can be obtained via student questionnaires and disaggregated in similar ways. Now that these data have been spelled out, school personnel need to think about what they are doing to teach reading at each of the different levels. Are they seeing a difference in scores based upon a difference in teaching approach? Other questions begin to emerge, such as—

- Are there differences in how reading is taught at the different grade levels and in different classrooms?
- What are the student characteristics that can be identified that will help predict the lack of reading at the third grade level?
- Which students did not meet end-of-year expectations?
- What methods need to be changed based upon what was learned from this analysis?
- What will it look like when a new approach is implemented?
- How will the impact of a new approach be measured?

Figure 52

Thinking Through the Data Analysis Process Flowchart
Problem: Not all Children are Reading at Grade Level by Grade 3.

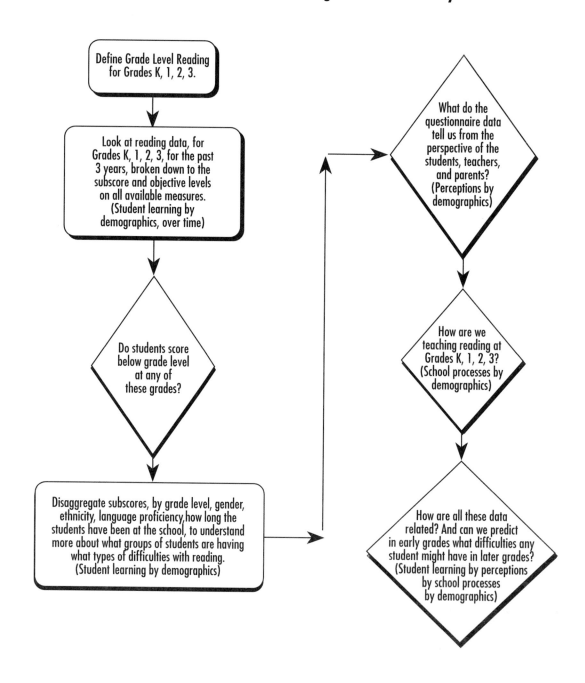

A flowchart could guide group processes that are focused on looking at the root causes of a problem. Similar flowcharts can be used to uncover the problem. One could also use the process flowchart to focus data questions, or to simply list the questions and data as Valley High did at the end of this chapter. It is important to understand that these processes do not have the *solutions*, per se. Teachers must conduct research and study different approaches to implement. Without new knowledge of processes, the same mistakes can be made again and again.

Analyze Multiple Measures of Data

Everyone on staff needs to understand and be able to use the data that is gathered about the school. There are many approaches to using group processes to this end. One approach to getting everyone to "own" the data is to get everyone involved in a systematic group discussion focused on the data. Steps in this approach follow:

1. Give everyone an opportunity to get familiar with each piece of data gathered about the school.

2. Focus the group on a piece of data, e.g., disaggregated questionnaire chart.

> *Seek first to understand and then to be understood.*
>
> Stephen R. Covey

3. Systematically go around the room and have each person say what they see in the chart that should be noted. With groups larger than 30, consider pairing people to examine the data first and note important observations. Then use a "fish bowl" approach in which the reporters sit in an inner circle surrounded by "listeners" who may move to an empty seat in the inside circle if they have observations that others are not reporting.

4. Record observations related to the data on chart paper.

5. Keep going around the room encouraging participants to look deeper and for connections with the previously observed data. Individuals should pass if they have nothing new to add.

6. Looking at the chart paper, the group looks for and classifies related issues.

7. Using the same process, ask the group, "What else do we need to know?" Other disaggregations of the data they want to see are then recorded.

8. The process continues with other pieces of data, e.g., disaggregated student achievement scores.

9. Eventually, the group looks at the relationship of the results of all the pieces of data and begins to brainstorm meanings and solutions. Guidelines for brainstorming were presented on page 147.

Figure 53 below shows the brainstorming of multiple measures placed in an affinity diagram. The data analyzed are used as headings and the teachers' brainstormings are listed under the appropriate heading.

Figure 53

Problem: All students are not reading at grade level by grade 3					
Student Learning by Demographics	Perceptions about Student Learning	Processes by Perceptions	Processes by Student Learning	Perceptions by Demographics	Perceptions by Processes by Student Learning by Demographics
Hmong students are not performing as well as other ethnicities.	Mien students feel responsible.	Students in the Reading Recovery Program feel that teachers care about them.	Most students are able to meet the standards for reading after Reading Recovery.	Mien students feel less positive than others that other children are nice to them.	Students who feel they can do the work and that teachers feel they can do the work, meet the standards.
A greater percentage of Hmong students are not meeting the standard.	Fewer Mien students than others feel that school work is challenging.	Students in the Reading Recovery Program feel they can do the work.	Supportive teachers' classrooms have the best success after Reading Recovery.	Fewer Mien students than others like coming to school.	Students who do not reach a Level 8 on Reading Recovery in grade 1 will not read on grade level by grade 3.
Hmong and Mien children have not been exposed to American customs.	Fewer Mien students than others feel that they know how to solve problems.		Teachers must assist students in understanding the meanings of words students have not been exposed to.	Mien students feel less positive than others that they are treated with respect.	Students who do well on Reading Recovery still must be supported by the classroom teacher.
Many students did not meet the CTBS standards.	Most students, regardless of ethnicity, feel that their families expect them to do well in school.			All American Indian students strongly agree that grown-ups treat them with respect.	
More students meet the standards when following cohorts.	American Indian students are bored with school.			All American Indian students strongly agree that their teacher thinks they can do well in school.	
All ethnicities are improving.					

Using the headings of the interaction analyses, we substitute the question in step 4 with this question, "What do the data tell us about this heading." The data analysis diagram in Figure 54, built as a variation of a cause and effect diagram, shows how data from different sources interacts to solve problems. We find it useful to place the negative results on one side and the positive results on the other side of the spines. We also move the problem statement to the left because the data can lead to the solution; we have the arrows lead to a solution.

Figure 54

**Cause and Effect Diagram
Built on Data
Analysis Results**

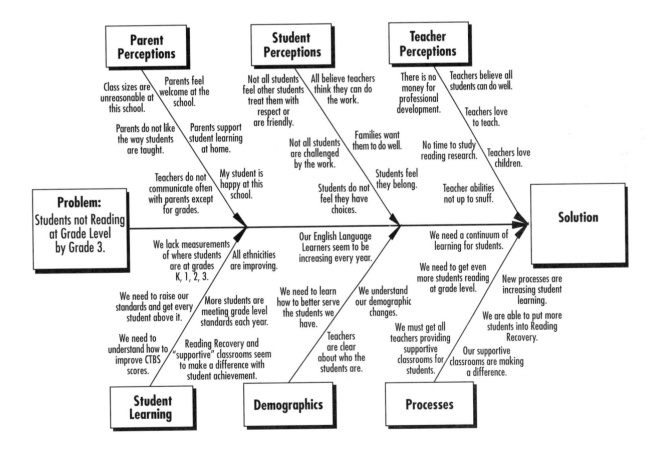

Analyze Political Realities

With all the analyses completed, we can again use an affinity diagram to understand the driving forces that can be strengthened and the restraining forces that can be deleted. The idea is to start gnawing away at the restraining forces, while strengthening the driving forces. Figure 55 shows Figure 51 reordered.

Figure 55

Reorder of Figure 51

Ideal state — All students reading at grade level by grade 3.

Driving Forces	Restraining Forces
What teachers want for kids	Families do not help with homework
We need better processes for teaching reading	Students are not native English speakers
Teachers want to improve	No agreement on what constitutes reading at grade level
We need strong measurements	
School board desires	
Fits with priorities	
Fits with the purpose of the school	

When reordering Figure 51, staff started planning for action immediately. They determined that because they wanted all students to read at grade level by grade 3, this had to become their highest priority. This desire was directly related to the purpose of the school and the vision—if all students weren't reading at grade level by grade 3, they would have limited options in life. With reading as their priority, there was no reason to not agree on what constitutes reading at grade level—this became an action item for their next staff meeting. It was no longer a restraining force.

One of the reasons teachers had not agreed up to this point was the lack of a rigorous look at past data. When past data are used, everyone can see what is possible and establish the standard together. A group of teachers worked with an outside consultant to get past data together for the staff meeting. They committed to continue conducting rigorous measurements in order to assess their progress with new processes. Teachers, working with administration, determined that professional development and teachers' abilities would no longer be restraining forces because, if reading at grade level by grade 3 is really the school priority, money cannot be an issue. Money has to first be allocated to the priorities that help everyone implement the vision. Time to prepare and learn about reading can no longer be an issue either. Time must be reallocated to the top priority issue. From this point forward, it was agreed that staff meetings would focus on this issue, and other items that tend to take up staff meeting time would be dealt with via electronic mail or memorandum. Staff determined that, with reading as a priority, every time teachers meet together, they must be working to that end.

As one can see, this group of teachers started sorting out what was really doable. By thinking through the pieces together, they began changing their thinking about the situation. They began to see that the way they were thinking about the children and their processes was at the root of the problem. The next important step would be for them to build a solid plan to ensure that everyone understands and implements the agreed upon action.

One reason forcefield analysis works is that teams select the targets for change. They are able to see those things that are changeable. Not all things can be changed, which brings up the difference between a "problem" and a "condition." A problem is something we can do something about, so we can focus time and energy in that direction. A condition is something that we cannot do anything about—we acknowledge it and go around it, but we do not waste time trying to change it. In most common situations, restraining forces would probably be reordered from condition to problem. In this case, families not helping with homework and students' home language are conditions.

Many people view change as a struggle between forces that seek to upset the status quo. We can build on the "driving forces" to implement change if we can remove "restraining forces." When the opposing forces are equal, or the restraining forces are too strong to allow movement, there is no change.

Forcefield analysis can also be used to align what the data show are the driving forces and the restraining forces. In other words, if you know what the interaction analyses show, those results can be ordered as driving and restraining results just like the other items above.

Develop an Action Plan

After analyzing for root causes of problems, and looking for solutions, the team must plan to put the solutions into action by first asking—

- Are our solutions congruent with the purpose of the school, and what are we trying to do ultimately for all students?

- Does our plan include a way to measure change?

- Does our plan include a specific date for implementation and review?

- Do our budget priorities line up with planned priorities?

- Does our plan truly represent an objective analytical look at the root causes of problems and solutions?

Action plans include what is to be done, who is responsible for making sure that it gets done, cost considerations, and timelines (i.e., by when the work will be done). An outline of an action plan is shown as Figure 56. A complete example is shown with the Valley Story on page 176.

Do not be dismayed if the problem analysis leads to the need to gather more data.

> *Not everything that is faced can be changed, but nothing can be changed until it is faced.*
>
> James Baldwin

Figure 56

Action Plan Outline

Task to be accomplished: _____

What is to be done?	Who is to do it?	Cost Consideration	SEPT	OCT	NOV	DEC	JAN	FEB	MAR	APR	MAY	JUN	JULY	AUG

Nominal Group Technique

When identifying a solution, often the person who speaks the loudest or has the most authority ends up making the decision. This could cause staff members to lose their commitment to change. When there are many solutions possible and consensus cannot be reached, the Nominal Group Technique is a way to make sure everyone in the group has an equal voice in solution selection. The steps in the process follow:

1. Have all group members write on a piece of paper or say the solution that they feel is most important.

2. Record the solutions on a flip chart, or somewhere where everyone can see them.

3. Let the team determine if a statement has been written twice. If so, combine the two into one item.

4. Ask members to write on a piece of paper the letters corresponding to the number of problem statements the team produced. For example, if the team ended up with five statements, everyone would write the letters A through E on the paper, and associate a letter with each statement.

5. Making sure that each problem statement has a letter in front of it, ask members to rank the statements according to their importance, with 5 being the most important.

6. Everyone completes the voting and combines their responses, which might look something like the following:

A.	2, 5, 2, 4, 1	D.	5, 2, 1, 1, 2
B.	1, 4, 5, 5, 5	E.	3, 3, 4, 2, 3
C.	4, 1, 3, 3, 4		

7. Add across each line. The item with the highest total number is the most important solution to the total team. In this case, the solution statement coded B is the most important, and C and E are the next important solutions.

A.	=	14	D.	=	11
B.	=	20	E.	=	15
C.	=	15			

Implement the action plan

After the quality action plan for implementing the solutions is developed, a commitment to implementation needs to be made by all staff members. Teachers must commit to adjusting their instructional and assessment strategies to meet the needs of their students, and they must be able to assess the impact of their actions on students. Leaders must do everything they can do, at all times, to make sure that the plan is implemented. The plan will need to be implemented in ways that reflect grade levels and subject areas, and must be congruent with the vision and overall strategic plan. A structure might need to be established to coordinate, implement, and support the plan.

Evaluate the implementation

All parts of the implementation need to be evaluated, using multiple measures, on an ongoing basis. A continuously improving learning organization uses evaluation to understand the impact and effectiveness of its actions; to ensure the congruence and synergy of the elements of its vision; and, to determine how well new strategies have been implemented, with the overall goal of improving processes, products, and procedures on an ongoing basis.

Improve the process

Understanding the impact each element has upon the other determines what to change. When evaluating on an ongoing basis, one can know what is working and what is not working. Improvements can and ought to be made, as they are necessary.

OUR EXAMPLE SCHOOLS

Problem Analysis at Valley High School

Forest Lane School's problem was detailed in Chapter 8. Valley High's example appears on the following pages.

THE VALLEY STORY

Valley staff wanted to address the issue of why so many freshmen were receiving F's in coursework. The staff brainstormed their hunches about this phenomenon and grouped the responses, as follows:

PROBLEM: Too many Valley freshmen have one or more F's

Hunches about why these students are failing:

THEIR FAMILIES

- Lack of family support for students
- Lack of family support for the school
- Parents don't volunteer at school
- Number of single parent families
- Number of students' families below the poverty line
- Are not native English speakers

STUDENTS

- Don't do homework
- Too many don't speak English
- Don't attend school regularly
- Have other problems that interfere with focusing on school
- Don't bring class materials (textbooks, pens, paper, etc.) to class
- Lack discipline
- Don't see the value of school
- Don't care about school
- Don't seek help from school support services
- Lack study skills
- Lack time management/organizational skills
- Some may schedule too many classes (i.e., eight-period day)

TEACHERS

- Lack of support for behavioral problems (students can only be legally suspended for x # days, then they're back in the classroom)
- No time to address problem, thoughtfully
- No time to plan
- No time for staff development
- Not enough training on how to work with limited and non-English-speaking students or heterogeneous classes

PROCESSES

- Grade level advisors don't have enough time to adequately track the D & F students
- Lack of course standards so that teachers are accountable for the same things
- No standardized measures of achievement in all subject areas
- No support from the school board to hold students back or to make them accountable before they graduate
- Beginning to have the process in place to identify root causes, but not enough experiences yet to have it be truly powerful.
- Middle School did not teach the prerequisite skills
- No substitute teachers are available due to sub shortage in district
- No funds for basic classroom supplies, let alone extras
- Some class sizes are too large
- Not enough administrative or district support
- There are not always solutions for every problem

THE VALLEY STORY (Continued)

Staff then listed the questions they wanted to answer with data that would help them understand the facts behind their hunches. They also made a list of the data they knew they had that could answer their questions.

	Questions	Data Needed to Answer Question
STUDENTS	Who are the students getting F's? How many students are getting F's?	Demographics by ethnicity, gender, language, attendance, age, retention, GPA, CAT scores, middle school attended
	What are the F's in?	F's by courses
	What are the students' perceptions of the school? Do their perceptions differ by where they went to middle school, by ethnicity, gender, or by the kinds of grades they are getting?	Questionnaire disaggregated by grades, ethnicity, gender, where they went to middle school
	What happens to the freshmen when they become 10th graders, and so on?	Check transcripts Look at test scores
	How did they do in elementary/middle school?	Check cumulative files
	Do they use support services?	Check files
	Do they schedule too many classes?	Check files
	Are they involved in extracurricular activities?	Check files
FAMILIES	Who are the families?	Demographics
	Do the parents think they are supporting their students?	Questionnaire
	What are parent perceptions of the school?	Questionnaire
TEACHERS	What are teachers' perceptions of the school?	Questionnaire
	What are class sizes?	Check files
PROCESSES	What are we doing to track D's and F's?	Describe Process
	How do teachers deal with the issue?	Describe Process
	What would we like the processes to look like?	Describe Process

THE VALLEY STORY (Continued)

Using existing data, Valley staff began making a list of what the data told them about their freshmen.

Valley Freshmen Get Too Many F's		
Student Data	**Students' Perceptions**	**Students' Perceptions, By GPA***
Of our 434 freshmen, 210 have a total of 767 F's at mid-year (48%). 152 freshmen are getting 2 or more F's (35%).	Feel safe.	Students feel good about the school overall.
The majority of students receiving F's are Hispanic males and Hispanic females, with 85 and 63, respectively.	Feel like they belong at Valley.	Students who get mostly A's, A's and B's, and B's and C's would not like help from a tutor.
Caucasian males had 27 F's and Caucasian females had 19 F's.	Feel treated with respect by staff, except for African American students.	Students who get mostly A's are not in strong agreement that teachers set high academic and behavioral standards in the classroom, do not feel the classwork is challenging, or that it is at their level.
Average number of F's for freshmen are 3.65.	Students feel relatively informed about the support services.	All students, except for the students getting mostly A's, do not feel that the classwork/ homework at Valley is easy.
54 students had one F; 46 had 2 F's; 22 had 3 F's; 16 had 4 F's; 16 had 5 F's; 18 had 6 F's; 12 had 7 F's; 8 had 8 F's; 8 had 9 F's; 4 had 10 F's; 2 had 11 F's.	Students do not want help from a tutor.	Students receiving C's and D's, and D's and F's do not have regularly scheduled quiet times to do homework at home.
F's are in a variety of courses and combinations.	Students feel classwork/ homework is challenging.	Students receiving C's and D's, and D's and F's do not feel academically prepared for their classes at Valley.
The students getting F's are attending school—they are not the ones absent.	Students agree that the work is at their level, except for the Asian students.	Students receiving C's and D's, and D's and F's do not feel students at Valley are friendly.

* As reported by students on the questionnaire.

THE VALLEY STORY (Continued)

Valley Freshmen Get Too Many F's

Student Data	Students' Perceptions	Students' Perceptions, By GPA*
178 sophomores had 588 F's. 146 juniors had 431 F's. 97 seniors had 243 F's.	Students do not feel that the classwork/homework at Valley is easy.	Students receiving C's and D's, and D's and F's would like help from a tutor.
Most of the freshmen receiving F's are English Language Learners.	Students are trying their best. All student ethnic groups are trying their best.	Students receiving A's and B's, B's and C's, C's and D's, and D's and F's feel that the work is challenging.
We do not know how many freshmen are retained for poor performance each year.	Students agree that teachers set high academic and behavioral standards.	Students receiving D's and F's do not feel that the classwork is easy and that they are treated with respect by staff.
Looking at the CAT V Reading quartiles for freshmen with 2 or more F's by gender and ethnicity, one can see that the majority of these students score in the 2nd quartile, followed by the 1st quartile. Because the largest numbers are Hispanic males and females, we need to look by language fluency to determine if the language is holding them back. CAT V scores for the past 3 years show about the same performance.	Students are friendly at Valley. Asian and African American students have regularly scheduled quiet time to do homework at home. Caucasian, Hispanic, and "Other" students do not have regularly scheduled quiet time to do homework at home.	There appears to be a difference in freshman student perceptions of Valley High based on where they attended middle school.

* As reported by students on the questionnaire.

170

THE VALLEY STORY (Continued)

Valley Freshmen Get Too Many F's

Parent Perceptions	Processes	Teachers' Perceptions
Parents feel welcome at Valley, and are encouraged to visit.		Feel lack of support to deal with the behavioral problems.
Parents feel informed about students' progress.	A database to track student progress is needed.	Do not have adequate instructional material and facilities.
Parents know what the teachers expect of the students.	Grade level advisors do not have time to adequately track the D and F students.	Feel instructional program is challenging.
Students are safe.	We need course standards.	School provides atmosphere where every student can succeed.
Parents respect the principal.	We do not agree on the processes for dealing with students who do not get the grades they need to move ahead.	Quality work is expected of all students at this school.
Parents feel teachers show respect for the students.	We need to understand the root causes of the problems.	The school vision is clear and shared.
School meets the academic needs of the students.	We do not have a way of measuring where the students are when they come to us.	Teachers think it is important to communicate often with parents.
School expects quality work of its students.		Teachers feel they communicate often with parents about students' progress, but not as often as they would like.
School has excellent learning environment.		Teachers do not often communicate with parents other than about grades.
There is adequate recognition of student successes.		Teachers feel they encourage parents to be involved in their student's learning.
Elective courses are important.		Morale is not so high for teachers, staff, administrators, and students.

THE VALLEY STORY (Continued)

Valley Freshmen Get Too Many F's

Parent Perceptions	Teachers' Perceptions
Amount of homework is appropriate.	Teachers believe outcomes are clear to them and to the students.
Class sizes are not reasonable.	Teachers are not communicating well with each other to make student learning congruent across grades.
Teachers do not communicate often with parents about their student's progress.	Teachers love to teach and feel that learning is stimulating in their classroom.
Teachers do not communicate with parents aside from grades.	Teachers are not so eager to team teach or to participate in extra curricular activities, or teach with a cross-curricular emphasis.
Parents do not volunteer at this school.	Almost all teachers want to continue teaching at Valley.
	Almost all teachers feel like they belong at Valley.
	Many teachers do not feel recognized for good work.
	Although teachers feel that administrators support them in their work with students, they do not feel strongly that administrators are effective instructional leaders, or that administrators are aware of what goes on in their classrooms.
	Teachers do not feel that they work effectively with special education and limited English speaking students.
	Teachers believe that students behave well.

THE VALLEY STORY (Continued)

STAFF "Ah-Hahs"

Staff studied the charts and what the data told them. There were many "ah-hahs":

- It is not just the freshmen that have F's—actually many sophomores, juniors, and seniors have F's.
- We need to communicate more with parents.
- Many of these students are attending school every day.
- Processes are not complete and not effective.
- Need to work with middle schools to know where the students are when they leave middle school.
- Valley High School and the feeder middle schools need to articulate their standards better so that there is a continuum of learning that makes sense for students.
- Our standards are not clear—they must be clarified.
- We need to treat students like we think they can do the work.
- We need to connect closer to students' interest—why they chose Valley in the first place.
- We need to read the research to find more effective strategies that have been proven to work with students in our highest failure groups.
- We have been more concerned with recruiting freshmen than in helping them meet standards.
- The Partnerships for Achievement Program is outstanding. Unfortunately, the students getting F's are not necessarily the ones in the program.
- We need to think about acceleration instead of remediation.
- There is nothing we can do about the families, except encourage them to support their children's learning and use this information to predict "at-risk" students to offer them options *before* they fail.
- We need to review how we grade homework. If students do not have a quiet place to work at home, they cannot compete with students who do.

THE VALLEY STORY (Continued)

The following are processes these teachers thought would help with the situation, followed by their plan of action (just one year is shown).

Valley staff decided what they wanted to do about the problem.

NEXT STEPS

Establish task forces in each content area to establish standards. Include middle school and elementary school teachers.

Sponsor a two day conference (with follow-up) of one elementary, middle, and high school to reestablish our essential student learnings, and begin to build a continuum of learning that makes sense for students.

Find assessments that we can use at the beginning of the freshman year to know where students are when they arrive at Valley, and that we can also use in the middle and at the end of the year.

Study how our classes are structured so all students feel like they know we expect them to do the work, that they can do the work, and that they feel nurtured in their learning.

Study the processes we are using to ensure English Language Acquisition. We have to get students speaking, reading, and writing in English as soon as possible, so they can be successful in high school and in the future.

When at all possible, students must be grouped in smaller groups to ensure learning takes place.

We need to look into self-assessment techniques that will give students the self-motivation and interest to improve.

Establish partnerships with our middle schools.

Continue to gather data on an ongoing basis to improve everything we do.

Continue to measure student growth in sophomore, junior, and senior years.

THE VALLEY STORY (Continued)

Valley High Action Plan

ACTION	Responsible Person	Due Date	JAN	FEB	MAR	APR	MAY	JUN	JUL	AUG	SEPT	OCT	NOV	DEC
Develop Standards														
Create task forces in each subject area	Cindy Jones	1/15	X											
Task forces meet	Dept. Chairs	Ongoing	X······					······X						
Task forces report to each other	Cindy Jones				X		X							
Report results	Cindy Jones	6/1						X						
Conference for Revisiting Essential Student Learnings														
Plan the conference	Sarah Ball	1/31	X											
Hold the conference	Principal Skinner	4/15				X								
Writing Assessments for Freshmen														
Locate appropriate assessment	Sandra Cooke	3/31			X									
Plan for implementation of assessment	Sandra Cooke	3/31			X									
Pilot the assessment	Sandra Cooke	5/1					X							
Report on the results of the pilot	Sandra Cooke	5/30						X						
Study current processes	Wendy Ken	3/31	X······	······X										
Recommend new processes for teaching writing	Wendy Ken	5/30						X						
Administer new assessment	Sandra Cooke	9/1,12/1									X			X
Report on results	Sandra Cooke	9/15,12/15										X		X
Implement new processes	Every teacher	Ongoing									X······			
Reading Assessments for Freshmen														
Locate appropriate assessment	Jamie Richmond	3/31			X									
Plan for implementation	Jamie Richmond	3/31			X									
Pilot the assessment	Jamie Richmond	5/1					X							
Report on the results of the pilot	Jamie Richmond	5/30						X						
Study current processes for teaching reading	Phil Jones	3/31	X······	······X										
Recommend new processes for teaching reading	Phil Jones	5/30					X							
Administer new assessment	Jamie Richmond	9/1, 12/1									X			X
Report on results	Jamie Richmond	9/15,12/15										X		X
Implement new processes	Every teacher	Ongoing									X······			
Improve Class Structures														
Study current approaches	Nicholas Shelton	4/1	X······			······X								
Study new approaches	Wen Nikko	4/1	X······			······X								
Report on new implementation plan	Wen Nikko	4/15					X							
Establish Database for Data Analysis	George Bonner	2/15		X										
Get classroom level data to teachers	George Bonner	4/15 & ongoing				X······								······
Review where we are as a school	George Bonner	5/15					X							
Celebrate Our Successes	Everyone		Last Day of School											

Summary

Problem analysis techniques help all staff members see the same processes and understand them in the same way. Group processes and tools are helpful for desensitizing the information and the discussion around problems and causes.

Each of the tools discussed in this chapter can be used to think through the data analysis and interactions discussed in the previous chapters. (See References and Resources for more information on this topic.)

The laying out of the information helps staff see the big picture of the school for the students. Next steps are evident immediately, and many issues are taken care of during the conversation.

Putting It All Together Questions

Step 1:

For your school, use the fishbone below to identify a problem and to document your hunches and hypotheses.

Use the—
- box on the right for the problem
- other boxes for headings for your hunches and hypotheses
- lines for the hunches and hypotheses

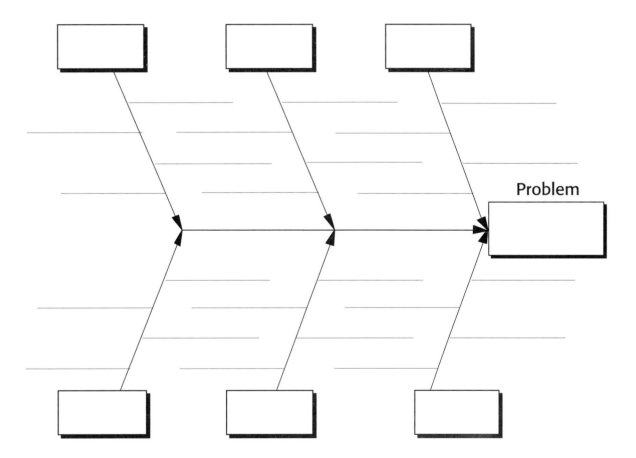

Putting It All Together Questions

Step 2:

    After identifying your hunches and hypotheses—

    • list the questions you need to answer to know if your hunches and hypotheses are fact or fiction

    • then list the data you would need to gather to answer the questions

QUESTIONS	DATA NEEDS

Chapter 10

COMMUNICATING THE RESULTS

Now that we have conducted the analyses and want others to understand our solutions and implementation approaches for continuous schoolwide improvement, we focus again on why we did the analyses in the first place.

Communicating the purpose and results of data analyses is critical if the analyses are going to affect decisions and if solutions are going to be implemented as intended. We can perform the most complex analyses in the world, but if we want others to use the data, they must be able to understand the analyses, their results, and their uses.

One of the first considerations in reporting data analysis results is the audience—the people who need to understand and use these data. Staff are the most important recipients of schoolwide data analysis results. These data tell them how they are doing and how they can improve what they are doing. We want staff to utilize the analyses to implement new ways of doing business, if needed.

We also want the community to understand the data analyses and resulting new approaches. What follows are ideas about communicating the data analysis results.

> *Analysis procedures that are employed should be appropriate to the data collected and analyses should always be done in a way that recognizes the evaluator's obligation to communicate to potential users. This communication should be in forms that are meaningful and likely to enhance the possibility of use. The evaluator's job is not to dazzle or to impress with sophisticated expertise, but rather to communicate.*
>
> Marvin Alkin

Communication Strategies

Many methods exist for reporting data results. It is important to match the method with the audience. For communication to a large audience, e.g., the public in general, you might want to use one or more of the following:

Article in the local newspaper by an education reporter. A prepared fact sheet or press release can help keep the facts straight. An example press release is shown at the end of this chapter.

Public meeting or news conference presented by the superintendent. Make sure the superintendent has all of the facts as well as a thorough understanding of the data. Also help the superintendent by thinking through typical questions that the public might ask. You might want to stage a practice news conference with staff to inform them and to rehearse for the real one.

Newsletters. Schools often send newsletters home to parents. The results of the data analysis could be described in the newsletter with information about the changes implied by the results.

Special events. If the data focus is on reading, for example, a special reading event might be set up for public participation. The results of the data could be reported that night in terms that will help parents understand what they can do differently, and what teachers are going to do differently, to improve reading at the school. Any handouts prepared for the audience could be sent home to those parents who were unable to attend.

School Portfolio. Other ways to communicate findings might include a school or district portfolio, telephone trees, speeches to service clubs, site council or leadership team briefings, and/or private meetings with business.

Web Sites. Many schools now have web sites that could be good communication vehicles for parents and community members with web access.

School Summary Report. Short school summary reports can be set up to let the public know how the school is doing and what it learned from recent analyses. An example is shown for Forest Lane at the end of this chapter.

Each of these methods for disseminating information will require slightly different approaches to presenting the data visually and discussing it in the text. An article for the local newspaper will need to sound objective and professional, while a newsletter can sound warmer and more casual. The pages for the school portfolio will need to include all the details behind the analyses, while a school summary report would generally summarize and highlight important results.

Whether communicating data analysis results to educators or non-educators, the person communicating the data analysis results has an obligation to interpret all of the data so pieces are not fragmented and so the data can be interpreted easily.

Communicating the Data Analysis Results

Graphs (or charts) are a powerful means of communicating data analysis results. Data graphics display multiple measures in terms of points, lines, bars, symbols, and pictures. Graphs set the stage for discussion, convey a message, or reinforce a central point. Graphs are designed to be concise in conveying data and be readily digestible.

A good graph deserves a thousand words.

The power of graphs comes from their ability to convey data directly to the viewer. Viewers use their spatial intelligence to retrieve data from a graph—a source of intelligence different from the language-based intelligence of prose and verbal presentations. The audience sees graphs. For most people, the communication process becomes more direct and immediate through graphic displays. Data become more credible and more convincing when the audience has direct interaction with it.

Graphs allow us to move easily from the analytical to the descriptive and vice versa. They also raise the motivation of the audience to access and use the data.

Graphs break up narrative in reports and encourage readers to engage in the material. Graphs encourage the eye to compare different pieces of data and to reveal the data at several levels of detail—from a broad overview to the fine points. Graphs can show test score data, for instance, with confidence limits or in comparison to norms or standards.

Graphs must be meaningful, interesting, and well designed. Graphs are meant to communicate information about relationships, especially where intensive inspection will deepen or induce understanding of the relationships. Readers should be able to make sense of a graph without reference to the text, and should be enticed to think about substance rather than methodology.

The previous chapters showed examples of graphs designed to provide overviews of a school (demographics), overviews of questionnaire results (perceptions), summaries of student achievement results (student learning), and their interactions. In each of these examples, the graphs did not rely on the text for interpretation. The key to creating excellent graphs is to convey the greatest number of ideas with the least ink in the smallest space.

Different Types of Charts and Graphs

There are many ways to chart or graph data. It is easy to choose a graph that can tell the comprehensive story of your data. It is just as easy to choose one that muddles the information. "Appropriate graphs" are simple—not complex—can stand alone, and are clear about the information they try to compare. The most common types of graphs used for displaying schoolwide data are pie, bar, and line charts.

> *I want to reach that state of condensation of sensations which constitutes a picture.*
>
> Henri Matisse

Pie Charts

Use pie charts to stress proportions or percentages of a population or category. Use no more than eight slices in any pie chart. When using color, do not use red and green together since 5 percent of the population can not distinguish between red and green. Also do not use patterns next to each other that result in optical illusions. Pie charts are outstanding for displaying the proportion of a school's enrollment for one year as in Figure 57 below.

Figure 57

Example Pie Chart

Enrollment for 1997-98
(N= 992)

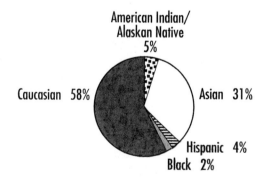

Bar Charts

Bar charts are the most highly recommended format for descriptive data. Bar charts can be shown horizontally or vertically. Bar charts typically show the relationship of the x-axis and y-axis, or frequency of events. These charts should be greater in length than height. Our eyes naturally look left to right and, therefore, horizontal charts are more accessible to the eye. It is wise to stay away from three-dimensional charts and stacked bar charts, because it is very difficult to comprehend the information being presented. Notice your personal preference as you look at the four identical bar charts, one set of flat charts set up vertically and horizontally, and one set of three-dimensional charts, set up vertically and horizontally (Figure 58).

Figure 58

Example Bar Charts

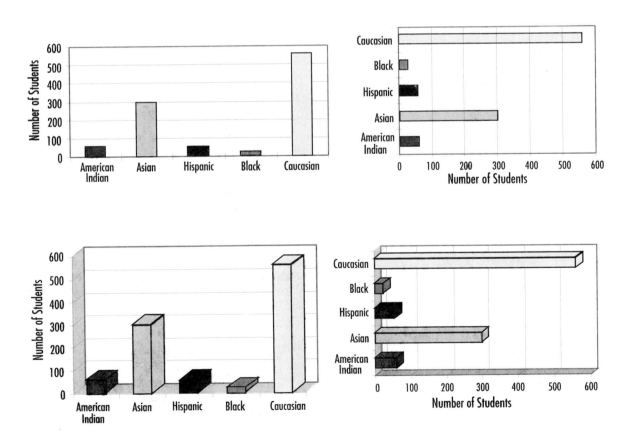

Figure 59, below, summarizes chart design considerations for bar charts.

Figure 59

**Design Considerations
for Bar Charts**

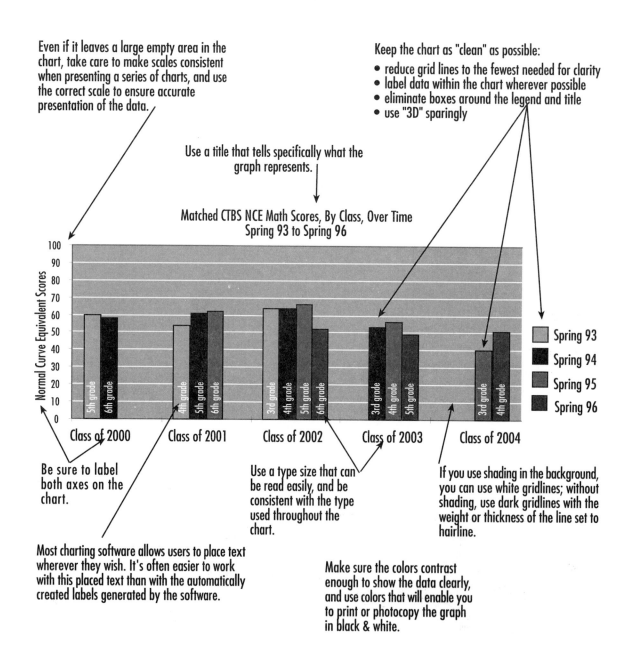

Even if it leaves a large empty area in the chart, take care to make scales consistent when presenting a series of charts, and use the correct scale to ensure accurate presentation of the data.

Keep the chart as "clean" as possible:
• reduce grid lines to the fewest needed for clarity
• label data within the chart wherever possible
• eliminate boxes around the legend and title
• use "3D" sparingly

Use a title that tells specifically what the graph represents.

Matched CTBS NCE Math Scores, By Class, Over Time
Spring 93 to Spring 96

Be sure to label both axes on the chart.

Use a type size that can be read easily, and be consistent with the type used throughout the chart.

If you use shading in the background, you can use white gridlines; without shading, use dark gridlines with the weight or thickness of the line set to hairline.

Most charting software allows users to place text wherever they wish. It's often easier to work with this placed text than with the automatically created labels generated by the software.

Make sure the colors contrast enough to show the data clearly, and use colors that will enable you to print or photocopy the graph in black & white.

Line Charts

Line charts give a lot of flexibility and are exceptionally good for showing a series of numbers over time. Line charts can display complex data more effectively than bar charts. If a bar chart was used to display the data in Figure 60, six bars would be needed for each item. Line charts are outstanding for showing how different groups responded to items on a questionnaire. For instance, Figure 60 shows an example of a disaggregated line chart that is helpful in data analysis for comprehensive schoolwide improvement. This chart would only be used in-house for problem finding. There are too many lines for an audience to read. Line charts enable a "big picture" look at the results of a questionnaire. One can see the overall response averages and individual group averages at the same time.

Design considerations are also found in Figure 60, on the following page.

Figure 60

Design Considerations for Line Charts

When charting large numbers of groups (usually eight or more) with very similar responses, the chart may become difficult or even impossible to read. Be nice to your audience—if you think the chart is hard to read, it is! Consider breaking the groups into two charts.

Be sure to include the number of people who make up each of the groups being charted. (Groups of 5 or less are generally considered to be too small to be considered in the chart.)

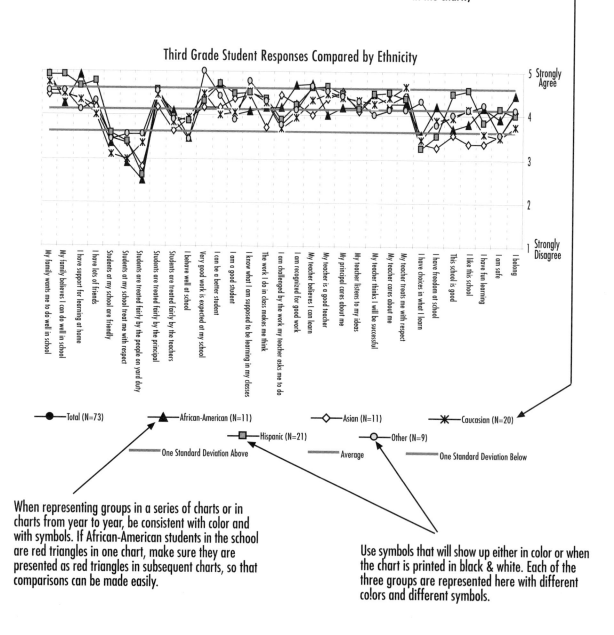

Third Grade Student Responses Compared by Ethnicity

When representing groups in a series of charts or in charts from year to year, be consistent with color and with symbols. If African-American students in the school are red triangles in one chart, make sure they are presented as red triangles in subsequent charts, so that comparisons can be made easily.

Use symbols that will show up either in color or when the chart is printed in black & white. Each of the three groups are represented here with different colors and different symbols.

It is just as important to describe questionnaire results as it is to describe student achievement test results. Be sure to—

1. include the purpose for administering the questionnaire in your description

2. explain that the results of the questionnaire are a snapshot in time that reflect where the school is right now

3. start with a general overview of the data

4. point out strengths and areas of concern

5. show how you dug deeper and deeper into the data to find answers

6. discuss how the school is going to use the data

The next three pages show a series of graphs that are designed to help you find the information that can be considered for communication to your various audiences. Whether you decide to present it in more or less detail will depend upon what you learn from the graph and how it needs to be presented to the audience in question.

The first graph (Figure 61) shows the total responses for a group of students that responded to a survey in 1997. The figure highlights various points of interest on the graph that should be considered when communicating the results of the survey to an audience.

Figure 61

Total Student Responses

The overall average across all items gives an idea of how much these respondents were in overall agreement with this set of items.

We look at the standard deviation as an indicator of the amount of variation within the averages.

The narrower the band formed by the standard deviation, the more the individuals agree. A wide band would indicate that the individual responses making up the overall averages varied considerably.

On items that are particularly important, it is good to view the standard deviation for that individual item.

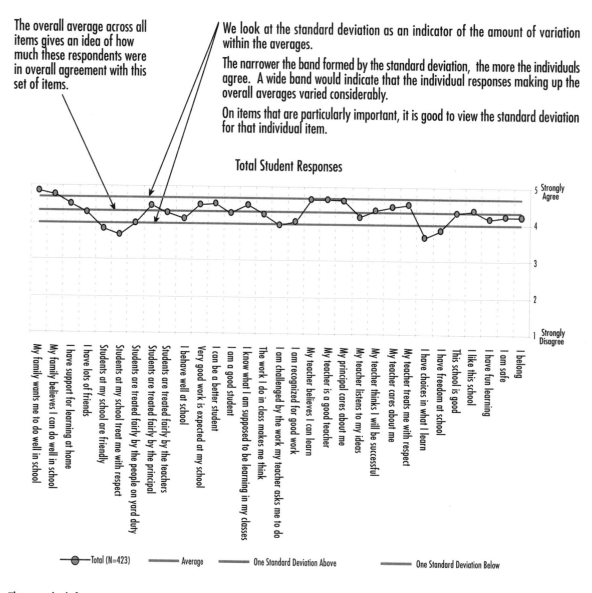

Total Student Responses

Things to look for:

- Overall, these students are in strong agreement with the set of items (overall average = 4.25)
- The narrow band created by the upper and lower standard deviation lines indicates the variation within the item averages were almost nonexistent.
- Highest averages or items in which these students were in most agreement were related to their families wanting and believing that students can do well in school.
- A couple of items show passion in the responses, i.e., every student stated that they <u>strongly agree</u> with the two highest items.
- Lowest averages were about having choices in school and other students treating them with respect, possibly unrelated, and still in agreement.
- Disaggregation is needed to understand more about the averages.
- No item averages were in disagreement.

The second graph (Figure 62) shows the same survey responses broken down by grade level. Again, the figure highlights various points of interest to consider and some recommendations for further problem analysis.

Figure 62

Student Responses by Grade Level

Average response of first graders to Item 29. (First grade responses are also reflected in the overall average.)

The lowest average for sixth graders is neutral. How that came about needs to be looked at (i.e., were agree and disagree responses equally distributed? Or, were all sixth graders indifferent to the question?)

Item averages for the total group responding to the questionnaire.

Line links first grade average item responses.

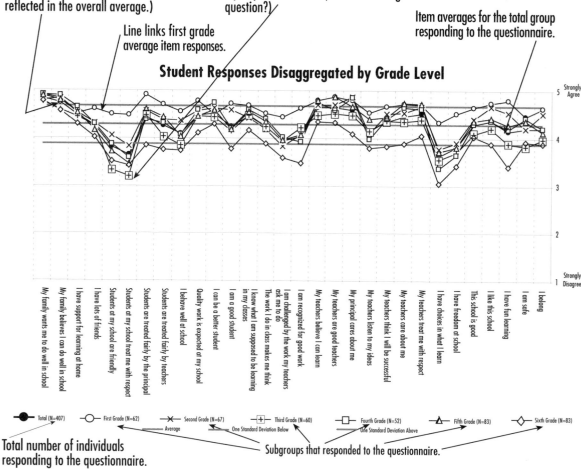

Student Responses Disaggregated by Grade Level

Total number of individuals responding to the questionnaire.

Subgroups that responded to the questionnaire.

Things to look for:

- Subgroups that "stick out" or look different from the others.
- Big gaps between one subgroup and the other subgroups.
- Differences in averages that result in opposite responses, such as agree-disagree.
- Subgroup trends that are unexpected.
- Size of subgroup that looks different from the other groups, although small numbers may still indicate issues that need to be addressed.
- Subgroups whose averages fall outside the standard deviation lines.
- Other analyses that would provide further understandings of the responses.

Things we found:

- There are some differences between group averages.
- First graders tend to be in strongest agreement with items on the questionnaire.
- Sixth graders tend to be in least agreement with questionnaire items.
- Third grade responses would be expected to consistently fall in the middle of all the subgroups.
- The third grade low scores appear as though they may be related.
- The lowest average for third grade is neutral. Might want to understand how that average came about (i.e., one-half of third graders agree and the other one-half disagree? Or, are all third graders indifferent to the question?) This issue, along with the possible relationship with the low scores, suggests we need to take a closer look at third grade.

The third graph (Figure 63) shows just the third grade responses, disaggregated by ethnicity. The items to consider are the same as those presented in the previous figure. This chart shows what the reader learns from looking at the data. What we learn from this level of data is normally what would be discussed with staff and not necessarily presented to the public at large, although it certainly could be used as a good example of getting your school to the root causes of a problem. In this particular case, there was a problem with a yard duty supervisor that was alleviated as soon as staff saw these survey results and talked to the children who responded negatively to the survey item.

Figure 63

Student Responses
by Ethnicity

African-American third grade students disagree that:
- Students at my school treat me with respect.

Looking at the third grade responses by ethnicity, one can see that:
- Caucasian third grade students agree that students are treated fairly by the people on yard duty.
- African-American, Hispanic, and Asian students disagree with that statement.

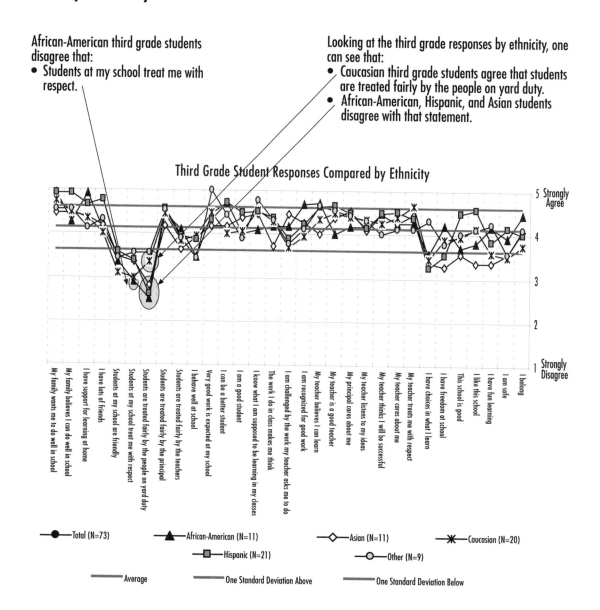

Things to look for:
- Issues that surface needing further investigation to understand the issues behind the responses. In this example, there are issues surfacing related to ethnicity. Teachers might interview the third grade classes or disaggregate further to pinpoint an even more specific subgroup, such as African American males.

If the medium for communicating the results of the survey is the portfolio, you would want to describe the survey results in detail, i.e., you would display the whole graph and describe in detail what you found in that graph that you consider important. More often than not, the best way to present questionnaire results in their entirety is to use a line chart for the reasons discussed earlier in this chapter. Specifically, with a line chart, it is easy to get an overall picture of positive or negative responses. It is easy to see where various subgroups fall, and you can get a lot of information on one page.

A detailed narrative description of a sample figure for Forest Lane Elementary students follows (Figure 64).

Figure 64

Interpreting Line Charts

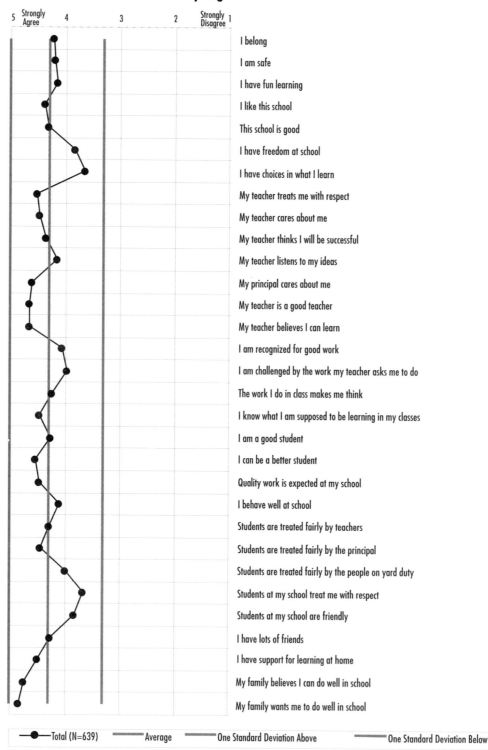

In Spring 1997, Forest Lane Elementary School students were asked to complete a survey regarding how they felt about the school. The 423 responses were charted for the overall student body, disaggregated by ethnicity and grade level.

The line graph on the previous page shows black dots that represent the average student response to each item labeled at the bottom; the overall average across all items is shown as the middle solid line; and the two additional lines indicate one standard deviation above and one standard deviation below the overall average.

The results show the overall average to be very positive—about a 4.39 on a five-point scale, with 5 representing "strongly agree" and 1 representing "strongly disagree." Average student responses for all survey items were in agreement. In other words, no item's average fell in the disagree category.

Overall results are described below. The line graph that displays these results appears on the previous page (Figure 64).

Students were in strongest agreement to:

- My family wants me to do well in school
- My family believes I can do well in school

The next most strongly agreed to items were:

- My teacher is a good teacher
- My principal cares about me
- My teacher believes I can learn

Although still in agreement, the items that received the lowest scores were as follows:

- Students at my school treat me with respect
- Students at my school are friendly
- I have choices in what I learn
- I have freedom at school

The lowest average was approximately 3.8.

Interpreting Line Graphs – Sample Narrative Analysis

If you are using a newsletter or a press release to communicate an important point that was revealed by the survey, or you are discussing one particular item with the school board, you might want to show a portion of the chart and include a brief summary statement of what was learned. In that case, you can present that questionnaire item as a little bar chart included in the text, such as the example below.

Parents and the board may wish to be aware that a greater percentage of students at this school do not feel their fellow students treat them with respect.

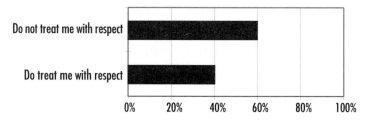

This is just another indication of the need for us to implement our new program.

There are also times when you want to show questionnaire data over time, to show positive change, or to compare responses. Again, a line chart is an excellent choice to present data as a whole, but bar charts can also be used to get a greater level of detail by charting the number responding to each response option.

Figure 65 shows a line chart comparing student responses to teacher predictions of student responses. In reporting these results, one needs to keep perspective. While there is a difference in responses to the item, "Students are treated fairly by the people on yard duty," it is not the only information that can be gleaned from this chart. Note the difference, along with the other information, make recommendations, and move on.

A sample of how the results of such a comparison might be described in a school portfolio follows.

Figure 65

Responses Compared to Teacher Predictions

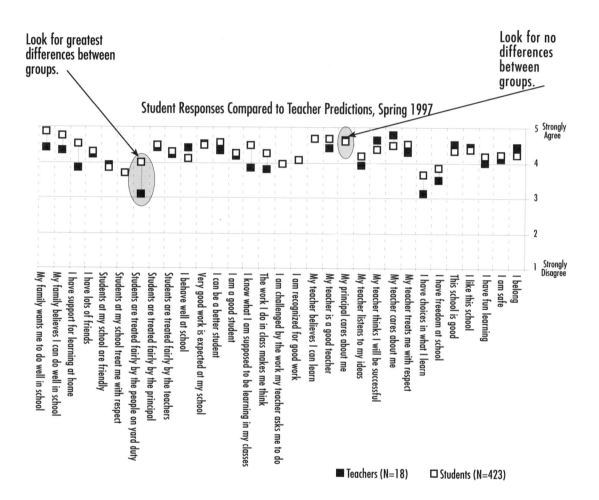

Look for greatest differences between groups.

Look for no differences between groups.

Student Responses Compared to Teacher Predictions, Spring 1997

■ Teachers (N=18)   □ Students (N=423)

Things to look for:
- Greatest differences
- No differences
- Relationships between (among) items with large (or no) differences
- Further analyses required to understand the differences

Interpreting Comparisons – Sample Narrative Analysis

The student and teacher responses were charted in distribution form from strongly disagree to strongly agree to look more closely at the patterns of the responses.

With this distribution we wanted to see in which areas either students or teachers felt strong passion about the items. In other words we wanted to see which responses were strongly agree or strongly disagree, as opposed to spread out over all of the categories. We also wanted to see how "in-tune" to the students the teachers were.

The areas in which the students were most positively passionate were the following:

- My family wants me to do well in school
- My family believes I can do well in school
- My teacher believes I can learn
- My teacher is a good teacher
- I have support for learning at home

Teachers predicted that the students would respond positively to these items, but not as strongly as the students actually responded.

The items in which there was most variety in the student responses and teacher predictions were:

- Students are treated fairly by the people on yard duty
- I have support for learning at home
- I know what I am supposed to be learning in my classes
- I have choices in what I learn

Teachers' closest prediction of student responses was with the following item:

- My teacher believes I can learn

If an item with differences in responses turns out to be educationally significant, you might want to look at the distribution of responses in a bar chart which will tell you how the individuals making up the average responded to the statement. (See Figure 66.)

Figure 66

Interpreting Bar Charts

Bar charts are a way to present numbers (or percentages) of individuals who chose each response option.

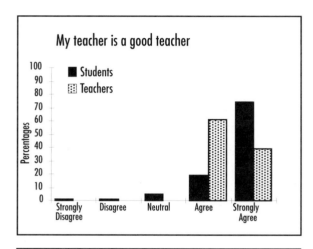

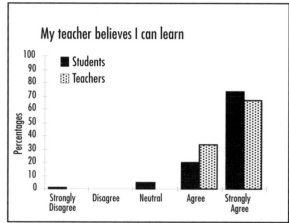

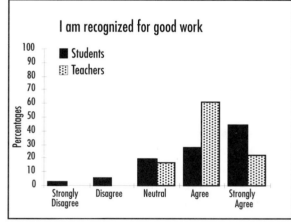

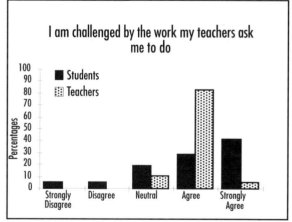

Students (N=187)
Teachers (N=24)

Things to look for:
- Where the average came from—if an average came from a variety of responses, or if the majority of respondents marked the response option that equals the average.
- Items in which respondents are passionate (all responses strongly agree or strongly disagree).
- Discrepancies in responses by groups completing the questionnaire.
- The story told by comparing two groups or two years on the same chart, provided the items are consistent.
  (The comparison of two groups can show how in tune the predicting group is to the predicted group.)
  (The comparison of two years can show how the attitudes changed or differences between two groups in different years.)

Interpreting Test Results

Many of us have been misquoted by reporters, or have heard horror stories of misinterpretations related to reporting school measures, especially standardized test scores. Below are concepts to remember when communicating assessment results, especially to people without testing backgrounds.

> *The ability to simplify means the ability to eliminate the unnecessary so that the necessary can speak.*
>
> Hans Hoffman

- Make sure everyone writing about assessments results understands your purposes for conducting the assessments in the first place.

- If you use norms to describe your performance, define for the non-educator what the results mean, as well as other scores that have importance to you on a daily basis. Remember that 50 percent of the children in the country are below average, and 50 percent are above average on norm referenced tests. The norm is set at the 50th percentile, the point at which half of the scores are above and half of the scores are below.

- Do not compare scores across different measures or across different versions of the same test unless conversion tables are provided by the test publishers. There are some derived test scores (such as the normal curve equivalents) that can allow you to look at the same measures, over time, and use these. Percentile ranks, although they may look the same on different tests, are different because they have been specifically calculated for each test.

- Make sure that the reporting of standardized or norm referenced tests—or any assessments of student learning—are reported within the context of many of the other variables that we know make a difference with standardized and norm referenced tests, such as demographics, perceptions, and processes used.

- Use a simple graph to display the information you want everyone to see.

- Provide data results in context, with detail, so they can be interpreted appropriately. Try to stay away from statements that can be used as "sound bites" and put you at risk of being quoted out of context.

- Emphasize progress.

- Provide easy to understand information.

- Never lie about the results or attempt to keep them from the public. The result will be worse.

- Stay away from excuses and blame.
- Remember, there is no such thing as "off the record." Pull together a professional summary of what you want the public to know and stick to it.
- Never speculate.

Sometimes educators do all these things and still feel that the newspapers "do them in." We believe the best defense is a strong offense. Here are some ideas, for the offense:

- As Americans we have a right to publish almost anything we want in the editorial section of the local newspaper—use that right to report what you want your community to know, if your education newspaper reporter does not do that for you.
- Hold a news conference.
- Create press releases that describe the context of the data and how you plan to use it.
- Publish annual reports in the format of a newspaper and distribute to the community. In some small town locations, your local newspaper will insert it with the local newspaper. They will most likely distribute it free of charge.
- Keep your data analysis with your school improvement documentation, such as a School Portfolio, that shows how you use data within the context of the school purpose and goals.
- Establish an action plan to discuss and make sure everyone understands the results and the actions to be taken based upon the results.
- Think through the questions you might get from the media or community and construct responses to—
  - Why haven't all students been achieving?
  - How many students are not achieving?
  - What are you going to do about it?
  - How do I know you are doing everything you can for my child?
  - Why doesn't our neighboring school district have the same problem?
  - Do the neighboring school districts have the same problems?
  - How are students taught reading?
  - Can you tell me the names of the students not reading at grade level?

- Are these children all of one ethnicity?
- How do you know your data are accurate?
- How do you know your standards are appropriate?

Chapter 6, Student Learning, contains a wide variety of examples of test results and student achievement data in graphic form. More often than not, these data have been presented in bar chart form, but it does not have to be. First determine what you want the chart to convey to the reader, then decide if a bar chart will be the best choice. Often, the software you work with makes a recommendation, and it almost always works to go with what the software recommends. Also, whether you choose to display those bars as horizontal or vertical depends upon the number of bars needed and how much text you need to include to make the chart clear to the reader.

Chapter 6 also covers in detail the types of scores to use when communicating results to an audience. Please refer to Figure 22 in that chapter.

The most important thing to remember is to keep what you are saying clear. If you want to show the reader that a subgroup everyone was worried about last year is now doing better, include the information that shows that data. Don't bury it in a chart that is more confusing then it needs to be.

Figure 67 was first seen in Chapter 6 (Figure 30). Here, it is used again to visually communicate the progress made by Forest Lane school staff in improving the reading abilities of their students in the primary grades. Note that the standardized test score results are based upon numbers of students who met the NCE standard set by the district, but are presented as percentages of students meeting the standards. The test level score results are based upon numbers of students who met the grade level standards at any given point, but, again, is presented as a percentage of students meeting the standards. Using data this way enables the school to talk to parents about how the students are doing on the standardized test subscores and on the text level, which is assessed in the classroom.

Figure 67

Impact of
New Reading Strategies

Percentage of Forest Lane Students Meeting Reading Standards
for the CTBS and Text Level Tests
From 1996-1998

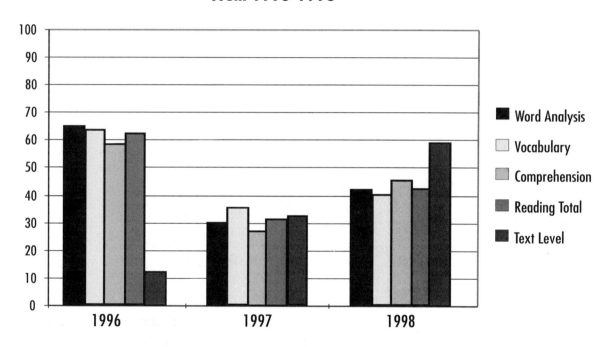

The description of Figure 67 could include the following:

In 1996, 1997, and 1998, Forest Lane student reading abilities were assessed on the CTBS Reading Standards and Text Level Tests. Approximately 60 percent of the students met the district standard on the three CTBS subtests and the Reading Total in 1996.

Those percentages dropped to approximately 30 percent in 1997. In 1998, each of those percentages increased to 40 percent, or higher. The percentage of students meeting the Text Level standards went from 12 percent to 31 percent to 59 percent between 1996 and 1998.

Explaining Demographics Results

While educators feel that demographics are important factors in student achievement, they are often reluctant to talk about them to the public. They sometimes feel that they will sound bigoted or biased, or that it is illegal to talk about demographics in public. If the discussion is important enough to be taking place within the school walls, the discussion needs to surface outside of the school in order to make a difference. For instance, teachers bemoan the fact that parents move their children during the school year because they know it makes learning more difficult for the children. Some parents do not have any idea of the impact location changes have on their children's education. They need to know. A chart of student achievement data can show parents the differences between students who have remained in the same school over time and those affected by moving in and out of different schools.

There are ways to describe demographic data within the context of the other data analysis that will provide clarity and direction to both staff and community. Figure 68, which also appears in Chapter 4 (Figure 6), is a classic example of a school population changing over time, and reflects the growing diversity of many of our cities. Using a chart like this will help you show your board and the people who vote for school bonds that the numbers of children who come to our schools needing help in learning to speak and read English are something that will continue to have an impact on staffing and budgeting. This type of chart will help your community predict how to meet the needs of these children, and enhance the educational experience of all students at the school.

Here, again, the thing to remember is to communicate your point. We can't show color in this book, but if the growing Asian population is what you want to make your audience aware of, make the Asian population bar stand out and make sure that the title says clearly what you want the audience to learn.

Figure 68

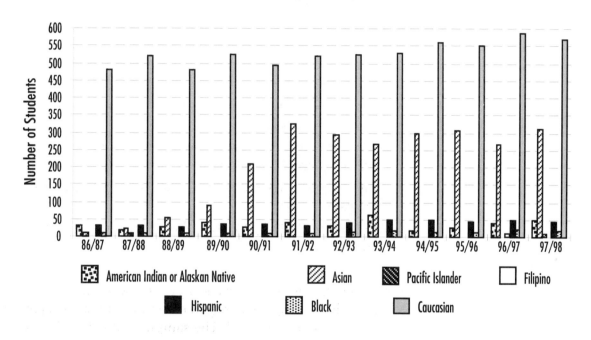

**Forest Lane Elementary School
Changes in Non-English-Speaking Population
1986/87 to 1997/98**

Reporting the Big Picture

improvement, we need to communicate the big picture to everyone by whom we want the results understood. The ideal report is two-to-four pages long with high quality graphics that convey the story.

A summary of steps in presenting your school's data analysis reports follow:

1. Determine the message you want to convey about your data analysis results.

2. Present the data as simply and clearly as possible to convey the message.

    • Develop charts and graphs with clear titles, legends, and numbers to convey the message.

    • Only compare your data to the nation, state, or other districts when appropriate.

    • Never display or provide data that will allow individuals to be identified.

3. Write a narrative interpretation of the charts and graphs to prevent misinterpretations.

4. State how parents and the community have helped and can continue to help.

5. Always state what your school is doing, or plans on doing, with the results.

The following pages contain a sample profile about Forest Lane Elementary School using the data gathered thus far that everyone in the community can understand. The sample profile is followed by another way to summarize the data via a press release.

Forest Lane Elementary School Profile

Forest Lane Elementary School   **Mountain Union Elementary School District**
5555 Pinetree Avenue • Mountain, CA 99555 • (500) 777-3715
Gary Smith, Principal   **Profile of the 1997-98 School Year**

INTRODUCTION

This school profile has been developed to provide you, the parents and community, with information about our school, our successes, and the areas in which we have plans to improve.

During the 1997-98 school year, our focus has been to get all students reading at grade level by grade three. This profile focuses on these efforts and offers suggestions about how you can assist. A review of the context of our school appears first.

We hope you enjoy this profile and find it to be a useful document. We would appreciate your comments and suggestions for improving both this report and our school.

Sincerely,
Gary Smith, Principal

MISSION

Our mission is to provide all students with a positive, secure, and supportive learning environment in which they can acquire the skills and attitudes that foster an enjoyment of learning; a respect for themselves and others; and the physical, emotional, and social competencies necessary to become responsible and productive citizens of the twenty-first century.

THE STUDENTS

Forest Lane Elementary School, the only elementary school in Mountain Union Elementary School District, served 992 students in 1997-98. Forest Lane's ethnic constituency is shown on this pie chart.

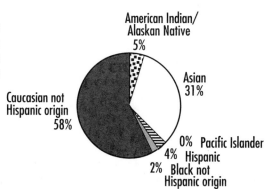

American Indian/
Alaskan Native
5%

Asian
31%

Caucasian not
Hispanic origin
58%

0% Pacific Islander
4% Hispanic
2% Black not
Hispanic origin

Page 1 of 5 pages

207

Forest Lane Elementary School Profile

Our population has increased over the past 10 years, from around 650 to the 992 students we have today. The graph below shows how the ethnic composition has changed during this time.

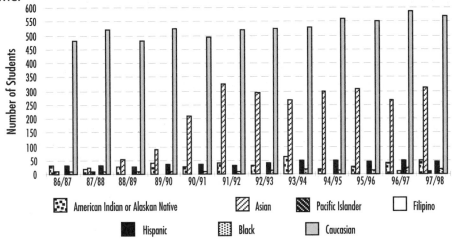

With the addition of new nationalities and languages, Forest Lane staff has worked hard to get all students speaking English as soon as possible. The chart on the left shows the number of students, by language spoken, who have had to learn English in the past 8 years.

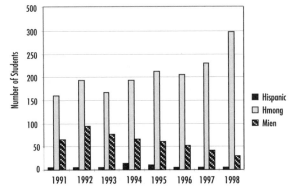

THE STAFF

Forest Lane's staff includes 49 teachers, 6 language resource teachers, and 3 bilingual teachers. The teachers have been teaching an average of 22 years, although we welcomed several new teachers this year.

Staff goals are to—

- Improve all students' academic performance in the school
- Cultivate an understanding of and respect for cultural diversity
- Strengthen parent and community support and involvement
- Utilize all school resources to support best classroom practices
- Implement an evaluation program to measure school effectiveness

Page 2 of 5 pages

208

Forest Lane Elementary School Profile

STUDENT ACHIEVEMENT IN READING

Literacy skills are assessed in many different ways at Forest Lane School depending upon grade level. Across all grade levels, the standardized test the district has adopted is the Comprehensive Tests of Basic Skills (CTBS). Teachers also use a mix of observations, performance assessment rubrics, and writing samples.

The district standards for reading include:

• A score of 35 NCE (Normal Curve Equivalent) on the CTBS total for third grade.

• A level of 8 for kindergarten, 16 for first grade, 20 for second grade, and 24 for third grade as measured by the text level subtest given at the beginning, middle, and end of each year.

The graphs that follow display the percentages of students meeting and exceeding these standards for the past three years. The subscores on the CTBS, word analysis, vocabulary, and comprehension are shown with the total battery and text level results.

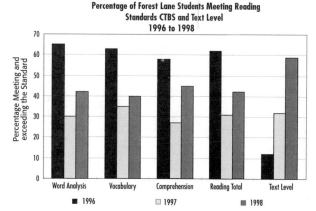

Percentage of Forest Lane Students Meeting Reading Standards CTBS and Text Level 1996 to 1998

Beginning in 1997, students who were not fluent English readers and speakers took the CTBS reading test, as required by law. The gains achieved between 1997 and 1998 with non-native speakers of English are educationally significant! Staff knows that the Reading Recovery Program has been extremely helpful in getting all students reading by the third grade. With Reading Recovery and classrooms designed to support the concept, almost twice as many second graders in 1998 have begun to meet the third grade standard at Grade 2 than in 1997 (see chart below). In fact, more of last year's second graders met the third grade standard than third graders—attributed to the first and second grade interventions and the move to lower class sizes.

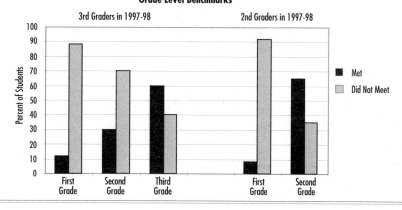

Text Level Scores Compared to Grade Level Benchmarks

Page 3 of 5 pages

209

Forest Lane Elementary School Profile

QUESTIONNAIRE ANALYSIS

During the 1996-97 and 1997-98 school years, Forest Lane staff administered questionnaires to students, staff, and parents. The purpose for administering the questionnaires was to understand from each constituency how they perceive the learning environment at Forest Lane, to help staff learn how to improve everything they do.

Overall, the students, staff, and parents responded very positively to most of the items on the survey. Our staff is happy with the students and their learning. The students are happy with their teachers and their learning, and the parents responses echoed the same degree of satisfaction.

We continue to want to do better in at least one area addressed by the survey, however, and would ask for your help with this. The responses given by the students to "Students at my school treat me with respect" and "Students at my school are friendly" are not as positive as we would like them to be. The parent responses to "The students treat other students well" were also not as positive as we would like to see.

The staff feels that these responses may come from misunderstandings that arise from cultural differences between the children. As many of you may know, we continue to work in the classroom with exercises designed to help all of the students learn more about a variety of cultures. This year we have begun mentor relationships ("buddies") with the middle school students, who are coming to the school and talking to the younger children about their immigrant experiences. The 7th and 8th graders have been interviewing our local elderly population as part of a service learning project, finding out where they came from and what life was like in the early 1900's. This has given them a new perspective on what it was like to be an immigrant in a new country, based on the stories told by some of our older community members about their own parents. The middle school students have found striking similarities between these stories and those told by our new Hmong and Mien community members and it has given them a wonderful perspective that we hope they can share as role models with the younger students.

Please ask you child about their buddy and let us know what you learn from that conversation.

GOALS FOR IMPROVEMENT FOR 1998-99

Staff will continue to study current and past results to understand what they can do to ensure that all students meet or exceed the district standards. Staff know that if they want to change the results they have been getting, they must study and change the processes that produced the results. They also recognize they need to continue to strengthen the partnerships between parents and the school. Changing the processes, based on data, has improved reading scores substantially last year. During 1998-99, staff will continue this research at an even more intensive level.

READING GOALS FOR 1999

As staff perfect the processes of teaching reading, they are learning more and more about what makes the difference in getting all students to read at grade level by grade three. One thing they know is that all students benefit from knowing as many words as possible. The more words a child knows well, the easier he or she will learn to read and will be able to read well. We are doing many things at Forest to help our students increase their vocabulary and word recognition, but we need your help.

Forest Lane Elementary School Profile

WHAT PARENTS CAN DO TO HELP

We continue to encourage parents to:

- Read, in English, to or with your children—regardless of age—at least 15 minutes each night. Children love to read with their parents. Make reading an enjoyable experience—something to look forward to. Teachers have sent home a list of books in our library that are at an appropriate level for your child.

- Engage your child in discussion as often as you can. Ask him or her what they did at school and if it was fun or not. Encourage your child to use new words as much as possible.

- Speak in English at home during the week. Early English language fluency will make a difference in each student's achievement results in early grades, which will make all other learning easier.

- Let teachers know when there are things you feel are needed to assist your child's learning. Together we can make the difference.

- Make sure your child does not miss school, unless she or he is ill. It is very hard for your child to catch up with the others, and it is difficult for the class to move ahead if every student is not progressing at similar rates.

- Please make sure there is a quiet, well-lit space and a consistent time for your child to do homework. Homework is assigned to help with the daily concepts. When all students in a class have completed their homework, teachers can, more easily, move all students to that next level of achievement.

- Parents are invited and welcome to attend all professional development days at the school. Come learn along with us.

- Come volunteer to help in your child's classroom. This will give you an opportunity to see first hand what teachers are trying to accomplish and for you to help make a difference in the learning of many children. Our teachers have a sign-up sheet posted next to their doors. We would love to have you with us.

- Stop by and read our School Portfolio that describes the Forest Lane vision, goals, and achievements. All data referred to in this profile are located in the portfolio.

- Staff are now offering English classes for parents in a supportive environment. If you have been wondering how to become fluent speakers of English as well, come give this class a try. The classes are offered free of charge. Child care is provided.

- Look for announcements. We will soon be offering parenting and technology classes.

Page 5 of 5 pages

211

Example Press Release

FOR IMMEDIATE RELEASE
Insert Date Here
Contact: Gary Smith, Principal
Forest Lane Elementary School
Mountain Union Elementary School District
(500) 777-3715

> **Announce your message and how the community was involved**

MOUNTAIN, CALIFORNIA — Forest Lane Elementary School announces the results of a recently completed analysis of the 1997-98 school year. "I am very pleased to announce that Forest Lane Elementary School of the Mountain Union Elementary School District has taken a comprehensive look at how well they are serving their students and how they can do an even better job in the future," said Superintendent Richard Long. "The school sought parent, student, administrator, and teacher input, including demographic data and student achievement results in their analysis."

> **Background**

As a part of their effort to continuously improve, Forest Lane committed to the hard work of measuring how well they are doing for children with their current approaches and thinking about what instructional strategies they need to change to get different results.

> **Data Analysis**

The data showed how the population of Forest Lane has changed during the past 10 years. Consequently, with population changes came changes in student achievement results. "As students with primary languages other than English arrived in our district, Forest Lane's average reading and writing scores on student achievement tests decreased," reported Superintendent Long." We studied our past scores to understand what skills needed to be improved; we looked at our data to understand learning styles and perceptions of students and what attitudes needed to be improved on the part of teachers, students, and community; and, then we analyzed how to improve our instructional and assessment strategies to meet all of our students' needs.

Page 1 of 2 pages

Example Press Release

Describe Plans for Improvement

Some tangible changes that are being implemented in the area of reading are—
- teachers will increase the minutes for daily K-3 reading instruction
- teachers will continue to encourage parents to read with their children for at least 15 minutes every night

Reference Attached Graphs

The attached charts and graphs show the changes in population and student achievement results for the past 5 years.

End on a Positive

Said the Superintendent, "I commend and am extremely proud of the Forest Lane Elementary School staff for committing to this hard work of understanding where they can improve what they do for all students. Within two years, all of us are looking forward to seeing striking increases in student achievement."

Summary

Gathering data and putting together a comprehensive data analysis is difficult for schools. Many schools have difficulty communicating data analysis results to the public largely because they do not have all of the pieces of the big picture—together. Once the data analyses are complete, a big picture report can be very informative and useful for all parties. This communication process must be planned and carefully written.

Communicating the Results Questions

The intent of the questions below is to help your school staff think through who you want to use the data and what message you want to give.

Who do you want to inform about your results?	What do you want them to know?	How will you get the message to them?	Who will be responsible for getting the message out?

Chapter 11

SCHOOL AND DISTRICT DATABASES

Throughout this book, the discussion has been focused on why data are important, what data to collect and analyze, the importance of interacting the data, and how to communicate the results. That work is fairly straightforward and logical.

Many of the barriers mentioned in Chapter 1 which keep schools from doing this work are related to the mechanics behind the data collection and analysis—specifically, the database. Although much of the information is reported by subgroups, the ability to retrieve that data is dependent upon the data being linked to each individual student.

The databases discussed in this chapter might typically contain a collection of student information which is organized by individual student for easy retrieval. For example, the database might include individual numbers for each student that are used to make up an average for a particular grade level, or individual student scores that constitute an ethnicity's subscore average. Databases can be very large and complex, or fairly simple, but *some* sort of database, consisting of individual student records, is necessary to conduct the analyses shown in the previous chapters. The ability to manipulate data in order to look at it by instructional program, by ethnicity—by any measure or combination of measures—is dependent upon being able to work with individual student records.

> *A superintendent I know spoke for 99 percent of the school districts in America today when he told me that his district had systems to manage money down to the dime, but no systems to manage the learning mission. This is the most critical challenge for school districts to meet.*
>
> Larry Lezotte

The Ideal Database for Comprehensive Data Analysis

Everyone in education wants schools to have the data they need to understand how well they are doing in order to meet the needs of *all* students. In an ideal scenario, districts could and would collect common and useful information for all their schools in a database that could be used at both the district and school levels. These data would also be accessible by, and useful to, teachers at the classroom level.

With these data easily available, along with staff development to implement models that demonstrate the effective use of data at the different levels, teachers and administrators would move teaching into a more scientific realm.

Where the Data Come From

Because federal and state regulations now require that student achievement data be disaggregated and reported by ethnicity, gender, and language proficiency, many districts are considering the necessary modifications to their databases. Until now, many small districts have been able to avoid using databases altogether. These districts are now looking for appropriate ways to build and use databases.

Because the databases required to generate mandated federal and state reports are essentially the same as those needed for school improvement, this is an excellent time for schools to work with districts to ensure that data collected at the student level is accessible and comprehensible to all who could profit from the valuable information it provides. If school districts will work to develop databases and assist teachers in the interpretation of data, they will end up with new knowledge that can be used for—

♦ assisting teachers in assessing the progress of their students, individually and by subgroups, in order to improve classroom instruction

♦ assisting school staff, and the district as a whole, in assessing progress toward achieving content and performance standards with all students and within all subgroups

♦ enabling principals, school staff, and individual teachers to do action research for the purpose of instructional improvement

♦ replacing the individual cumulative record folders

♦ reporting to the community what students know and are able to do.

The work required to create a good student achievement database differs greatly depending upon the size of the district. If you are part of a large district, most of the data you will need is probably already available in existing databases.

Large school districts typically maintain basic databases with the following information:

- student demographic information
- student attendance
- standardized test data
- other data which must be reported for purposes such as categorical funding

Some districts have more contemporary systems in place, and are able to respond quickly and easily to school requests for data at the individual student level. More often, however, districts use different software systems, or offices in the same district maintain data on separate, sometimes incompatible, systems making the use of data to analyze student needs very difficult. For these districts, responding to school requests for data is often time-consuming and involves substantial programmer time.

The majority of small districts do not maintain an ongoing database, other than for specific programs or funders, and depend upon receiving information from the schools.

In either a large district or small district, school processes data are very unlikely to exist in computerized form. However, it is important that these data be gathered and linked to individual student records to be able to look at the impact of school processes on student outcomes.

District-level Databases

In some cases, working with the district is just too difficult, or the district's computer system is not useful at the site level as a tool to assist in school improvement. If this situation is not likely to change in the near future, schools may want to plan to set up their own databases.

While home-grown databases may not be elegant, or serve schools' purposes well in the long run, they do allow schools to put all student information in one place and begin using that data for the continuous improvement of their instructional program. The district must help by providing data from its database—demographic and test score data—in a format that allows easy import into the school's database. If the school later needs a more elaborate database,

School-level Databases

or the district gets a school-friendly system, the data the school has collected in the interim could be transferred back to the larger district database.

In a small district where no existing databases have been established, the data typically come from a variety of sources. Student demographic information can usually be obtained from the established attendance system at the school level, although the process of importing these data to a new database may not be intuitively obvious to the person operating the system. Standardized test scores, as well as any demographic and program information submitted at the time of testing, can be obtained on disk from most of the test publishers. Most districts capture data for individual students for specific programs such as Migrant Education. Although these data are spotty, they can add important information to, or be used as the basis for, the database.

The hardest part in creating a schoolwide database is to figure out what fields are needed in order to produce the desired reports, especially when the intention is to analyze data over time. For example—

- If school staff want to know how well students who transferred into the school during the current school year are doing on a math assessment compared to students who have been in the school for one or more years, the school would need fields to identify when the student entered the district, entered the school, and the math assessment scores received.

- If school staff want to know how students did on the district math assessment disaggregated by ethnicity, for the past three years, the school would need an ethnicity field and fields for the matched scores.

When beginning to establish a new database, careful thought about what fields will be needed can prevent spending a great deal of time modifying the database later. The difficulty, of course, is that most schools are still quite new to the concept of action research and may not have sufficient experience to recognize all the fields that will be needed at future points. The fields of a database must be thought out very carefully with curriculum and school improvement leaders, federal and state program directors, the district technology person, teachers, administrators, and someone knowledgeable about databases.

If all this seems like one more impossible task for school level personnel, particularly if there is no help available from the district, start by cutting out the work you are currently doing by hand. Every time someone makes a handwritten list of students, work is duplicated. If the district has a writing assessment, for example, that information can be entered *once* in a database, as opposed to being rewritten several times in teachers' records, student portfolios, and office records. As you begin using databases, your understanding of what you will need in the future will improve, and you will be in a better position to make the hard decisions in choosing the right database for the long-term. You are likely to find that using a database is like using word processing—once you get started and begin to see the benefits, you will wonder how you lived without it.

While a specific software program cannot be recommended in this type of publication, generally speaking the type of software program one would need in order to do the type of work we refer to here would be cross-platform and easy to learn and use. *Cross-platform* means that the program files can work on most common operating systems in the same way.

Further, software that provides the option of designing a *relational* database might be beneficial. A relational database is able to combine two or more databases to make a more comprehensive database (i.e., linking files of standardized test score data from different years, so that longitudinal student achievement data could easily be accessed). School and district personnel need to be sure the database is easy to learn and use or it will not be viewed as a functional tool.

There are many different types of software available that can be used for entering data that will be used for later data analysis. Work with your district and school personnel, and involve knowledgeable school partners or parents to help you determine the best solution for your school. Look for database software that—

- has a fast learning curve
- easily imports and exports data
- customizes (i.e., add fields, change layouts)
- can link data with different sources
- makes producing reports non-threatening
- is cross-platform
- has good technical support

- is able to be secured so that only authorized people can use the database
- is not expensive
- has understandable documentation

Summary

The data analysis examples that have been shown throughout this book have all been created with one or more individual student-level databases. This level of analysis links student information together to form subgroupings that allow us to understand the impact of different programs and processes on achieving school success, and identify any differences that may occur related to subgroupings (e.g., gender or ethnicity).

Database software is available for this type of work. School districts should start by studying what already exists at the district or school levels, carefully think about what specific data are needed (this determines the necessary fields to use in a database), and clarify what types of reports would be helpful in finding answers to their questions.

Database Questions

The intent of the questions below is to help your school think about a database that will support your uses of the data analyses performed thus far.

What data does your district collect in a database that would be helpful to your comprehensive data analysis efforts?

What data does your school need to collect, that your district does not currently have, in a database that would be helpful to put in *your* database?

Just replace the word "evaluation" with comprehensive data analysis for schoolwide improvement and the quote below sums up everything we are trying to do in this book—pull all the pieces together into a meaningful whole to tell school personnel how they are doing, to help them understand how they can do what they are doing better, and to inform them of what changes they can make to get better results.

The aim of data analysis is not to gather more data, but to gather and use meaningful data. Data help us understand where we are right now, where we want to go in the future, and what it is going to take to get there. Just like designing questionnaires, we have to *begin with the end in mind.*

Chapter 12

CONCLUSION: USING THE RESULTS

Determine the Purpose

As you begin your comprehensive data analyses, clarifying how the data will be used, and the purposes for conducting the analyses will guide your efforts and ensure the use of the results.

Focus the Data Analyses

Focus the analyses on the guiding principles of the school. Even if problems have been identified and are the focus of specific data analysis work, the overall guiding principles of the school will still provide necessary grounding. Without this focus, data results could lead to random acts of improvement. Just about every school in the United States has developed mission and vision statements. A solid data analysis will show within 15 minutes if those mission and vision statements are valid.

It's easy to make judgments—that's evaluation. It's easy to ask questions about impact—that's evaluation. It's easy to disseminate reports—that's evaluation. What's hard is to put all those pieces together in a meaningful whole which tells people something they want to know and can use about a matter of importance. That's evaluation.

Halcolm

Get Everyone on Staff Committed

Getting everyone on staff committed to comprehensive data analyses at the beginning can help ensure the results will be used by them when the analyses are complete. One way to gain that commitment is to have staff lay out their hunches and hypotheses about the area(s) of focus.

Identify Questions

Think logically about the questions that will help you know more about the problem being analyzed. In other words, what questions do you need to ask to know more about the problem, or what questions do you need to ask to know if your school is meeting its guiding principles.

Identify Data Sources

Identify data sources that will help you answer the questions. These logically follow the data questions.

During the Analysis

Include Everyone

Using data for improvement is most successful when everyone understands that the purpose is not to criticize or blame individuals, but to move the school forward—using data. We need everyone to understand the results of the data analysis and to implement the implications of the results. If group processes are used, such as those described in Chapter 9, everyone will be involved in finding the meaning of the data analysis results. Teachers will be more inclined to change the way they do business when they are a part of identifying the problems and solutions.

Determine What the Data are Telling You

Look at the results of each of the analyses included in the larger comprehensive analysis. Use all the data together to predict what needs to be done differently to get different results. One piece of information will not tell the whole story and could lead to faulty reasoning. Bad data is worse than no data at all. Piecemeal data is bad data.

Dig Deeper

Determine additional analyses that are necessary, such as further disaggregations or data collection, to thoroughly understand the issues. Avoid jumping to conclusions. Student, teacher, or parent questionnaire data may need to be followed up with focus group discussions to fully understand what the data mean. Student achievement data may need to be further disaggregated to fully understand all aspects of the learning environment. Make sure you are getting to the root causes of the problems.

Keep the Process Positive

Never use the data analysis process to "beat-up" on individuals. Allow staff to understand the data, and to take responsibility for giving it meaning in each of their classrooms, while guiding the meaning across the classrooms. Give every staff an opportunity to understand what they can do differently to get different results. If the data become a negative, the results will never be used to benefit children.

Make Sure Everyone Understands How They Have to Work Differently

Make sure everyone on staff understands the results that current processes are getting now. If staff have worked with the data, they will be able to see clearly that the results they are getting now are directly related to what teachers are doing in their classrooms and to the school's support systems for students. They will also see that if they want to create different results, they will have to change the system that created the results.

Solutions to Problems

Look for solutions to problems only after you are sure that all the questions about the problems and the analyses are thorough.

After the Analysis

Establish a Plan of Action

Lay out a plan of action that clarifies what needs to be done, who is responsible for completing each task, and when it is to be completed. Describe what each staff member is expected to do to implement the action plan that evolves from the data analysis results and solutions to identified problems. Make sure every element of the action plan is understandable to everyone in the same way, and that there is an expectation that the plan will be monitored.

Make Implementation of the Plan a Part of Everything You Do at the School Site

It may take some time to implement a complete plan of action. If the current processes are not getting the results teachers want, it may require studying different approaches, visiting other schools using different approaches, and multi-year staffwide professional development to implement new strategies that will get different results. It will also require constant reinforcement and support. Staff meetings need to focus on the use of the data and the implementation of new approaches. All professional development days need to be focused on what will make the system more effective for all students.

Evaluate Using the Same Data Analysis Processes Every Year

If a school can put together a solid student assessment system and database, and update it each year, three-fourths of the battle is won. It is impossible to be reliant on data if there is no consistent system or process available. Use the same questionnaires over time. Assess students in the same way every year. Clarify your processes so you know what you are measuring. Collecting the same data each year allows schools to know whether the solutions being implemented are causing the intended impact.

Document

Document the results you are getting now based upon the processes used. Document the changes implemented in the processes so everyone can understand how the new results came about. Without documentation, staff will not know what to keep doing and what to stop doing.

Keep the Momentum Going

One of the best ways to keep the schoolwide improvement momentum proceeding is to document the results in a school portfolio. A school portfolio is a great way to report the data, to show how the data are used for continuous schoolwide improvement, and to document the importance of new processes and procedures. The school portfolio encourages measurement on an ongoing basis, provides feedback, and communicates progress to everyone. The school portfolio also keeps the purpose and guiding principles of

> **What happens is not as important as how you react to what happens.**
>
> Thaddeus Golas

the school the focus of everything the school does, including the data analysis. Seeing progress that makes a difference for every student will keep staff implementing new approaches, when needed.

Using the Results Questions

The intent of the questions below is to help your school staff plan for the use of the data analysis results.

The data analyses conducted so far show the results your school is getting based upon what you are doing now.

Are there still missing data elements? How and when will you get them?

Has everyone been included in coming to an understanding of the data? If not, how and when will you include everyone in examining the data?

Has the school community examined the interactions among the different data, looked for patterns, and followed up on gathering additional sources of data which were identified as necessary (such as focus groups)? If not, how and when will this happen?

Has the school identified the results that you would like to get, such as student standards? If not, how and when will you identify these results?

Using the Results Questions (Continued)

What does the staff/school have to do differently to get these results?

Within each classroom

Across classrooms

With respect to how teachers interact with children

With respect to parents and the community

For professional development

If answering the previous questions is difficult, what resources (current literature, visiting other sites, etc.) do you need to answer the questions?

What support do you need to do this work? How will you get the needed support?

How questionnaires are used and the type of information sought will vary from purpose-to-purpose and from school-to-school. Your staff might solicit information from teachers to understand if you truly have a shared vision. You might want to ask students or parents about their perceptions of the school, what they think are the strengths of the school, or what they feel needs to be improved. You might want to understand shifts in parent attitudes about the way you teach "new math" before Family Math Night and after Family Math Night.

Appendix A

QUESTIONNAIRE DESIGN

Basically, a questionnaire is a system for collecting information to describe, compare, and explain knowledge, attitudes, perceptions, or behavior. According to Arlene S. Fink (1995), the best surveys have the following features:

- specific objectives
- straightforward questions
- sound research design
- sound choice of population or sample
- reliable and valid survey instruments
- appropriate analysis
- accurate reporting of survey results
- reasonable resources

Whatever type of questionnaire you decide to use for data gathering, the questionnaire must be based upon an underlying assumption that the respondents will give truthful answers. To this end, you must ask questions that are—

- valid
- reliable
- understandable
- quick to complete
- able to get the first response from the respondent
- able to get what you want in the end

Requiring respondents to read questions over and over again in order to understand what we are talking about, or making it necessary for the respondents to gather information before they can complete the survey, will increase the possibility of inaccurate responses or no response at all.

Begin With the End in Mind

The diagram which follows (Figure A-1) outlines useful steps for thinking through and selecting the most appropriate criteria when designing questionnaires for your particular purpose.

Plan for the Questionnaire

It is next to impossible to put together a valid, understandable questionnaire that is easy to complete and analyze without thinking through the elements of questionnaire construction and analysis before starting. Notice that as you go through the elements profiled in Figure A-1, one answer could impact previous elements. That is why it is important to go through these questions before writing a questionnaire. There are many issues that need to be taken into consideration, with a lot of rethinking needed along the way.

Determine the Purpose

What do you really want to know? Why are you administering a questionnaire? To what end are you asking these questions? You might want to know perceptions of parents, students, teachers, and administrators to understand where the school is right now with respect to a shared vision—what each constituency values and believes about school, education, teaching, and learning. These might also be questions that you want to continue to ask over time to watch the responses change as new ideas and innovations are being implemented. Questionnaires that have been used with Education for the Future Initiative schools are offered as examples in Appendix B. The results of these questionnaires are used to understand the perceptions of students, teachers, and parents to help us get to root causes of problems (discussed in Chapter 9) and to get everyone's input into the vision for the school.

To what end is this data collection activity directed? How will the information be used? How do you want to disseminate the findings? Do you need to present this information to a funding agency, to your school board, or to staff for improving instructional practices? The intended use of the information collected has a major impact on the steps used to construct the questionnaire.

Identify How the Information Will Be Used

Another important question to ask yourself, as you begin the arduous task of putting together a questionnaire, is: Can we get this information without doing a questionnaire? Too often, inexperienced staff will want to ask questions that can be answered through other means. Consider a parent survey example: "Did you attend Back to School Night?" If the purpose for asking the question is to find out how many parents came to Back to School Night, there are other ways to know that information which might, in fact, produce more accurate data. Usually there is a guest book at Back to School Night functions, or someone is put in charge of counting the number of attendees. Use that source of information, and reserve questionnaires for important questions that cannot be answered in other ways.

As you think through the purpose, also consider whether the questionnaires will be given out anonymously, or if you will code them to link them with other databases. If you want honest, non-threatened responses, you might consider not asking for names or information that could identify the respondents.

Check for Existing Data

With respect to the purpose for administering the questionnaire and how it will be used, who or what are the logical sources of information? Who can answer these questions? When at all possible, we want to go directly to the source, i.e., if we want to know what parents are thinking, we need to ask parents.

Identify Sources of Information

Figure A-1

Begin With the

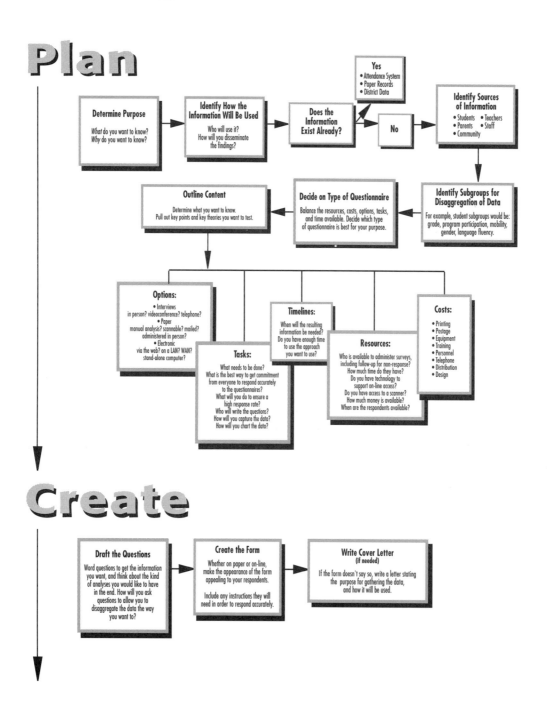

Plan

Determine Purpose	Identify How the Information Will Be Used	Does the Information Exist Already?		Identify Sources of Information
What do you want to know? *Why* do you want to know?	Who will use it? How will you disseminate the findings?		No	• Students • Teachers • Parents • Staff • Community

Yes
• Attendance System
• Paper Records
• District Data

Outline Content	Decide on Type of Questionnaire	Identify Subgroups for Disaggregation of Data
Determine what you want to know. Pull out key points and key theories you want to test.	Balance the resources, costs, options, tasks, and time available. Decide which type of questionnaire is best for your purpose.	For example, student subgroups would be: grade, program participation, mobility, gender, language fluency.

Options:
• Interviews
in person? videoconference? telephone?
• Paper
manual analysis? scannable? mailed?
administered in person?
• Electronic
via the web? on a LAN? WAN?
stand-alone computer?

Tasks:
What needs to be done?
What is the best way to get commitment
from everyone to respond accurately
to the questionnaires?
What will you do to ensure a
high response rate?
Who will write the questions?
How will you capture the data?
How will you chart the data?

Timelines:
When will the resulting
information be needed?
Do you have enough time
to use the approach
you want to use?

Resources:
Who is available to administer surveys,
including follow-up for non-response?
How much time do they have?
Do you have technology to
support on-line access?
Do you have access to a scanner?
How much money is available?
When are the respondents available?

Costs:
• Printing
• Postage
• Equipment
• Training
• Personnel
• Telephone
• Distribution
• Design

Create

Draft the Questions	Create the Form	Write Cover Letter (if needed)
Word questions to get the information you want, and think about the kind of analyses you would like to have in the end. How will you ask questions to allow you to disaggregate the data the way you want to?	Whether on paper or on-line, make the appearance of the form appealing to your respondents. Include any instructions they will need in order to respond accurately.	If the form doesn't say so, write a letter stating the purpose for gathering the data, and how it will be used.

End in Mind

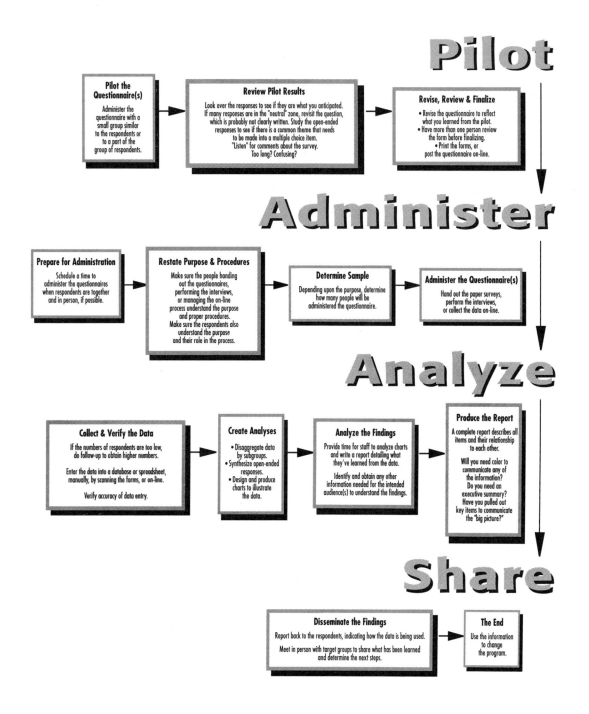

Pilot

Pilot the Questionnaire(s)

Administer the questionnaire with a small group similar to the respondents or to a part of the group of respondents.

Review Pilot Results

Look over the responses to see if they are what you anticipated. If many responses are in the "neutral" zone, revisit the question, which is probably not clearly written. Study the open-ended responses to see if there is a common theme that needs to be made into a multiple choice item. "Listen" for comments about the survey. Too long? Confusing?

Revise, Review & Finalize

• Revise the questionnaire to reflect what you learned from the pilot.
• Have more than one person review the form before finalizing.
• Print the forms, or post the questionnaire on-line.

Administer

Prepare for Administration

Schedule a time to administer the questionnaires when respondents are together and in person, if possible.

Restate Purpose & Procedures

Make sure the people handing out the questionnaires, performing the interviews, or managing the on-line process understand the purpose and proper procedures. Make sure the respondents also understand the purpose and their role in the process.

Determine Sample

Depending upon the purpose, determine how many people will be administered the questionnaire.

Administer the Questionnaire(s)

Hand out the paper surveys, perform the interviews, or collect the data on-line.

Analyze

Collect & Verify the Data

If the numbers of respondents are too low, do follow-up to obtain higher numbers.

Enter the data into a database or spreadsheet, manually, by scanning the forms, or on-line.

Verify accuracy of data entry.

Create Analyses

• Disaggregate data by subgroups.
• Synthesize open-ended responses.
• Design and produce charts to illustrate the data.

Analyze the Findings

Provide time for staff to analyze charts and write a report detailing what they've learned from the data.

Identify and obtain any other information needed for the intended audience(s) to understand the findings.

Produce the Report

A complete report describes all items and their relationship to each other.

Will you need color to communicate any of the information? Do you need an executive summary? Have you pulled out key items to communicate the "big picture?"

Share

Disseminate the Findings

Report back to the respondents, indicating how the data is being used.

Meet in person with target groups to share what has been learned and determine the next steps.

The End

Use the information to change the program.

Identify Subgroups for the Disaggregation of Data

After you decide to whom you want to administer the questionnaire, it is advisable to think of ways you will want to use the information in the end. If you want to disaggregate the data, as mentioned in the previous chapters, think about the different subgroups you will want to split out for the analysis. For example, if you think there will be a difference in student responses by grade level and gender, you will want to ask students' grade level and gender on the questionnaire. This is information we cannot recapture after the questionnaire is administered. If you want to know this information in your analyses, you have to ask it on the questionnaire. You will need to match this to the database items, or use student identification numbers.

Decide on the Type of Questionnaire

There are many issues to consider when determining the type of questionnaire you will use, in addition to the ones already discussed. Think about the best way to get the information. Is it through interviews—either in-person, through videoconference, or by telephone—or would it be through a questionnaire that the respondents actually get to look at, feel, think about, and respond to on their own time? A lot of what will help you decide depends upon—

- your timelines
- the purposes for administering the questionnaire
- how much money you have available
- who is going to be completing the questionnaire and their availability

Time considerations will definitely impact whether or not you want to mail out a survey because you will also need ample time to send out a follow-up for any non-responses. In addition, it takes time to put the survey together, write the questions, create the form, get reviews, and pilot the survey. If you are planning to conduct in-person interviews, the questions need to be written very clearly and consistently, especially if more than one person is going to do the interviewing. In this case, you will also need precise instructions for interviewing. How the questionnaire will be analyzed in the end is another time consideration.

Table A-1 profiles advantages and disadvantages of different types of questionnaires. Table A-2, Figure A-2, and Table A-3 show data collection considerations. The approach determined in the beginning will determine how it can be analyzed in the end. If a questionnaire is set up for manual analysis—in other words, the completed questionnaires are not set up to be machine-scanned or entered directly into the computer by respondents—someone will have to figure out how to put the coded responses into a spreadsheet on the computer, or tally the responses by hand in order to get aggregated and disaggregated results. This process could take months to complete. We recommend that you not use this approach with over twenty respondents in a group. The exception would be if you can set up a database that looks like your questionnaire on the computer and someone can enter the responses into the database quickly and accurately. The database will then take care of some of the analysis and data error issues (discussed below). (Databases are discussed later in this appendix.)

Everyone has experienced fill-in-the-bubble kinds of questionnaires that can be read by a machine scanner. Many people are stunned to find out their scanner will not read a questionnaire they have administered. Not every scanner can read every bubble form. There are many details to take into consideration when setting up a scannable form. First of all, you will want to ensure that the completed questionnaire can be scanned with the scanner you are going to use. Secondly, the questionnaire responses need to be imported into a database that will allow analyses to be done quickly and easily. If you have the appropriate software and equipment, you can set up your own scannable forms, print them on a laser printer, scan them, and import the results into a database. This requires time to understand the scanner software, the scanner, and databases.

If you feel your school does not have the capacity to set up and analyze forms, bubble questionnaires can be sent to an outside contractor to set up for administration and analyses. With either approach, you must be very sure of the questions you want to have answered before they print out a machine-scannable questionnaire. If you want the outside contractor to do the analyses once the responses are returned, you must also be clear on the kinds of analyses you want as an end result. An approach between these two options would be to use a pre-printed scannable sheet in addition to a sheet with the questions. However, that would mean having respondents deal with two different pieces of paper, which is not desirable.

The fastest, most cost-effective approach is to collect the data electronically—on a stand-alone computer, in a computer laboratory, or through on-line processes. Costs for printing, postage, and telephone are eliminated, and the accuracy is increased significantly. This approach, of course, requires that someone know how to work with databases, questionnaires, and servers in this manner. We highly recommend that, whenever possible, you gather your data electronically. The trade-offs of the different methods of data collection are described in Table A-3.

Table A-1

Types of Questionnaires

Types of Questionnaires	Advantages	Disadvantages	Appropriate When—
Interview (face-to-face)	• Allows for in-depth person-to-person exchanges • Might be the most appropriate way to get information from people with disabilities • Can see evidence of change as well as hear about it	• Cost prohibitive; often need to pay interviewers and sometimes interviewees • Requires extensive training and quality control to standardize • Collating the responses is tedious, time-consuming, and difficult • Easy for the interviewers to change the questions	• physical changes are a result of the program—need to understand all aspects of change from the individuals • persons you seek to know about are physically or language impaired • you have people trained to standardize questions • the length of the survey requires over an hour of a respondent's time
Telephone Interview (person-to-person)	• Allows for the personal contact of face-to-face interviews, at a lower cost • Can be done relatively cheaply • Interviewers can enter responses into an electronic database as they interview • Can hear individual perspective, while still using standardized questions	• Requires extensive training and quality control • Might require interviewers to be able to speak different languages • People do not like to be called for questionnaire responses • Easy for the interviewers to change the questions slightly or greatly • Interviewees might not answer all questions before they hang up the telephone	• people do not speak or read English • you use the survey as a win-win and want to connect closer to the community to get people talking and add an element of public relations to your questions • you have people trained to standardize questions • you need fast results • the technology is available • need less than 20 minutes of respondent's time (some say 10 minutes)
Mailed	• Flexible • Can gather a large number of responses • Individuals can respond at their convenience • Relatively inexpensive • Respondents can look up information if necessary	• It is sometimes difficult to get an adequate return rate • Must be able to write a compelling cover letter/request to complete questionnaire • Probably need to send twice • Can be expensive • Takes a long time to get to the point where you are ready to analyze the results	• all perspective respondents are not present in one location at a particular time • you need to ensure anonymity • respondents live out of the immediate area • you have time • you are not asking time-certain questions

Table A-1

Types of Questionnaires

Types of Questionnaires	Advantages	Disadvantages	Appropriate When—
Paper	• Can give classes or groups oral instructions and guide them through the questionnaire • Can be mailed • Can easily include different types of questions and graphics to make it aesthetically appealing • Responses can be scanned	• Requires knowledge about scanning, databases, and analysis of data to make easy analyses of responses • Can be difficult and time-consuming to score, if automation is not an option • Requires time to check the accuracy of the scanning procedure on every questionnaire response	• documented comparisons of groups are desired • anonymity is desired • surveying large numbers of people • respondents are in many locations • a large number of questions is required
Computer	• Least expensive to administer and analyze of all methods • It is unique and has an element of appeal • Students love to complete questionnaires using computers • Can do with computers networked to the Internet, in a lab, or on stand-alones • Database can be automatically completed as individuals submit responses • Do not have to type open-ended responses • Easy to check for double submissions	• It is not always possible to get parents and community to complete computer questionnaires (although not impossible) • Not everyone has a computer at their disposal • It is difficult to complete in large schools with few computers • Not everyone likes the approach • Need people to set up the survey on-line that are trained to do it right	• school / organization has computer laboratories or a doable number of computers • —ever possible, since the advantages far outweigh the disadvantages • you need quick return of responses

Data Collection Considerations

Using an on-line method of data collection is usually the most cost effective in terms of time and personnel required to process the data, and offers the best option for data accuracy.

Collecting Data	
Time for Design and Production	Scannable questionnaires produced by a contracting firm will generally require six to eight weeks of production time after the questionnaire items have been identified. If the questionnaire needs to be administered in a very short period of time, it is best to go with an in-house form (either manual data entry or scannable), or an on-line questionnaire.
Number of Respondents	Scannable questionnaires produced by a contracting firm or produced in-house and sent to the printer are most cost effective when more than 500 people are being surveyed, or when the questionnaire will be administered again. For smaller numbers of respondents, questionnaire responses can be entered cost effectively using either manual or on-line data entry.
Age of Respondents	Generally speaking, the younger the respondent, the more likely they will want to use a computer. Assistance should be provided to respondents who do not yet have mouse skills and are expected to complete an on-line questionnaire.
Literacy of Respondents	Assistance should be provided to respondents who do not have the literacy skills required to understand the questions being asked of them, either by providing a written translation or an interpreter.
Availability of Respondents	Captive audiences—teachers, students—usually are better situated to complete questionnaires, written or on-line, at school. Community members may find it easier to take and complete a paper questionnaire at home, although a better response rate may be realized if the questionnaires are completed at parent-teacher conferences or open houses.
Availability of Equipment	Using an on-line questionnaire requires an adequate number of computers to service the number of respondents at each site. Using scannable forms requires the availability of a scanner. The use of either is only helpful if a computer with a database is available for analysis.
Time for Analysis and Reporting	If the time available from response to analysis is very short, try to go with an on-line or scannable option. If manual data entry is being used, administer a few and enter data for "test" questionnaires in order to predict the time required to enter the expected number of responses.

Figure A-2

Data Collection Options

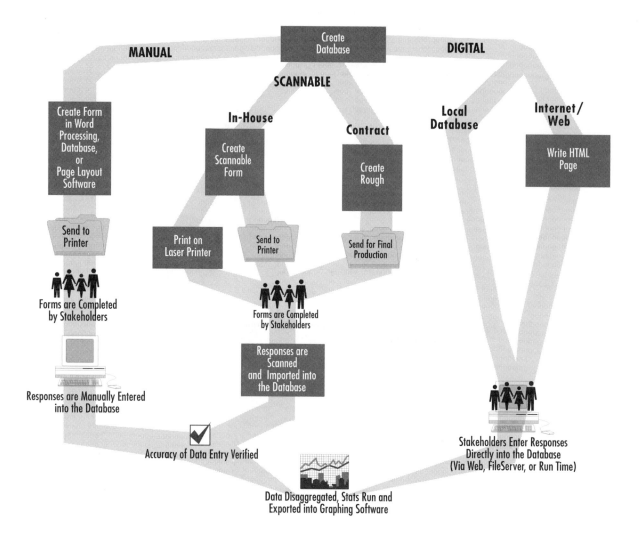

Table A-3

Data Collection
Trade-Offs

There are always trade-offs in terms of personnel and production costs. Here are some of the pros and cons of the options we've presented:

Data Collection Options	Description	Pros/Cons
Manual Data Entry (Non-scannable Forms)	This option requires the least technical expertise and equipment. Once the questionnaire items are written, the survey form is produced in word processing, database, or desktop publishing software and photocopied or printed. After the forms come back, the responses are manually entered into a database package. The downside to this option is the time required for data entry and the possibility for human error during the data entry process.	
In-House Produced Scannable Forms	Scannable questionnaires can be produced in-house and printed on a laser printer or sent to a printer. This option requires the knowledge and use of a software package that will create a master digital file that is either sent out of the office (off-site) to be printed on an offset printing press or printed to a laser printer, in-house.	Advantages — • producing the form can be done faster than contracting the job out • can accommodate small groups on a cost-effective basis • scanning the forms is much faster than manual data entry
Purchased Scannable Forms	Companies such as Scantron and NCS offer scannable (bubble) forms for purchase. You need to add the questions. Some forms allow you to print questions on the form. Others require the use of two sheets of paper.	
Contracted Scannable Forms	Scannable questionnaires can be roughly designed and sent to companies like Scantron or NCS for final production. This option takes the most time; however, it is a good option on a per-unit basis when there is adequate lead time and large numbers of forms are needed.	Advantages — • contracting companies usually guarantee that all forms will scan properly • no need for in-house expertise in publishing design • scanning the forms is much faster than manual data entry Downside to this option is that it generally takes from six to eight weeks to have the forms produced, and is not cost-effective for small numbers of completed forms.
Digital Data Collection	Collecting questionnaire responses on-line is the best option for speed, flexibility, and accuracy.	Advantages — • no paper—no printing or distribution costs • questionnaires can be modified for different groups at minimal cost • people tend to "write" more in response to open-ended questions • opportunities for human error in scanning or manual data entry are eliminated • data are available immediately Disadvantages are that this option does require in-house or contracted technical expertise and related equipment

Create the Questionnaire

Creating the questionnaire can be an arduous task. Many people who want to design questionnaires often stop when it comes to writing the questions. It is definitely one of those tasks that looks much easier than it actually is.

Outline Content

Begin by thinking about what you want to know and pulling out key points or key theories that you want to test through the questionnaire. For example, the Education for the Future Initiative student questionnaire in Appendix B was designed by teachers who wanted this questionnaire to ask questions related to what they wanted their students to be able to say by the time they had implemented their vision—that they feel safe at school, have freedom, fun, and like school— theories from William Glasser's *The Quality School* (1990). Once you determine what you want to know, outline the key points and jot down ideas in the outline.

Draft the Questions

Formulate questions that address issues based upon what you want to know. There are many different ways to ask questions. Table A-4 describes different types of questions, advantages and disadvantages for each type, and when it is appropriate to use each type of question. You can create forms that will allow you to use different types of questions; however, it is probably not wise to use more than two or three different types of questions in a form. The key is to make the questionnaire interesting and fun to complete.

The types of questions that might be appropriate for a school working toward building a quality learning organization aligning parts to create a whole system—are those related to whether or not this objective is being met. It would follow that student, parent, and teacher questions would focus on their perceptions of the learning organization, creating questions that are a part of the hypotheses of how the quality learning organization should look. Be sure to:

- ask purposeful questions—don't just ask questions for the sake of asking questions
- make sure the questions will be interpreted the same way by many different people

Think about the impact of every question on your respondent. Will it offend anyone? Hints in developing the questions are summarized below.

Helpful hints include—

◆   Simple is best
◆   Short (definitely less than 20 words)
◆   Free of jargon and bureaucratic wording
◆   Phrased to not suggest a response
◆   Logical sequence (general to specific)
◆   Ask questions that everyone understands in the same way
◆   Make sure that, if necessary, your questions will allow you to disaggregate responses in your analyses

Avoid—

◆   Trying to assess a little bit of everything
◆   Conjunctions in questions
◆   Leading questions
◆   Jumping around content-wise

Table A-4

Types of Questions

Types of Questions	Advantages	Disadvantages	Appropriate when you—
Written (open-ended) Example: What do you like about this school? (Write your response in the space provided below.)	• Spontaneity of the response • Can really understand what the respondent thinks • Can get deep into the topic • Can use to build multiple choice items • Sometimes respondents provide quotable material • Can ask all types of individuals, regardless of language differences	• Must pay for someone's time to transcribe and synthesize • Takes time—on everyone's part • Coding can be unreliable • Cannot always read the response • Some handicapped people might have difficulty responding • Language translations are expensive • Difficult to interpret	• are not sure about what a population is thinking and feeling about a topic • want to gain insight into the population's thinking • design closed-ended questions • want to supplement or better understand closed-ended responses
Multiple Choice (ordinal) (closed-ended) Example: Suppose you are a school board member. On what one thing do you think the school should focus to ensure well-prepared students? (Circle the one response option below that best represents your position.) 1. Basic skills 2. Computers 3. Problem-solving skills 4. Lifelong learning 5. Flexibility	• Fast to complete • Respondents do not need to write • Relatively inexpensive • Easy to administer • Easy to score • Can compare groups and disaggregate easily • Responses can be scanned and interpreted easily	• Unless one has thought through how the items will be scored and has the capabilities of scoring items mechanically before sending out the questionnaires, it can be expensive to do, time-consuming, and easy to make mistakes • Lose spontaneity • Don't always know what you have as results • Respondents are not always fond of these questionnaires • Some respondents may resent the questioner's pre-selected choices • Questions are more difficult to write than open-ended • Can make the wrong assumption in analyzing the results when response options are not the same as what respondents are thinking	• want to make group comparisons • know some of the responses that the sample is considering, and want to know which option they are leaning toward • have large samples • want to give respondents finite response choices
Ranking (closed-ended) Example: Why did you choose to enroll your child in this school? (Mark a 1 by the most important reason, 2 by the second most important reason, etc.) • It is our neighborhood school • Reputation as a quality school • Know someone else who attends • I went there when I was in elementary school • My child needs more challenge • My child needs more personal help	• Allows understanding of all reasons in priority order	• More than seven response items will confuse respondents • May leave out important item response options	• want to know all responses in an order • are clear on common response options • do not want people to add to list

Types of Questions	Advantages	Disadvantages	Appropriate when you—
Rating (closed-ended) Example: (Circle the response that best represents your feelings.) I feel like I belong at this school. Strongly Neutral Strongly Disagree Agree 1 2 3 4 5	• Allows you to see the passion behind respondents' feelings, i.e., Strongly Agree / Strongly Disagree • Easy to administer • Easy to score • Can compare group responses	• Do not always know if every respondent is reading the question and response options in the same way • Do not always know what you have when neutral is circled—might be a bad question or the respondent doesn't care • Unless one has thought through how the items will be scored and has the capabilities of scoring items mechanically before sending out the survey questions, it can be expensive to do, time-consuming, and easy to make mistakes • Questions are more difficult to write than open-ended • If charted together, questions must be written so the desired responses all fall in the same direction	• want respondents to rate or order choices, such as: strongly disagree to strongly agree, or rank • want to make group comparisons • have large samples • want to understand where problems are in the organization
Yes — No (closed-ended) Example: Yes No I like this school. ☺ ☹	• Very young children can answer questions with these response options • Very easy to score, analyze, and chart	• Not sure how meaningful the data are when used generally • Responses do not give enough information	• want all or nothing responses • have a sample that would have difficulty responding to more options

Nominal
(categorical)
 	
Example: I am—
        Male
        Female
	• Factual: have no values attached to the questions
	• Useful for disaggregating other questions by groups
	• Lets you know if sample is representative of the total population
		• Some people will not respond to these types of questions
		• Some people could respond falsely to these questions
		• With small groups, one might be able to identify the respondent on an anonymous questionnaire because of the demographic information given
			• want to disaggregate data by male / female, age, height, program
			• want to know the impact of a program on different types of individuals
			• want to know if respondents resemble the population

Scales

Questionnaires are collections of items intended to reveal levels of information not readily observable by direct means. We develop scales when we want to measure phenomena that we believe to exist because of our theoretical understanding of the world, but which we cannot access directly.

Scales, or response options to questions in questionnaires, are developed to measure underlying constructs.

Most items have a stem (the question) and then a series of response options. How many response categories should an item have? The number of response options could be anywhere from one to a hundred. If we want to see discrimination in our analyses, we need to allow discrimination in our options, considering the following:

- How many response options does it take to discriminate meaningfully?

- How many response options will bore or confuse our respondents?

- Presented with so many response options, will respondents use only those responses that are multiples of five, for instance, reducing the number of options anyway?

There are several kinds of response options. The response option chosen depends upon the purpose for considering the questionnaire and the types of questions desired. For the majority of surveys, five-point options are adequate. Possible labels include—

- Endorsement: strongly disagree, disagree, neutral, agree, strongly agree

- Frequency: never, almost never, sometimes, very often, always

- Intensity: really apprehensive, somewhat apprehensive, mixed feelings, somewhat excited, really excited

- Influence: big problem, moderate problem, small problem, very small problem, no problem

- Comparison:
    - much less than others, less than others, about the same as others, more than others, much more than others
    - much worse than others, worse than others, no difference, better than others, much better than others

The scale you use is determined by personal preference. The example questionnaires provided in Appendix B utilize a five-point endorsement scale. Each item is presented as a declarative sentence, followed by response options that indicate varying degrees of agreement with the statement—from strongly disagree to strongly agree. The questionnaires go from strongly disagree to strongly agree because it is our opinion that this direction is left to right—like our brains work. That is also why our response options are on the right.

People often ask about the center option. They worry that most individuals will use the middle response option if it is made available. Experience tends to show that people will not automatically choose the middle response. If they commit to responding to the questionnaire, they will typically respond with precision. When responses on a questionnaire do appear in the middle, the questionnaire constructor needs to examine the questionnaire to determine if it is the question causing indecision, if the response option and the statement do not go well together, or if, indeed, the respondent does not have a definite response to the question. One of the first things to check is whether there is a conjunction in the statement that would cause people to say: "Well, I agree with this part of the question and I disagree with that part of the question." Researchers often add the middle response to give respondents a legitimate response option for opinions that are divided or neutral. If you prefer to force your respondents to make a decision, you can always use an even point scale that has no middle point.

An often-neglected but very important factor that must be taken into consideration when establishing a scale and format for the questionnaire is the age and attention span of the respondent.

What about offering "don't know" or "not applicable" as a response option? Some researchers say that "don't know" does not affect the proportion of responses. Depending upon the question, a "not applicable" response might give you more information than getting no response.

Create the Form

Appearance and arrangement of the survey frequently determine whether respondents will complete it. In fact, research shows that individuals determine within five seconds whether or not they will respond to a questionnaire. Think about what would get you to psychologically commit to completing a questionnaire, and build in those same considerations for your respondents. The good news is that once respondents take the effort to read a questionnaire, they make a psychological commitment to complete it.

Upon first glance, we definitely want the questionnaire to be appealing to the eye. We want to have white space. We want to keep the questionnaire consistent. Never split questions, instructions, or the responses from the questions between pages. Use an easy-to-read, equally spaced font for the questions themselves. Avoid italics. Try to make it look as professional as possible. We typically want to end the questionnaire by giving each respondent a chance to comment on the topic. Figure A-3 offers tips to consider when creating the form. Take the time to make the appearance pleasing and the instructions clear to the respondent.

Begin with the end in mind. If you are planning to scan the survey responses, you must begin by setting up the survey so that it is scannable. You cannot expect to scan something that was not set up for scanning in the beginning.

Questionnaire constructors differ on where demographic information should be placed in a questionnaire. The majority feel that the personal information needs to go at the end. Occasionally, if people see personal questions first, they may find these kinds of questions worrisome and might decide to not complete the questionnaire. Of course some people believe in putting the demographic questions first because they are easy to respond to. Respondents can answer them quickly, feel accomplished, and will, therefore, keep going. Wherever you decide to place these important questions, always group them together.

Figure A-3

Design Considerations

The appearance and arrangement of the survey frequently determines whether or not the respondents will complete it. Try to fit the questions and answers onto one page, if possible. You want the survey to be quick to complete, so that the respondent will answer all of the questions.

Your respondents read from left to right. If the layout of the questions and responses is consistent with this pattern, it will increase the accuracy, and will be easier and faster for your respondent to complete.

Placing response options close to the questions decreases the chance of error due to respondents mismatching lines.

If the questions are worded so that the answers fit into one scale, it will be easier to analyze the data and make charts later.

Make it obvious where respondents should make their mark.

Begin with more general questions and lead up to the more specific.

Write instructions that tell your respondents what you would like them to do.

Leaving white space makes the survey easier to read.

Do not use questions that have conjunctions. Use two separate questions instead.

Ask questions to address the issues that are based on what you want to know, and that cannot be gathered from other sources.

Think about the impact of every question on your respondent. Will it offend anyone?

Make the questions simple, short and jargon/bureaucratic word free.

Avoid:
- trying to assess a little of everything
- leading questions
- jumping around content-wise

parents

Please complete this form for your family. Please use a No. 2 pencil and completely darken the circle that corresponds to your answer. Thank you!

Scale: Strongly Disagree, Disagree, Neutral, Agree, Strongly Agree

I feel welcome at my child's school.
I am informed about my child's progress.
I know what my child's teacher expects of my child.
My child is safe at school.
My child is safe going to and from school.
There is adequate playground supervision during school.
There is adequate supervision before and after school.
The teachers show respect for the students.
The students show respect for other students.
The school meets the social needs of the students.
The school meets the academic needs of the students.
The school expects quality work of its students.
The school has an excellent learning environment.
I know how well my child is progressing in school.
I like the school's report cards/progress report.
I respect the school's teachers.
I respect the school's principal.
Overall, the school performs well academically.
The school succeeds at preparing children for future work.
The school has a good public image.
The school's assessment practices are fair.
My child's teacher helps me to help my child learn at home.
I support my child's learning at home.
I feel good about myself as a parent.
I enjoy being a parent.

Number of Children in This School: ①②③④⑤⑥⑦⑧⑨
Number of Children in Household: ①②③④⑤⑥⑦⑧⑨

Children's Grades:
○ Kindergarten
○ First
○ Second
○ Third
○ Fourth
○ Fifth
○ Sixth
○ Seventh
○ Eighth

My Native Language Is:
○ Chinese
○ Eastern European
○ English
○ Japanese
○ Korean
○ Spanish
○ Vietnamese
○ Other

Ethnic Background:
(Darken all that apply)
○ African-American
○ American Indian
○ Asian
○ Caucasian
○ Hispanic
○ Other

© Bernhardt, V.L. (1993-95) San Francisco: Telesis Foundation

Make sure that however you wish to disaggregate the data later, that the information is captured on the form.

In other words, if you want to know the difference between males and females on their responses to particular questions, ask your respondents their gender in the questionnaire.

Figure A-3

Design Considerations
(Continued)

Only ask a few open-ended questions because of the length of time it takes respondents to reply and because of the difficulty of analyzing the responses.

Place open-ended section at the end of the survey.

What are the strengths of your child's school?

What needs to be strengthened at your child's school?

Leave enough space for respondents to comment.

What would make the school better?

Do not use lines.
Lines limit feedback.

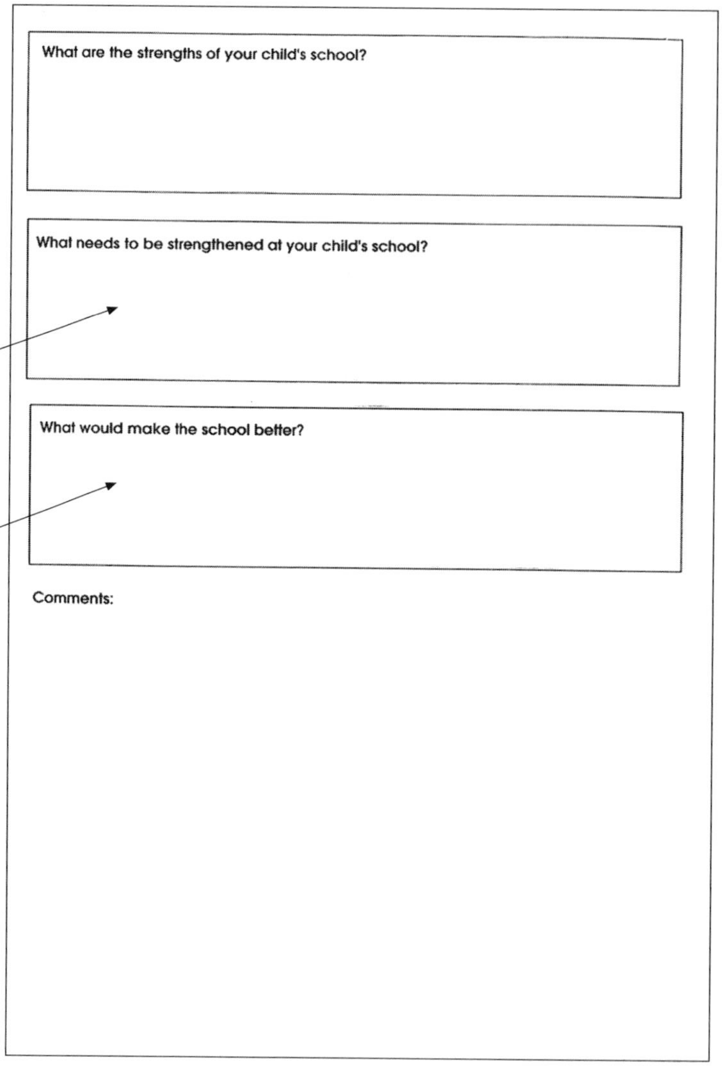

Comments:

Write a Cover Letter (if needed)

If you must mail a questionnaire, it is important to include a cover letter. Most of the time when schools want questionnaires completed, there are ways to get them completed in person. For example, student and teacher questionnaires can be administered during school hours or during a staff meeting. Parent questionnaires can be administered at parent-teacher conferences. This is the ideal—to administer the questionnaires when you can gather all responses in person and at the same time. The chances of getting a good response rate are tremendously increased when you administer a questionnaire in person. Just make sure that you receive most, if not all, responses from your target group. Cover letters should include what the questionnaire is about, why the respondent's response is important, how long it will take to complete the questionnaire, and when the results can be seen. Table A-5 shows an example cover letter.

Table A-5

Example Cover Letter

Date

Name
Address
City, State Zip

Dear Parent:

The enclosed questionnaire has been developed to assist Forest Lane Elementary School in examining its effectiveness for students. As a parent of a Forest Lane student, your input about our effectiveness is important to us.

The questionnaire consists of 25 statements. After you read a statement, please fill in the bubble that represents the first response that comes to mind which is the closest to what you think or how you feel. Responses range from strongly disagree to strongly agree.

It takes approximately 15 minutes to complete the questionnaire. All of your responses are confidential and will be combined with other parent responses for reporting purposes.

Please return the completed questionnaire in the envelope provided as soon as you can, or no later than (Date). If you have any questions, call (Name) at (Telephone Number). The results of the survey will be reported at Back to School Night in May.

Thank you for your cooperation and valuable response.

Sincerely,

Name

Enclosures
    Questionnaire
    Return Envelope

Pilot the Questionnaire

No matter how many times you go over the individual questions, and look at the questions collectively, you don't know how the questions will actually perform until you administer them to a small number of respondents in your target group as a pilot test. We highly recommend piloting the questionnaire and then analyzing the data to understand if you are asking questions, first of all, that respondents understand, and secondly, that provide responses which lead to your purpose.

To pilot the questionnaire, you need a small group of respondents who are similar to the larger target group. Administer the questionnaire and analyze the results. Include questions on the pilot questionnaire to help you know if the pilot group understood everything on the questionnaire, if they thought the questions were relevant, if there are other questions they feel you should be asking, if they feel the questionnaire was easy to respond to, and solicit their general overall comments.

Review Pilot Results

After the pilot responses come in, look over those responses to see if they are what you anticipated. If there are many responses that fall within the neutral zone, "not applicable," or are blank—

- look at each of the questions to see if it is understandable
- look for conjunctions
- look at the open-ended responses for clues
- ask respondents, if they are available, to tell you why particular questions were hard to understand

Revise, Review Again, and Finalize

After you study the responses from the pilot group, revise the questionnaire to reflect what you have learned. If you feel that the questions need to be piloted again, do so. It is much better to try a questionnaire out on a small group again than to administer a poor questionnaire to a large group.

Have several people review the questionnaire once it has been put into its final form to ensure there are no typographical errors and to ensure that the content flow is as you intend. When you feel that all of the bases have been covered, print the forms or post them on-line for the "real" questionnaire administration.

Administer the Questionnaire

Prepare for Administration

When at all possible, administer the questionnaire when people are together, in person. Schedule a time for the administration. For example, if you want all students in your school to complete the questionnaire, work with the teachers to have them administer the questionnaires to the students during first period. State the purpose and procedures, making sure the people handing out the questionnaires, performing the interviews, or managing the on-line process understand clearly the purpose for giving out the questionnaire and the proper procedures for administering and collecting the information. Also, make sure respondents understand the purpose and the importance of their role in the process, and that their honest responses are desired and necessary.

Restate Purposes and Procedures

Teachers and administrators often ask how to get the students and teachers to take the questionnaire seriously. You must have a clear purpose for doing the questionnaire, clear instructions for completing it, and assurance that the information will be used to understand more about a program or its impact on students. It is the job of the person in charge to make sure that the people administering the questionnaire understand the purpose and can relay that purpose to the respondents.

Sometimes providing input for continuously improving programs is incentive enough for people to respond to a questionnaire. Other times it is not enough. If you have a nice budget you might want to offer a small gift or cash incentive.

In some elementary schools, students are encouraged to get their parents' responses to the questionnaire by offering them a pencil in return for a completed questionnaire. Response rates have improved from non-pencil days to pencil-incentive days, from 40 percent to 85 percent and 90 percent. Middle and high schools have offered raffle tickets for a $25 gift certificate to all students returning their completed parent questionnaires. Classes of high school students are awarded pizza parties for 100 percent return rates.

The downside of giving incentives is that you may have to keep giving incentives in the future to get responses.

Determine Sample

A common question about questionnaire administration is how do we sample? A sample is a portion or subset of a larger group called a population. Surveys often use samples rather than populations. A good sample is a miniature version of the population—just like it, only smaller.

Let's think first about why we would sample. Who you send your questionnaire to has to be dependent upon your purpose for doing the questionnaire in the first place. If one reason is to find out how all of your parents are thinking about your school, you will want to send the questionnaire to every parent. There is nothing wrong with trying to look for the win-wins. You could receive parents' perceptions of the school and, at the same time, you could be informing them about things that are going on—building your public relations.

If your purpose leads you to sample instead of administer to the population, there are methods to use and references to study, some of which are listed in the reference section of this book. Although the lengthy discussion of sampling is beyond the scope of this book, methods of sampling are briefly described below.

> A *stratified random sample* is one which divides the population into subgroups and then a random sample is selected from each of the groups. You would use this approach when you want to make sure that you hear from all the groups of people you want to study. You might want to sample parents with low, medium, and high socioeconomic status; number of children in the household; or number of children at that school in order to feel that every condition of parenthood is heard.

> A *simple sample* is a smaller version of the larger population that can be considered representative of the population. One classroom of students can be a simple sample, or one school in the district. This is typically used when administering a very large questionnaire.

> One might use a *split questionnaire* design if you have a very large sample and a very long questionnaire. It is possible to split the questionnaire and to give one part to one and another part to another group.

Convenience sampling is done when you want to survey people who are ready and available, and not hassle with trying to get everyone in the population ready and willing to complete the questionnaire.

Snowball sampling relies on members of one group completing the questionnaire to identify other members of the population to complete the questionnaire.

Quota sampling divides the population being studied into subgroups such as male and female, or young, middle, and old, to ensure that you set a quota of responses.

Administer the Questionnaire

Hand out the paper questionnaire, perform the interviews or collect the data on-line. It is very important that the people assisting with the administration of the questionnaire take their jobs seriously and do a professional job of explaining the questionnaire's importance.

Collect and Verify the Data

Consider the number of people who were given the questionnaire and the number of responses received. If the number of responses is low—for example, a response of 60 percent—look to see if the responses are representative of the total population. If not, do a follow-up to get more responses. A response rate of 60 percent may or may not be low. For instance, if the questionnaire was administered during school, 60 percent is low. If it was mailed, and is representative of the population, it could be high.

For each of the approaches to gathering questionnaire data, you will need to verify the accuracy of the data entry. In other words, you want to make sure that each of the dots were scanned into the right location in your database (if you are using a scannable form), or entered into the correct location, if they are manually tallied. If the numbers were analyzed manually, every number must be verified for accuracy by preferably more than one person. For electronic gathering of questionnaire data, you will want to make sure there are no duplicate responses.

It is best to set up a database that will handle the questionnaire responses early in the process—preferably when you check your scanning process. It is an excellent double-check for your questionnaire and questions.

Create Analyses

After you are 100 percent confident that the data you are going to analyze is accurate and representative of the population you want to assess, begin using whatever software program you choose to design the analyses. Look at the total group and subgroup responses, synthesize the open-ended responses, and design and produce charts to illustrate the data (see Figures 59 through 62 in Chapter 10).

Analyze the Findings

Someone has to analyze the charts and write a report that explains what the data tell us. It is very important for other people to be able to read words that relate to charts as well as see charts. There might be additional information to be taken into consideration in order for your audience to understand the responses. If some of the questions relate to specific issues that aren't mentioned in the questionnaire, you need to discuss that issue in the report and discuss how the questionnaire information relates. In Chapter 10, Figures 65, 66, 67, and 68, show examples of chart interpretation and sample analyses.

Analysis of questionnaires depends upon what you want to know and why you are doing the survey in the first place.

One of the first things you might want to do is take a look at the average responses, by item, for students who took the survey. We chart our questionnaire results to show the group average to each item, which helps us get a "big picture" of the results, as shown in Figure 61 in Chapter 10. Standard deviations help us understand the range of individual responses that make up the averages. A wide standard deviation tells us that there is considerable variation in the responses that make up the averages. A small standard deviation would tell us the respondents were more or less in agreement with each other with respect to these items.

If you diligently set up the variables by which to disaggregate questionnaire results, charts can also display disaggregated information. In Chapter 10, Figures 62 and 63, show how disaggregating information can lead deeper and deeper into the issues.

Many people who conduct analyses of questionnaire results often feel they do not know enough about statistics. They have a perception that statistical significance must be calculated. Our belief is that descriptive statistics are very powerful for what we want to know about a school. We want to know how students are doing, and if different groups are responding to the processes in the same or different ways. Comparisons between groups in terms of statistical significance really say less than descriptive statistics. Statistical significance tells you very little about what you need to do differently in order to improve your program. What we really want to know is how we can better do what we do for kids. Descriptive statistics can help us understand that.

Produce the Report

It is very important to chart work done so everyone can see a picture of the results. It is equally important to document the findings and to list next steps that come out of the analyses. There is something psychological about documentation that keeps groups from repeating what they have already done. The documentation of where they are right now helps them plan for and begin next steps.

A complete report describes all items and their relationship to each other, and to the questionnaire itself.

In reporting on a questionnaire, the following are important to include:

- Why the questionnaire was done
- The setting in which it was administered
- Unique features of the questionnaire
- Type of questionnaire
- Number of respondents (total and sample populations)
- Response rate
- How long the questionnaire took to complete
- General content of questionnaire
- Analysis and charts
- Results
- Recommendations

262

Disseminate the Findings

Once the report is written, you will need to determine the best way in which to get a summary of the analyzed results to the respondents and other interested parties. You may need to meet in person with target groups to share what was learned and to discuss next steps together. Think about what was promised when the questionnaire was administered— follow through on your word.

Graphs, as previously mentioned, can set the stage for discussion, convey a message, or reinforce a central point. Graphs must display the data, be concise in conveying the information, and be easily digestible to all readers.

The power of graphs comes from their ability to convey data directly to the viewer. Viewers use special intelligence to retrieve data from a graph—a source different from the language-based intelligence of prose and verbal presentations.

The audience sees data. Data become more credible and more convincing when the audience has direct interaction with them.

The communication process becomes more direct and immediate through graphic displays.

Just as important as getting the questionnaire constructed and analyzed appropriately is the use of the questionnaire results. It is important never to use one piece of data in isolation of the numerous other pieces of data available to schools. It is also important, whenever in doubt of what the data say, to ask respondents to clarify meaning.

Whether the meaning of the results is analyzed by a small group or by the entire staff, the results must be distributed back to staff with agreed upon next steps.

The End

As you think through all the steps in setting up and completing a questionnaire, remember this: You are taking an individual's time and energy, as well as your own time and energy, to put a questionnaire together and to analyze it. Think through all the steps, research the topics, and think about the people involved before you begin. Treat each questionnaire as a scientific instrument, not as just a list of questions to ask people.

Congratulations! You have now completely thought through your questionnaire administration and analysis.

Appendix
B

SAMPLE
QUESTIONNAIRES

On the pages that follow are student, teacher, and parent questionnaires that schools working with Education for the Future have used since 1991. We offer them here as examples of questionnaires that work.

Please note that they cannot be copied and scanned as they are right now. One would need to set them up to be scanned, or to be administered on line. Appendix A includes details of questionnaire administration and analysis.

Figure B-1

Student Questionnaire
Grade 1-6   Page 1

students

I AM IN:
- ○ First Grade
- ○ Second Grade
- ○ Third Grade
- ○ Fourth Grade
- ○ Fifth Grade
- ○ Sixth Grade

I AM: Boy ○
       Girl ○

I AM: (Darken all that apply.)
- ○ African-American
- ○ American Indian
- ○ Asian
- ○ Caucasian
- ○ Hispanic
- ○ Other: _____

Strongly Disagree — Disagree — Neutral — Agree — Strongly Agree

When I am at school, I feel:

	Strongly Disagree	Disagree	Neutral	Agree	Strongly Agree
I belong.	①	②	③	④	⑤
I am safe.	①	②	③	④	⑤
I have fun learning.	①	②	③	④	⑤
I like this school.	①	②	③	④	⑤
This school is good.	①	②	③	④	⑤
I have freedom at school.	①	②	③	④	⑤
I have choices in what I learn.	①	②	③	④	⑤
My teacher treats me with respect.	①	②	③	④	⑤
My teacher cares about me.	①	②	③	④	⑤
My teacher thinks I will be successful.	①	②	③	④	⑤
My teacher listens to my ideas.	①	②	③	④	⑤
My principal cares about me.	①	②	③	④	⑤
My teacher is a good teacher.	①	②	③	④	⑤
My teacher believes I can learn.	①	②	③	④	⑤
I am recognized for good work.	①	②	③	④	⑤
I am challenged by the work my teacher asks me to do.	①	②	③	④	⑤
The work I do in class makes me think.	①	②	③	④	⑤
I know what I am supposed to be learning in my classes.	①	②	③	④	⑤
I am a good student.	①	②	③	④	⑤
I can be a better student.	①	②	③	④	⑤
Very good work is expected at my school.	①	②	③	④	⑤
I behave well at school.	①	②	③	④	⑤
Students are treated fairly by teachers.	①	②	③	④	⑤
Students are treated fairly by the principal.	①	②	③	④	⑤
Students are treated fairly by the people on yard duty.	①	②	③	④	⑤
Students at my school treat me with respect.	①	②	③	④	⑤
Students at my school are friendly.	①	②	③	④	⑤
I have lots of friends.	①	②	③	④	⑤
I have support for learning at home.	①	②	③	④	⑤
My family believes I can do well in school.	①	②	③	④	⑤
My family wants me to do well in school.	①	②	③	④	⑤

Figure B-2

Student Questionnaire
Grade 1-6   Page 2

What do you like about this school?

What do you wish were different at this school?

What do you wish I would have asked you about your school?

Figure B-3

Student Questionnaire
High School   Page 1

High School Student Questionnaire

Please complete this form using a No. 2 pencil.
Be sure to completely darken the circle that best corresponds
to your thoughts about the following statements.
Thank you!

	Strongly Disagree	Disagree	Neutral	Agree	Strongly Agree
I feel safe at this school	1	2	3	4	5
I feel like I belong at this school	1	2	3	4	5
I feel challenged at this school	1	2	3	4	5
I have opportunities to choose my own projects	1	2	3	4	5
I understand how to apply what I learn at school to real-life situations	1	2	3	4	5
I feel like I am in charge of what I learn	1	2	3	4	5
Teachers encourage me to assess the quality of my own work	1	2	3	4	5
This school is preparing me well for what I want to do after high school	1	2	3	4	5
I assess my own work	1	2	3	4	5
I am treated with respect by teachers	1	2	3	4	5
I am treated with respect by school administrators	1	2	3	4	5
I am treated with respect by campus supervisors	1	2	3	4	5
I am treated with respect by the office staff	1	2	3	4	5
I am treated with respect by other students at this school	1	2	3	4	5
The people most responsible for what I learn are my teachers	1	2	3	4	5
The work at this school is challenging	1	2	3	4	5
I find what I learn in school to be relevant to real life	1	2	3	4	5
I feel successful at school	1	2	3	4	5
The person most responsible for what I learn is myself	1	2	3	4	5
School is fun here	1	2	3	4	5
I like this school	1	2	3	4	5
I think this is a good school	1	2	3	4	5
I like the students at this school	1	2	3	4	5
Students at this school like me	1	2	3	4	5
I like to learn	1	2	3	4	5
Doing well in school makes me feel good about myself	1	2	3	4	5
I am doing my best in school	1	2	3	4	5
Students at this school have opportunities to learn from each other	1	2	3	4	5
Students at this school have opportunities to learn about each other	1	2	3	4	5
Participating in extracurricular activities is important to me	1	2	3	4	5
Students at this school respect other students who are different than they are	1	2	3	4	5

Figure B-4

Student Questionnaire
High School   Page 2

My teachers:	Strongly Disagree	Disagree	Neutral	Agree	Strongly Agree
expect students to do their best	1	2	3	4	5
expect me to do my best	1	2	3	4	5
are understanding when students have personal problems	1	2	3	4	5
set high standards for achievement in their classes	1	2	3	4	5
help me gain confidence in my ability to learn	1	2	3	4	5
have confidence in me	1	2	3	4	5
know me well	1	2	3	4	5
listen to my ideas	1	2	3	4	5
care about me	1	2	3	4	5
make learning fun	1	2	3	4	5
are excited about the subject they teach	1	2	3	4	5
give me individual attention when I need it	1	2	3	4	5
challenge me to do better	1	2	3	4	5

I am ready for the real world in reference to:

	Strongly Disagree	Disagree	Neutral	Agree	Strongly Agree
my ability to write	1	2	3	4	5
my ability to read	1	2	3	4	5
my ability with mathematics	1	2	3	4	5
my ability to present information	1	2	3	4	5
my technology skills	1	2	3	4	5

In my classes, time is spent:

	Strongly Disagree	Disagree	Neutral	Agree	Strongly Agree
listening to the teacher talk	1	2	3	4	5
in whole-class discussions	1	2	3	4	5
working in small groups	1	2	3	4	5
reading	1	2	3	4	5
answering questions from a book or worksheet	1	2	3	4	5
working on projects or research	1	2	3	4	5
doing work that I find meaningful	1	2	3	4	5
using computers	1	2	3	4	5

I work well when:

	Strongly Disagree	Disagree	Neutral	Agree	Strongly Agree
I am working on projects or research	1	2	3	4	5
the teacher is leading a discussion with the whole class	1	2	3	4	5
I am working in a small group	1	2	3	4	5
I am working by myself	1	2	3	4	5

Figure B-5

Student Questionnaire
High School   Page 3

What do you like about this school?

What do you wish were different at this school?

What do you wish I would have asked you about your school?

———————— Student Demographic Data ————————

I am: (darken all that apply)
- ○ African-American
- ○ American Indian
- ○ Asian
- ○ Caucasian
- ○ Filipino
- ○ Hispanic/Latino
- ○ Middle Eastern
- ○ Pacific Islander
- ○ Other _____

I am a:
- ○ Freshman
- ○ Sophomore
- ○ Junior
- ○ Senior

I am a:
- ○ Female
- ○ Male

I participate in: (darken all that apply)
- ○ Athletics (includes cheerleading and Flag Team)
- ○ School clubs
- ○ Instrumental music
- ○ Vocal music
- ○ Drama
- ○ Speech/Debate
- ○ Not connected to any school club or regular extracurricular activity

I came to this school:
- ○ This year
- ○ Last year
- ○ Year before last
- ○ Three years ago

Immediately after graduation, I plan to:
- ○ go to a 2-year community college
- ○ go to a 4-year college
- ○ enter a training or apprenticeship program
- ○ get a full-time job
- ○ join the military
- ○ get married
- ○ other _____

Figure B-6

Staff Questionnaire
Page 1

Education for the Future	*Staff Survey*

Please darken the circle that best describes your beliefs and feelings, using the rating scale to the right.

Rating scale:
Strongly Disagree (1), Disagree (2), Neutral (3), Agree (4), Strongly Agree (5)

I feel:

	Strongly Disagree		Neutral		Strongly Agree
like I belong at this school	1	2	3	4	5
that staff care about me	1	2	3	4	5
that learning can be fun	1	2	3	4	5
that learning is fun at this school	1	2	3	4	5
recognized for good work	1	2	3	4	5
intrinsically rewarded for doing my job well	1	2	3	4	5

I work with people who:

treat me with respect	1	2	3	4	5
listen if I have ideas about doing things better	1	2	3	4	5

My administrator:

treats me with respect	1	2	3	4	5
is an effective instructional leader	1	2	3	4	5
facilitates communication effectively	1	2	3	4	5
supports me in my work with students	1	2	3	4	5
supports shared decision making	1	2	3	4	5
allows me to be an effective instructional leader	1	2	3	4	5
is effective in helping us reach our vision	1	2	3	4	5

I have the opportunity to:

develop my skills	1	2	3	4	5
think for myself, not just carry out instructions	1	2	3	4	5

I love:

working at this school	1	2	3	4	5
seeing the results of my work with students	1	2	3	4	5

I work effectively with:

special education students	1	2	3	4	5
limited English-speaking students	1	2	3	4	5
an ethnically/racially diverse population of students	1	2	3	4	5
heterogeneously grouped classes	1	2	3	4	5
low-achieving students	1	2	3	4	5
I believe that every student can learn	1	2	3	4	5

I believe student achievement can increase through:

hands-on learning	1	2	3	4	5
effective professional development related to our vision	1	2	3	4	5
integrating instruction across the curriculum	1	2	3	4	5
thematic instruction	1	2	3	4	5
cooperative learning	1	2	3	4	5
multi-age classrooms	1	2	3	4	5
student self-assessment	1	2	3	4	5
authentic assessment	1	2	3	4	5
the use of computers	1	2	3	4	5
the use of varied technologies	1	2	3	4	5
providing a threat-free environment	1	2	3	4	5
close personal relationships between students and teachers	1	2	3	4	5

Figure B-7

Staff Questionnaire
Page 2

	Strongly Disagree	Disagree	Neutral	Agree	Strongly Agree

I believe student achievement can increase through: (continued)

	1	2	3	4	5
addressing student learning styles	○1	○2	○3	○4	○5
effective parent involvement	○1	○2	○3	○4	○5
partnerships with business	○1	○2	○3	○4	○5
teacher use of student achievement data	○1	○2	○3	○4	○5
The instructional program at this school is challenging	○1	○2	○3	○4	○5
The school provides an atmosphere where every student can succeed	○1	○2	○3	○4	○5
Quality work is expected of all students at this school	○1	○2	○3	○4	○5
Quality work is expected of me	○1	○2	○3	○4	○5
Quality work is expected of all the adults working at this school	○1	○2	○3	○4	○5
The vision for this school is clear	○1	○2	○3	○4	○5
The vision for this school is shared	○1	○2	○3	○4	○5
We have an action plan in place which can get us to our vision	○1	○2	○3	○4	○5
This school has a good public image	○1	○2	○3	○4	○5
I think it is important to communicate often with parents	○1	○2	○3	○4	○5
I communicate with parents often about their child's progress	○1	○2	○3	○4	○5
I communicate with parents often about class activities	○1	○2	○3	○4	○5

Morale is high on the part of:

	1	2	3	4	5
teachers	○1	○2	○3	○4	○5
students	○1	○2	○3	○4	○5
support staff	○1	○2	○3	○4	○5
administrators	○1	○2	○3	○4	○5
I am clear about what my job is at this school	○1	○2	○3	○4	○5
I feel that others are clear about what my job is at this school	○1	○2	○3	○4	○5

Items for teachers and instructional assistants only:

	1	2	3	4	5
The student outcomes for my class(es) are clear to me	○1	○2	○3	○4	○5
The student outcomes for my class(es) are clear to my students	○1	○2	○3	○4	○5
Teachers in this school communicate with each other to make student learning consistent across grades	○1	○2	○3	○4	○5
Learning is fun in my classroom	○1	○2	○3	○4	○5
I love to teach	○1	○2	○3	○4	○5

For each item, please check the description that applies to you. Demographic data, which is used for summary analysis, will not be reported if individuals can be identified.

I am a(n):
- ○ classroom teacher
- ○ instructional assistant
- ○ certificated staff (other than a classroom teacher)
- ○ classified staff (other than an instructional assistant)

Ethnicity: (darken all that apply)
- ○ African-American
- ○ Asian
- ○ Caucasian
- ○ Latino/Hispanic
- ○ Other _____

Gender:
- ○ Male
- ○ Female

Items for teachers only:

I teach:
- ○ primary grades
- ○ upper elementary grades
- ○ middle school grades
- ○ high school grades (9-10)
- ○ high school grades (11-12)

I have been teaching:
- ○ 1-3 years
- ○ 4-6 years
- ○ 7-10 years
- ○ 11 years, or more

I am part of a formal teaching team:
- ○ Yes ○ No

Figure B-8

Parent Questionnaire
Page 1

parents

Please complete this form for your family.
Please use a No. 2 pencil and completely
darken the circles. Thank you!

	Strongly Disagree	Disagree	Neutral	Agree	Strongly Agree
I feel welcome at my child's school.	①	②	③	④	⑤
I am informed about my child's progress.	①	②	③	④	⑤
I know what my child's teacher expects of my child.	①	②	③	④	⑤
My child is safe at school.	①	②	③	④	⑤
My child is safe going to and from school.	①	②	③	④	⑤
There is adequate playground supervision during school.	①	②	③	④	⑤
There is adequate supervision before and after school.	①	②	③	④	⑤
The teachers show respect for the students.	①	②	③	④	⑤
The students show respect for other students.	①	②	③	④	⑤
The school meets the social needs of the students.	①	②	③	④	⑤
The school meets the academic needs of the students.	①	②	③	④	⑤
The school expects quality work of its students.	①	②	③	④	⑤
The school has an excellent learning environment.	①	②	③	④	⑤
I know how well my child is progressing in school.	①	②	③	④	⑤
I like the school's report cards/progress report.	①	②	③	④	⑤
I respect the school's teachers.	①	②	③	④	⑤
I respect the school's principal.	①	②	③	④	⑤
Overall, the school performs well academically.	①	②	③	④	⑤
The school succeeds at preparing children for future work.	①	②	③	④	⑤
The school has a good public image.	①	②	③	④	⑤
The school's assessment practices are fair.	①	②	③	④	⑤
My child's teacher helps me to help my child learn at home.	①	②	③	④	⑤
I support my child's learning at home.	①	②	③	④	⑤
I feel good about myself as a parent.	①	②	③	④	⑤
I enjoy being a parent.	①	②	③	④	⑤

Number of Children in This School:
① ② ③ ④ ⑤ ⑥ ⑦ ⑧ ⑨

Number of Children in Household:
① ② ③ ④ ⑤ ⑥ ⑦ ⑧ ⑨

Children's Grades:
- ○ Kindergarten
- ○ First
- ○ Second
- ○ Third
- ○ Fourth
- ○ Fifth
- ○ Sixth
- ○ Seventh
- ○ Eighth

My Native Language Is:
- ○ Chinese
- ○ Eastern European
- ○ English
- ○ Japanese
- ○ Korean
- ○ Spanish
- ○ Vietnamese
- ○ Other

Ethnic Background:
(Darken all that apply)
- ○ African-American
- ○ American Indian
- ○ Asian
- ○ Caucasian
- ○ Hispanic
- ○ Other

© *Education for the Future Initiative (1997) San Francisco: Pacific Bell Foundation*

Figure B-9

Parent Questionnaire
Page 2

What are the strengths of your child's school?

What needs to be strengthened at your child's school?

What would make the school better?

Comments:

These Education for the Future Initiative Continuous Improvement Continuums, adapted from the Malcolm Baldrige Award Program for Quality Business Management, provide an authentic means for measuring schoolwide improvement and growth. In conjunction with a school portfolio, schools use these continuums as a vehicle for ongoing self-assessment. They use the results of the assessment to acknowledge their accomplishments, to set goals for improvement, and to keep school districts and partners apprised of the progress they have made in their school improvement efforts.

Appendix C

CONTINUOUS IMPROVEMENT CONTINUUMS

The Education for the Future Initiative Continuous Improvement Continuums are a type of rubric that represents the theoretical flow of systemic school improvement. The continuums are made up of seven key, interrelated, and overlapping components of systemic change — Information and Analysis, Student Achievement, Quality Planning, Professional Development, Leadership, Partnership Development, and Continuous Improvement & Evaluation.

The continuums are made up of seven key, interrelated, and overlapping components of systemic change

These rubrics, extending from *one* to *five* horizontally, represent a continuum of expectations related to school improvement with respect to an *approach* to the continuum, *implementation* of the approach, and the *outcome* that results from the implementation. A *one* rating, located at the left of each continuum, represents a school that has not yet begun to improve. *Five*, located at the right of each continuum, represents a school that is one step removed from "world class quality." The elements between *one* and *five* describe how that continuum is hypothesized to evolve in a continuously improving school. Each continuum moves from a reactive mode to a proactive mode—from fire fighting to prevention. The *five* in *outcome* in each continuum is the target.

Understanding the Continuums

Vertically, the *approach, implementation , and outcome* statements, for any number *one* through *five*, are hypotheses. In other words, the *implementation* statement describes how the *approach* might look when *approach.* If the hypotheses are accurate, the outcome will not be realized until the approach is actually implemented.

Using the Continuums

The most valuable way to use the continuums is to have all staff rate the school together. First have each member of the staff make their personal rating of where they feel the school as a whole is on each continuum. Take a quick count of how many feel this school is a *one* in *approach* to Information and Analysis, a *two*, and so on. If all staff agree on the same number, record the number and rationale, and move on. If there is a discrepancy, ask for discussion. The discussion clarifies what is happening schoolwide with respect to the continuum. The goal is to get a number that represents the rating that everyone can live with. The discussion and documentation of next steps are more important than the actual number that results. The ultimate goal is to make all aspects of the school consistent and congruent with the vision. Assessing your school on the Continuous Improvement Continuums at least twice each year is recommended.

> *The ultimate goal is to make all aspects of the school consistent and congruent with the vision*

Using these continuums will enable you and your school to stay motivated, to shape and maintain your shared vision, and assist with the continuous improvement of all elements of your school.

Remember that where your school is at any time is where it is. The important thing is what you do with this information. Continuous improvement is a never-ending process which, when used effectively and for the right purpose, will ultimately lead your school to providing a quality program for all children.

The Education for the Future Initiative Continuous Improvement Continuums and the School Portfolio are described in *The School Portfolio: A Comprehensive Framework for School Improvement*, Second Edition, published by Eye on Education, 6 Depot Way West, Suite 106, Larchmont, NY 10538, Tel: (914) 833-0551.

Table C-1

Information & Analysis

	ONE	TWO	THREE	FOUR	FIVE
APPROACH	Data or information about student performance and needs are not gathered in any systematic way; there is no way to determine what needs to change at the school, based on data.	There is no systematic process, but some teacher and student information is collected and used to problem-solve and establish student learning standards.	School collects data related to student performance (e.g., attendance, achievement) and conducts surveys on student, teacher, and parent needs. The information is used to drive the strategic quality plan for school change.	There is systematic reliance on hard data (including data for subgroups) as a basis for decision making at the classroom level as well as at the school level. Changes are based on the study of data to meet the needs of students and teachers.	Information is gathered in all areas of student interaction with the school. Teachers engage students in gathering information on their own performance. Accessible to all levels, data are comprehensive in scope and an accurate reflection of school quality.
IMPLEMENTATION	No information is gathered with which to make changes. Student dissatisfaction with the learning process is seen as an irritation, not a need for improvement.	Some data are tracked, such as dropout rates and enrollment. Only a few individuals are asked for feedback about areas of schooling.	School collects information on current and former students (e.g., student achievement and perceptions), analyzes and uses it in conjunction with future trends for planning. Identified areas for improvement are tracked over time.	Data are used to improve the effectiveness of teaching strategies on all student learning. Students' historical performances are graphed and utilized for diagnostics. Student evaluations and performances are analyzed by teachers in all classrooms.	Innovative teaching processes that meet the needs of students are implemented to the delight of teachers, parents, and students. Information is analyzed and used to prevent student failure. Root causes are known through analyses. Problems are prevented through the use of data.
OUTCOME	Only anecdotal and hypothetical information is available about student performance, behavior, and satisfaction. Problems are solved individually with short-term results.	Little data are available. Change is limited to some areas of the school and dependent upon individual teachers and their efforts.	Information collected about student and parent needs, assessment, and instructional practices are shared with the school staff and used to plan for change. Information helps staff understand pressing issues, analyze information for "root causes," track results for improvement.	An information system is in place. Positive trends begin to appear in many classrooms and schoolwide. There is evidence that these results are caused by understanding and effectively using data collected.	Students are delighted with the school's instructional processes and proud of their own capabilities to learn and assess their own growth. Good to excellent achievement is the result for all students. No student falls through the cracks. Teachers use data to predict and prevent potential problems.

Table C-2

Student Achievement

	ONE	TWO	THREE	FOUR	FIVE
APPROACH	Instructional and organizational processes critical to student success are not identified. Little distinction of student learning differences is made. Some teachers believe that not all students can achieve.	Some data are collected on student background and performance trends. Learning gaps are noted to direct improvement of instruction. It is known that student learning standards must be identified.	Student learning standards are identified and a continuum of learning is created throughout the school. Student performance data are collected and compared to the standards in order to analyze how to improve learning for all students.	Data on student achievement are used throughout the school to pursue the improvement of student learning. Teachers collaborate to implement appropriate instruction and assessment strategies for meeting student learning standards articulated across grade levels. All teachers believe that all students can learn.	School makes an effort to exceed student achievement expectations. Innovative instructional changes are made to anticipate learning needs and improve student achievement. Teachers are able to predict characteristics impacting student achievement and to know how to perform from a small set of internal quality measures.
IMPLEMENTATION	All students are taught the same way. There is no communication with students about their academic needs or learning styles. There are no analyses of how to improve instruction.	Some effort is made to track and analyze student achievement trends on a schoolwide basis. Teachers begin to understand the needs and learning gaps of students.	Teachers study effective instruction and assessment strategies to increase their students' learning. Student feedback and analysis of achievement data are used in conjunction with implementation support strategies.	There is a systematic focus on the improvement of student learning schoolwide. Effective instruction and assessment strategies are implemented in each classroom. Teachers support one another with peer coaching and/or action research focused on implementing strategies that lead to increased achievement.	All teachers correlate critical instructional and assessment strategies with objective indicators of quality student achievement. A comparative analysis of actual individual student performance to student learning standards is utilized to adjust teaching strategies to ensure a progression of learning for all students.
OUTCOME	There is wide variation in student attitudes and achievement with undesirable results. There is high dissatisfaction among students with learning. Student background is used as an excuse for low student achievement.	There is some evidence that student achievement trends are available to teachers and are being used. There is much effort, but minimal observable results in improving student achievement.	There is an increase in communication between students and teachers regarding student learning. Teachers learn about effective instructional strategies that will meet the needs of their students. They make some gains.	Increased student achievement is evident schoolwide. Student morale, attendance, and behavior are good. Teachers converse often with each other about preventing student failure. Areas for further attention are clear.	Students and teachers conduct self-assessments to continuously improve performance. Improvements in student achievement are evident and clearly caused by teachers' and students' understandings of individual student learning, linked to appropriate and effective instructional and assessment strategies. A continuum of learning results. No students fall through the cracks.

Table C-3

Quality Planning

	ONE	TWO	THREE	FOUR	FIVE
APPROACH	No quality plan or process exists. Data are neither used nor considered important in planning.	The staff realizes the importance of a mission, vision, and one comprehensive action plan. Teams develop goals and timelines, and dollars are allocated to begin the process.	A comprehensive school plan to achieve the vision is developed. Plan includes evaluation and continuous improvement.	One focused and integrated schoolwide plan for implementing a continuous improvement process is put into action. All school efforts are focused on the implementation of this plan that represents the achievement of the vision.	A plan for the continuous improvement of the school, with a focus on students, is put into place. There is excellent articulation and integration of all elements in the school due to quality planning. Leadership team ensures all elements are implemented by all appropriate parties.
IMPLEMENTATION	There is no knowledge of or direction for quality planning. Budget is allocated on an as-needed basis. Many plans exist.	School community begins continuous improvement planning efforts by laying out major steps to a shared vision, by identifying values and beliefs, the purpose of the school, a mission, vision, and student learning standards.	Implementation goals, responsibilities, due dates, and timelines are spelled out. Support structures for implementing the plan are set in place.	The quality management plan is implemented through effective procedures in all areas of the school. Everyone knows what she/he needs to do, and when it needs to be done to accomplish the school goals.	Schoolwide goals, mission, vision, and student learning standards are shared and articulated throughout the school and with feeder schools. The attainment of identified student learning standards is linked to planning and implementation of effective instruction that meets students' needs.
OUTCOME	There is no evidence of comprehensive planning. Staff work is carried out in isolation. A continuum of learning for students is absent.	The school community understands the benefits of working together to implement a comprehensive continuous improvement plan.	There is evidence that the school plan is being implemented in some areas of the school. Improvements are neither systematic nor integrated schoolwide.	A schoolwide plan is known to all. Results from working toward the quality improvement goals are evident throughout the school.	Evidence of effective teaching and learning results in significant improvement of student achievement attributed to quality planning at all levels of the school organization. Teachers understand and share the school mission and vision, the impact and importance of quality planning, and accountability.

Table C-4

Professional Development

	ONE	TWO	THREE	FOUR	FIVE
APPROACH	There is no professional development. Teachers, principals, and staff are seen as interchangeable parts that can be replaced.	The "cafeteria" approach to professional development is used, whereby individual teachers choose what they want to take, without regard to an overall school plan.	The school plan and student needs are used to target appropriate professional development for all employees. Staff is inserviced in relevant instructional and leadership strategies.	Professional development and data-gathering methods are used by all teachers and are directed toward the goals of continuous improvement. Teachers have ongoing conversations about student achievement research. Other staff members receive training in their roles.	Leadership and staff continuously improve all aspects of the school structure through an innovative and comprehensive continuous improvement process that prevents student failures. Professional development is appropriate for implementing the vision, supportive, collegial, effective, systemic, and ongoing. Traditional teacher evaluations are replaced by collegial coaching and action research focused on student learning standards.
IMPLEMENTATION	Teacher, principal, and staff performance is controlled and inspected. Performance evaluations are used to detect mistakes.	Teacher professional development is sporadic and unfocused, lacking an approach for implementing new procedures and processes. Some leadership training begins to take place.	Teachers are involved in year-round quality professional development. The school community is trained in shared decision making, team building concepts, and effective communication strategies.	Teachers, in teams, continuously set and implement student achievement goals. Leadership considers these goals and ensures appropriateness of professional development. Teachers utilize effective support approaches as they implement new instruction and assessment strategies.	Teams passionately support each other in the pursuit of quality improvement at all levels. Teachers make bold changes in instruction and assessment strategies focused on student learning standards and student learning styles. A teacher as action researcher model is implemented. Staffwide conversations focus on systemic reflection and improvement.
OUTCOME	No professional growth and no performance improvement. There exists a high turnover rate of employees. Attitudes and approach filter down to students.	The effectiveness of professional development is not known or analyzed. Teachers feel helpless about making schoolwide changes.	Teachers, working in teams, feel supported and begin to feel they can make changes. Evidence shows that shared decision making works.	A collegial school is evident. Effective classroom strategies are practiced, articulated schoolwide, and are reflective of professional development aimed at ensuring student achievement.	True systemic change and improved student achievement result because teachers are knowledgeable of and implement effective teaching strategies for individual student learning styles, abilities, and situations. Teachers are sensitive to and apply approaches that work best for each student.

Table C-5

Leadership

	ONE	TWO	THREE	FOUR	FIVE
APPROACH	Principal as decision maker. Decisions are reactive to state, district, and federal mandates.	A shared decision making structure is put into place and discussions begin on how to achieve a school vision. Most decisions are focused on solving problems and are reactive.	Leadership team is committed to continuous improvement. Leadership seeks inclusion of all school sectors and supports study teams by making time provisions for their work.	Leadership team represents a true shared decision making structure. Study teams are reconstructed for the implementation of a comprehensive continuous improvement plan.	A strong continuous improvement structure is set into place that allows for input from all sectors of the school, district, and community, ensuring strong communication, flexibility, and refinement of approach and beliefs. The school vision is student focused, based on data and appropriate for school/ community values, and meeting student needs.
IMPLEMENTATION	Principal makes all decisions, with little or no input from teachers, the community, or students. Leadership inspects for mistakes.	School values and beliefs are identified; the purpose of school is defined; a school mission and student learning standards are developed with representative input. A structure for studying approaches to achieving student learning standards is established.	Leadership team is active on study teams and integrates recommendations from the teams' research and analyses to form a comprehensive plan for continuous improvement within the context of the school mission. Everyone is kept informed.	Decisions about budget and implementation of the vision are made within teams, by the principal, by the leadership team, and by the full staff as appropriate. All decisions are communicated to the leadership team and to the full staff.	The vision is implemented and articulated across all grade levels and into feeder schools. Quality standards are reinforced throughout the school. All members of the school community understand and apply the quality standards. Leadership team has systematic interactions and involvement with district administrators, teachers, parents, community, and students about the school's direction.
OUTCOME	Decisions lack focus and consistency. There is little staff buy-in. Students and parents do not feel they are being heard. Decision-making process is clear and known.	The mission provides a focus for all school improvement and guides the action to the vision. The school community is committed to continuous improvement. Quality leadership techniques are used sporadically.	Leaders are seen as committed to planning and quality improve-ment. Critical areas for improvement are identified. Faculty feel included in shared decision making.	There is evidence that the leadership team listens to all levels of the organization. Implementation of the continuous improvement plan is linked to student learning standards and the guiding principles of the school. Teachers are empowered.	Site-based management and shared decision making truly exists. Teachers understand and display an intimate knowledge of how the school operates. Teachers support and communicate with each other in the implementation of quality strategies. Teachers implement the vision in their classrooms and can determine how their new approach meets student needs and leads to the attainment of student learning standards.

Table C-6

Partnership Development

	ONE	TWO	THREE	FOUR	FIVE
APPROACH	There is no system for input from parents, business, or community. Status quo is desired for managing the school.	Partnerships are sought, but mostly for money and things.	School has knowledge of why partnerships are important and seeks to include businesses and parents in a strategic fashion related to student learning standards for increased student achievement.	School seeks effective win-win business and community partnerships and parent involvement to implement the vision. Desired outcomes are clearly identified. A solid plan for partnership development exists.	Community, parent, and business partnerships become integrated across all student groupings. The benefits of outside involvement are known by all. Parent and business involvement in student learning is refined. Student learning regularly takes place beyond the school walls.
IMPLEMENTATION	Barriers are erected to close out involvement of outsiders. Outsiders are managed for least impact on status quo.	A team is assigned to get partners and to receive input from parents, the community, and business in the school.	Involvement of business, community, and parents begins to take place in some classrooms and after school hours related to the vision. Partners begin to realize how they can support each other in achieving school goals. School staff understand what partners need out of the partnership.	There is a systematic utilization of parents, community, and businesses schoolwide. Areas in which the active use of these partnerships benefits student learning are clear.	Partnership development is articulated across all student groupings. Parents, community, business, and educators work together in an innovative fashion to increase student learning and to prepare students for the 21st Century. Partnerships are evaluated for continuous improvement.
OUTCOME	There is little or no involvement of parents, business, or community at large. School is a closed, isolated system.	Much effort is given to establishing partnerships. Some spotty trends emerge, such as receiving donated equipment.	Some substantial gains are achieved in implementing partnerships. Some student achievement increases can be attributed to this involvement.	Gains in student satisfaction with learning and school are clearly related to partnerships. All partners benefit.	Previously non-achieving students enjoy learning, with excellent achievement. Community, business, and home become common places for student learning, while school becomes a place where parents come for further education. Partnerships enhance what the school does for students.

Table C-7

Continuous Improvement and Evaluation

	ONE	TWO	THREE	FOUR	FIVE
APPROACH	Neither goals nor strategies exist for the evaluation and continuous improvement of the school organization or for elements of the school organization.	The approach to continuous improvement and evaluation is problem solving. If there are no problems, or if solutions can be made quickly, there is no need for improvement or analyses. Changes in parts of the system are not coordinated with all other parts.	Some elements of the school organization are evaluated for effectiveness. Some elements are improved on the basis of the evaluation findings.	All elements of the school's operations are evaluated for improvement and to ensure congruence of the elements with respect to the continuum of learning students experience.	All aspects of the school organization are rigorously evaluated and improved on a continuous basis. Students, and the maintenance of a comprehensive learning continuum for students, become the focus of all aspects of the school improvement process.
IMPLEMENTATION	With no overall plan for evaluation and continuous improvement, strategies are changed by individual teachers and administrators only when something sparks the need to improve. Reactive decisions and activities are a daily mode of operation.	Isolated changes are made in some areas of the school organization in response to problem incidents. Changes are not preceded by comprehensive analyses, such as an understanding of the root causes of problems. The effectiveness of the elements of the school organization, or changes made to the elements, is not known.	Elements of the school organization are improved on the basis of comprehensive analyses of root causes of problems, client perceptions, and operational effectiveness of processes.	Continuous improvement analyses of student achievement and instructional strategies are rigorously reinforced within each classroom and across learning levels to develop a comprehensive learning continuum for students and to prevent student failure.	Comprehensive continuous improvement becomes the way of doing business at the school. Teachers continuously improve the appropriateness and effectiveness of instructional strategies based on student feedback and performance. All aspects of the school organization are improved to support teachers' efforts.
OUTCOME	Individuals struggle with system failure. Finger pointing and blaming others for failure occurs. The effectiveness of strategies is not known. Mistakes are repeated.	Problems are solved only temporarily and few positive changes result. Additionally, unintended and undesirable consequences often appear in other parts of the system. Many aspects of the school are incongruent, keeping the school from reaching its vision.	Evidence of effective improvement strategies is observable. Positive changes are made and maintained due to comprehensive analyses and evaluation.	Teachers become astute at assessing and in predicting the impact of their instructional strategies on individual student achievement. Sustainable improvements in student achievement are evident at all grade levels, due to continuous improvement.	The school becomes a congruent and effective learning organization. Only instruction and assessment strategies that produce quality student achievement are used. A true continuum of learning results for all students.

REFERENCES AND RESOURCES

Mapping the Route to Education Excellence

The references used in this book along with other resources that will assist busy school administrators and teachers in conducting quality data analyses appear, below, categorized by topic for easy use.

Assessing Perceptions

Bourque, L. B., & Fielder, E. P. (1995). *How to conduct self-administered and mail surveys*, *The survey kit*, v. 3. Thousand Oaks, CA: SAGE Publications, Inc.

DeVellis, R. F. (1991). *Scale development: Theory and applications*. Newbury Park, CA: SAGE Publications, Inc.

Fink, A. (1995). *How to analyze data: The survey kit*, v. 8. Thousand Oaks, CA: SAGE Publications, Inc.

Fink, A. (1995). *How to ask survey questions*: *The survey kit*, v. 2. Thousand Oaks, CA: SAGE Publications, Inc.

Fink, A. (1995). *How to design surveys: The survey kit*, v. 5. Thousand Oaks, CA: SAGE Publications, Inc.

Fink, A. (1995). *How to report surveys: The survey kit*, v. 9. Thousand Oaks, CA: SAGE Publications, Inc.

Fink, A. (1995). *How to sample surveys: The survey kit*, v. 6. Thousand Oaks, CA: SAGE Publications, Inc.

Fink, A. (1995). *The survey handbook: The survey kit*, v. 1. Thousand Oaks, CA: SAGE Publications, Inc.

Frey, J. H. & Oishi, S. M. (1995). *How to conduct interviews by telephone and in person: The survey kit*, v. 4. Thousand Oaks, CA: SAGE Publications, Inc.

Fowler, Floyd J. (1995). *Improving survey questions: Design and evaluation*. Thousand Oaks, CA: SAGE Publications, Inc.

Fowler, Floyd J. (1990). *Standardized survey interviewing*. Newbury Park, CA: SAGE Publications, Inc.

Greenbaum, L. (1998). *The handbook for focus group research*. Thousand Oaks, CA: SAGE Publications, Inc.

Jorgensen, D. L. (1989). *Participant observation: A methodology for human studies*. Newbury Park, CA: SAGE Publications, Inc.

Lavrakas, P. J. (1993). *Telephone survey methods: Sampling, selection, and supervision*. Newbury Park, CA: SAGE Publications, Inc.

Litwin, M. S. (1995). *How to measure survey reliability and validity: The survey kit, v. 7*. Thousand Oaks, CA: SAGE Publications, Inc.

Mangione, T. W. (1995). *Mail surveys: Improving the quality*. Thousand Oaks, CA: SAGE Publications, Inc.

Oppenheim, A. N. (1992). *Questionnaire, design, interviewing, and attitude measurement*. New York, NY: Pinter Publishers.

Patten, U.L. (1998). *Questionnaire research: a practical guide*. Los Angeles, CA: Pyrczak Publishers.

Payne, S. L. (1951). *The art of asking questions: studies in public opinion*. Princeton: Princeton University Press.

Ragunathan, T. E., & Grizzle, J. E. (1995). A split questionnaire survey design. Journal of the American Statistical Association, v. 90.

Assessing Student Learning

Angoff, W. H. (1984). *Scales, norms, and equivalent scores*. Princeton: Educational Testing Service.

Bird, L. B. (1995). *Assessing continuous learning*. Los Angeles, CA: The Galef Institute. Association for Supervision and Curriculum Development. *Questioning our motives*, Education Update, v. 38, p.5.

Interpreting the Reports: A Guide, published by the Psychological Corporation, Harcourt Brace Jovanovich, Inc., 1991, Stanford Achievement Test Series, 8th Edition.

United States Department of Education (1996). *Technical issues in large-scale performance assessment*. Washington, DC: U.S. Department of Education Office of Educational Research and Improvement.

Henry, G. T. (1995). *Graphing data: Techniques for display and analysis.* Thousand Oaks, CA: SAGE Publications.

Silverman, D. (1993). *Interpreting qualitative data: Methods for analyzing talk, text, and interaction.* Thousand Oaks, CA: SAGE Publications, Inc.

Tufte, E. R. (1983). *The visual display of qualitative information.* Cheshire, CT: Graphics Press.

Communicating Results

Deming, W. E. (1993). *The new economics for industry, government, education.* Cambridge, MA: Massachusetts Institute of Technology Center for Advanced Engineering Study.

Deming, W. E. (1982). *Out of the crisis.* Cambridge, MA: Massachusetts Institute of Technology Center for Advanced Engineering Study.

Mann, N. R. (1989). *The keys to excellence: The story of the Deming philosophy.* Los Angeles, CA: Prestwick Books.

Scherkenbach, W. (1991). *Deming's road to continual improvement.* Knoxville, TN: SPC Press, Inc.

Continuous Improvement

Gruenewald, P. J. Treno, A. J., Taff, G., & Klitzner, M., (1997). *Measuring community indicators.* Thousand Oaks, CA: SAGE Publications, Inc.

Demographics

Herman, J. L. & Winters, L. (1991). *Sensible school-based evaluation.* Washington, D.C.: Office of Educational Research and Improvement.

Herman, J. L., & Winters, L. (1992). *Tracking your school's success: A guide to sensible evaluation.* Newbury Park, CA: Corwin Press.

Patton, M. Q. (1986). *Utilization-focused evaluation.* Newbury Park, CA: SAGE Publications, Inc.

Patton, M. Q. (1981). *Creative evaluation.* Beverly Hills, CA: SAGE Publications, Inc.

Patton, M. Q. (1980). *Qualitative evaluation methods.* Beverly Hills, CA: SAGE Publications, Inc.

Popham, J. W. (1993). *Educational evaluation.* Needham Heights, MA: Simon & Schuster, Inc.

Evaluation

Sanders, J. R. (1992). *Evaluating school programs: The program evaluation guide for schools*. Newbury Park, CA: Corwin Press, Inc.

Scriven, M. (1991). *Evaluation thesaurus*. Newbury Park, CA: SAGE Publications, Inc.

Yin, R. K. (1989). *Case study research: Design and methods*. Newbury Park, CA: SAGE Publications, Inc.

Learning Organizations

Costa, A. & Kallick, B. (1995). *Shifting the assessment paradigm: The role of assessment in the learning organization*. Alexandria, VA: Association for Supervision and Curriculum Development.

Senge, P. (1990). *The fifth discipline: The art and practice of the learning organization*. New York, NY: Doubleday Currency.

Senge, P. (1994). *The fifth discipline fieldbook: Strategies and tools for building a learning organization*. New York, NY: Doubleday Currency.

Needs Assessment

McKillip, J. (1987). *Need Analysis: tools for the human services and education*, v. 10. Newbury Park: SAGE Publications.

Sampling

Henry, G. T. (1990). *Practical Sampling: Applied social research methods*. Newbury Park, CA: SAGE Publications, Inc.

School Improvement

Bernhardt, V. (1998). *The school portfolio: A comprehensive framework for school improvement*. Second Edition, Larchmont, NY: Eye on Education.

Berliner, D.C. & Biddle, B.J. (1995). *The manufactured crisis: Myths, fraud, and the attack on America's public schools*. Reading, MA: Addison-Wesley Publishing Company.

Glasser, W. (1990). *The quality school*. New York, NY: Harper Perennial.

Lezotte, L. W., (1997). *Learning for all*. Okemos, MI: Effective Schools Products, Ltd.

Lezotte, L. W. & Jacoby, B. C. (1992). *Sustainable school reform: The district context for school improvement*. Okemos, MI: Effective Schools Products, Ltd.

Schmoker, M. (1997). *Results: the key to comprehensive school improvement*. Alexandria, VA.: Association of Supervision and Curriculum Development.

National LEADership Network Study Group on Restructuring Schools, U.S. Department of Education (1993). *Toward quality in education: The leader's odyssey*. Washington, D.C.: United States Department of Education.

Setting Standards

Glass, G. V., & Stanley, J. C. (1970). *Statistical methods in education and psychology*. Englewood Cliffs, NJ: Prentice-Hall, Inc.

Ward, A. W., Stoker, H. W., & Murray-Ward, M. (1996). *Educational measurement: Origins, theories and implications*. Lanham, Maryland: University Press of America.

Statistical Methods

Patten, M. L. (1997). *Understanding research methods: an overview of the essentials*. Los Angeles, CA: Pyrczak Publishing.

Ravid, R. (1994). *Practical statistics for educators*. Lanham, Maryland: University Press of America, Inc.

Total Quality Management

Brassard, M. (1989). *The memory jogger plus+: Featuring the seven management and planning tools.* Methuen, MA: GOAL/QPC.

Lynch, R. & Werner, T. (1992). *Continuous improvement: Teams & tools*. Atlanta, GA: QualTeam, Inc.

McCloskey, L., & Collett, D. (1993). *A primer guide to total quality management*. Methuen, MA: GOAL/QPC.

Sashkin, M. & Kiser, K. (1993). *Putting total quality management to work: What TQM means, how to use it & how to sustain it over the long run*. San Francisco, CA: Berrett-Koehler Publishers.

Trucker, S., Oddo, F., and Brassard, M. (1993). *The educators' companion to the memory jogger plus+*. Methuen, MA: GOAL/QPC.

(1995). *Problem solving machine for the memory jogger II*. Methuen, MA: GOAL/QPC and Compact Publishing Co.

INDEX